*A Midrash on
American Jewish History*

Table of Contents

A Midrash on
American Jewish History

HENRY L. FEINGOLD

State University of New York Press

ALBANY

Published by
State University of New York Press, Albany

© 1982 State University of New York

All rights reserved

Printed in the United States of America

For information, address State University of New York Press,
State University Plaza, Albany, N.Y., 12246

Library of Congress Cataloging in Publication Data
Feingold, Henry L., 1931Ñ
A midrash on American Jewish history.

(SUNY series in modern Jewish history)
Includes index.
1. Jews—United States—Politics and government—Addresses, essays, lectures. 2. Judaism—United States—Addresses, essays, lectures. 3. United States—Ethnic relations—Addresses, essays, lectures. I. Title. II. Series.
E184.J5F376 305.8'924'073 82-5527
ISBN 0-87395-637-0
ISBN 0-87395-638-9 (pbk.)

*For Vera and my daughters
Margo and Duffy whose insights
reach beyond historical truth.*

Preface

THIS book examines the several historical processes which together compose the Jewish experience in America. But, like so many recent writings about American Jewry, its underlying preoccupation is with the question of Jewish survival. It seeks out those fortuitous factors that assured Jewish continuance and success in the past. That preoccupation is brought up to date in the concluding chapter, which wonders aloud whether history has not disarmed American Jewry by facing it with a survival challenge posed by a society beckoning it to enter completely.

After so many millenia of paying witness to other civilizations entering on and departing the historical stage, one would imagine that Jews would take their survival more for granted. If the Jewish historic persona is anything, it is that of survivor. Yet Jewish survivalists seem unaware of how anomalous their insistent alarums regarding an impending demise seem to the ear of the historian. The threat of absorption into a benevolent culture seems in the end no less ominous than the threat of physical destruction. For survivalists the consequences are identical.

The Jewish preoccupation with survival in America today is amplified, perhaps even irrationally. Having lived in the time–space between Kishinev and Auschwitz, some Jews feel that they do not strain the bounds of credulity by sensing that, at least in some parts of the Western world, there was a conspiracy against their survival. That it was not true in America does not allay their fears, since Jews also take cues from the general flow of Jewish history. One suspects that the manipulation of despair has in itself become part of a survival strategy. When joined with messianic hope, which lies at the root of the Western assumption of progress, hope and despair of survival together form a polarity, one of several that inform Jewish history. They are told by their prophets, ancient and contemporary, that they will either survive and prosper or slip into the abyss of history to be forgotten. The threat of perdition, of lostness, is in fact highly prescriptive. What a paradox: Jews—who, for the most part, have had little control of their history—are more concerned than most people regarding not only the possibility of inventing themselves through history but their place in it. The preoccupation with survival has mythic as well as real dimensions. That is the reason why American Jewry, to the extent that its members are identified as Jews, possess a growing anxiety about survial even in a benevolent host culture.

Historians, who, by training, if not by inclination, eschew the prescriptive and apocalyptic, cannot really understand the use of history itself as part of a survival strategy. They are prepared only to acknowledge that for an idiosyncratic group like the Jews one does not predict demise for light and transient reasons. That perception is made more possible because, more than those in other disciplines in the social sciences, historians are prepared to accept the anomalous on its own terms wherever it appears, in a specific event, person, or community. They seek out the particular rather than the commonality. The appreciation of the idiosyncratic, the nonrepetitive unique datum, gives historians a better vantage point from which to view the Jewish condition. They are not taken up with grouping and classifying seemingly like things, which is the first step of the "scientific" approach. They understand that the mystery of millenial Jewish survival lies not in what it shares with other cultures but precisely in what makes it different. Had it been otherwise, Jewish civilization would have gone the way of all flesh long ago.

With such a sensibility it should not surprise the reader that the author is comparatively optimistic concerning the contemporary American Jewish condition. He assumes that American Jewry is exceptional and therefore will be able to resist being

merged into the general American culture. To be sure, those
who anxiously monitor the life-signs of American Jewry are not
mistaken when they note a decline of the distinct Jewish enterprise in America. Yet, that anxious vision fails to note the new
sprouts, which often take entirely new forms, buttressing the
American Jewish presence.

There is a suspicion that those who insist that American
Jewry will somehow defy the normal fate of all subcultures in
the American environment are whistling in the dark. So powerful are the tie-dissolving solvents released by the secular pluralistic American society that one can readily note a weakened
religious core, which we here call Judaism, and also an erosion
of the characteristic ethnic-peoplehood bonds which we desig-
nate as Jewishness. Is it possible to insist that there is a special
element in American Jewish culture, a tie to a separate historical stream, which magically exempts it from the full completion of the acculturation process? There is bound to be suspicion of insufficient detachment when a historian who belongs to
the group he is studying speaks of "exceptionalism" or
"uniqueness." That occurs partly because the reader automati-
cally assumes that the remarkable American Jewish economic
achievement is to be used as evidence of exceptionality. But
that is not the case here. Every American subgroup seeks out
elements of its uniqueness to serve as a rationale for retaining a
separate identity. Members of such groups know instinctively
that if one is to withstand the impact of the host culture, the
touting of inspirational group achievement is requisite. Members of subgroups must be taught what they once learned with
their mother's milk—that their culture is worth preserving. All
subgroups have found such elements of uniqueness. Irish–
Americans might lay claim to a notable mastery of the "game"
of American politics, as well as to having added some new
wrinkles to it. Japanese–Americans appear to possess an even
faster mobility rate than Jews. Each group searches out and
finds something distinctive.

But while they deserve the attention of the historian, these
"achievements" are not what makes for exemption from the
acculturation process. They actually are often the result of suc-

cessful acculturation, and are themselves accelerators of that acculturation. What sets American Jewry apart is the particular way it has come to terms with the demands of the host culture. It acculturates on different terms than other subgroups. What makes that possible is its enduring link with a separate religious civilization with whose history and culture it also identifies. Jews recognize this mystical tie to other Jewish communities by referring to *k'lal Yisrael*, the universal community of Jewry. Should they forget the mystical dimension, there is the physical reality of Jewish communities in every area of the globe to remind them. No other American subgroup has anything quite like it in its arsenal, a separate religious civilization with its own history and its own claims. The normal subgroup is territorially anchored. Strong sentiments for the "old country" may persist for generations. But, in truth, by the act of emigration its members have stepped out of its space in the cultural as well as physical sense. That is not true of Jews, who could lay no claim to belonging to a culture which often despised them.

Instead, Jews developed a strong sense of kinship with Jewish communities elsewhere. How abiding that link is in American Jewry can be gleaned historically from the persistence of its concern for Jewish communities abroad, and today from its agenda and the flow of the philanthropic dollar. First place on the American Jewish agenda is the concern for the welfare and the security of Israel. Not far behind is a similar concern for Soviet Jewry and other beleaguered Jewish communities. The historian soon discovers that the most distinguishing characteristics of American Jewry are inevitably linked to the broader stream of Jewish history. What happens to American Jewry is a historical echo of what has happened to Jews elsewhere. One can see it in the triangulation of American Judaism into Conservative, Orthodox, and Reform branches. It is reflected in the unique development of the Jewish labor movement, which resonates a parallel development in Europe. It can be noted in the ocean commerce developed by Sephardic Jews during the Colonial period, and in the distinctive commercial banking nexus developed by German Jews in the late nineteenth century. Both were anchored in links with related Jewish communities in other areas. Today that facing outward is symbolized by the "Zionization" of American Jewry. It defines itself by an overriding concern for a "foreign" sovereignty which cannot by its very nature ever be "foreign" to American Jewry. Finally, we must take note of the fact that the way American Jewish history is periodized on the basis of three separate waves of Jewish immigration directly links American Jewish history to the broader stream of Jewish history. Like all Jewries of the diaspora, American Jewry has an inherent duality. It is part of American civilizatin, whose successes and travails it shares. It is also a part of the millenial flow of Jewish history, another diaspora community in a history full of diasporas. Living in the interstices of two cultures, its principal problem stems from the tensions generated by conflicting demands, and its stability rests on finding acceptable strategies for balancing one against the other. It is for that reason, too, that the acculturation of Jews in America is not comparable to other groups. From the outset being Jewish was peculiarly a thing of the spirit. Jewish group identity formation is uniquely internalized and anchored in time rather than space. It can be gradually worn away and made meaningless but it cannot overnight be stepped away from or out of. The realization of vulnerability makes the benevolent absorbency of American culture a source of survival anxiety. There is no American subgroup more enthusiastic for the benefits offered by a free and open secular society. But at the same time the longing for k'lal Yisrael, (the universal community of Jewry) which is the other anchor point of their new civil religion, continues to exercise a powerful pull. Survivalists slowly become aware that strategies fashioned on the notion of an enduring antagonism of the host culture are simply not applicable to America. Reneged upon almost everywhere in the world, the promise of emancipation is here fulfilled and even overfulfilled. The personal liberation and autonomy which is at the heart of the modernization process poses a new kind of threat to all ethno–religious corporations, especially if they trace their binding ties to the premodern period. The Jewish corporation finds itself compelled to rely on voluntarism, and since in America it never possessed the power to order a Jew to his Judaism it can adjust to that. It is, however, far more difficult for American Judaism to go to the marketplace with its wares to convince "modern" Jews of the usefulness of the Judaic ethos and tradition for their personal fulfillment. The accommodation that the "marketing" approach requires is somehow desacrilizing. It is perhaps asking too much from a belief system which, at its heart, demanded of the faithful that they recognize the sacredness of a force outside of themselves. It went far beyond the self-fortification modern humanity endlessly requires and can be squeezed into such a form only at a price. The question is whether Judaism and its ethnic–cultural component, Jewishness, can remain vital in a society with such highly personalized requirements, a society in which the laity has far more needs and demands than the deity.

These essays, each focused on a distinct historical episode, originated as a series of half-hour radio lectures sponsored by the Jewish University of the Air. The programs were then packaged in tape cassette form for nation-wide distribution. The idea that the lectures could serve as the basis of a book on American Jewry occurred to me when many listeners and friends told me how exceptionally clear the lectures made the subject at hand. That impression was reinforced when I spoke to a group of students who were using the taped lectures as the basis for a full-credit course in American Jewish history. It proved no easy task to rewrite and rework the twenty-one original programs to become fourteen distinct essays, and sometimes I wished that I had not taken the many kind remarks on the lectures so seriously. But when the process was done I was gratified with the results. Rather than a textbook history of the American Jewish experience, what emerged is a narrative based on the application of a historical intelligence to the culture, dilemmas, and foibles of American Jewry. It presents a historical perspective on why that strange and passionate tribe is the way it is.

I am grateful to Jacob Katzman, who conceived of and implemented the cassette program, for enlisting me in a worthwhile project. He constantly reminded me that an audience can be won only if it is addressed in language it understands, about issues which are potentially of deep concern to it. I also owe a word of thanks to Daria Martin, who typed the manuscript and corrected sundry errors. Those which remain, errors of fact and of perception, are, of course, completely my responsibility. In a historical narrative covering a three-hundred-year period, there are bound to be some errors. Nevertheless, I have the hope that the reader will find the synthesis and the conceptualization sufficiently compelling that they will hardly detract from the narrative.

Henry L. Feingold
New York City
9 May 1981

A Midrash on
American Jewish History

CHAPTER I /

Beginnings

H AD this book been written a generation ago the title of this first chapter might well have been something like "Present at the Creation" rather than simply "Beginnings." The writing of history was used then to help legitimate the Jewish presence in America. Historians were doing so by reminding us that Jews were among the first to arrive in the New World. Some went much further and claimed that the discovery was based on Jewish imagination and capital. A measure of how secure Jews have become in America is that the writing of apologetic history, writing designed to prove that Jews have earned the right to be here, is no longer in fashion.

We will, of course, probe that contribution to the discovery and development of early America, not to prove anything, but because it is necessary for us to do so. If a fitting description of the American–Jewish relationship pertains to its mutual benevolence, then surely that did not spring forth full-blown in the second half of the twentieth century. We must seek out its roots in an earlier time. That search for the beginnings of the American Jewish connection, how things got that way, is the objective of this chapter. Is there historical precedent for the bridging role between the core economy and the periphery Jews seem to play in the early decades of the twentieth century? Has the tendency to seek out new nonpreempted areas of the economy a historical precedent? Much of America's benevolence is more extended to Judaism, the religion, than to Jewishness, the characteristics of the people. Does that remarkable religious tolerance of Judaism so characteristic of contemporary American society find its roots in the dynamics of Colonial

I

American life? Finally, the perceptive observer cannot fail to note the continuities between American Jewish political culture today, its liberal bias and its broad approach to its group interest, and Jewish political behavior during the period of the American revolution and thereafter. Are these contemporary echoes fortuitous or is there a connection to the past?

Let us turn first to the relationship of Jews to the discovery and settlement of the New World. It has three distinct aspects: the first is demographic and concerns the origins of the Jewish population stock that settled in the New World; the second is economic and concerns the Jewish role in the commercial revolution that contained the historical forces impelling Europe to reach out to "discover" new areas to establish its system; and the third concerns the discovery and transmission of the nautical technology and lore that made the "discovery" of these areas possible.

The sources of Jewish settlers for the western hemisphere is well known. One stream of settlers stems from the Iberian dispersion and a second was triggered by the disintegration of the so-called Polish refuge in Eastern Europe. The first is a tragic story of progressive insecurity and threat of community dissolution by forced conversion of the Jews of Spain. The persecution of the Jews by the Christian princes after the defeat of the Moors in the thirteenth century stood in stark contrast to the Jewish condition under the Moors. There Jews had a subservient but secure place in society and some of their number did rise to great heights. But by 1212 only the kingdom of Granada in the southeastern part of the peninsula remained in Moorish hands. Under the hegemony of the xenophobic, militantly religious, Christian warrior–princes, the Golden Age of Sephardic Jewry could not sustain itself. Technically, the Inquisition, which was installed to assure religious conformity, did not persecute Jews per se. Rather, it targeted *marranos* or *conversos*, former Jews who had either been coerced—or, more likely seduced—into accepting Christianity only to slip back to Judaism, thereby becoming heretics. A good many of these *conversos*, aware of their unacceptability in Catholic society and

2

of the dangers they faced, made their way to distant outposts of the Spanish empire. Once resettled in Spanish America, some, not all, chose to reconvert to Judaism. They were joined by a greater number of Jews compelled to leave Spain in 1492 when the Spanish monarchs Ferdinand and Isabel, after the defeat of the Moors, decided that there would be no place for the 150,000 Jews in Catholic Spain.

By an eerie coincidence Christopher Columbus, whose voyage was destined to discover a new "haven" for Spanish Jewry, was also scheduled to leave Spain the first day of August 1492. The admiral was forced to use the port of Palos because the more convenient port of Cadiz was too crowded with hapless Jews praying that the expulsion order would be rescinded. (We shall have more to say regarding the strange interaction between Columbus and the Jews presently.) One of the many havens which these Jews found was Recife in Brazil. Under tolerant Dutch rule the original marranos, now joined by Jews who had not converted, became prosperous. But in January 1654, Recife was recaptured by the Portuguese, and the Jews were again compelled to flee for their lives. It was a remnant of this community which, after much misadventure, sailed into the spacious harbor of the Dutch colony of "Nieuw Amsterdam" to establish the first Jewish community of appreciable size in North America.

The second and latter source of Jewish immigration originated in Eastern Europe, when the Polish refuge originally established by Boleslav in 1246 and extended by Cassimir in 1334 disintegrated as a result of internal and external pressure. Under the tolerant conditions provided by these two early Polish kings, the Jewish community prospered and developed perhaps the most intense Jewish identity in Jewish history. Its faint echoes still nurture the traditional branch of Judaism today. After the Polish haven evolved into a Polish hell, the Jews began an east–west migration that continued for more than three centuries. In times gone by, when the religious spirit informed life, Jewish historians saw a divine hand in the fact that precisely at the juncture when the situation became untenable, first in Spain, then in Poland, new havens were discovered and developed where Jewish energies and talents could find full expression.

Historians of similar mystical inclinations have also made much of the Jewish origins of Christopher Columbus. They were convinced by dint of the fragmentary evidence available that Columbus was in fact a *marrano* who, for practical reasons, expended considerable energy in concealing that fact. These historians, among whom there are some well-known non-Jews, demonstrate that the discoverer had many Jewish friends and sponsors; one has suggested that he "looked" Jewish, while another has discovered that the name Colombo is one traditionally borne by *marranos*. One historian has traced Columbus's ancestry to a *marrano* family who fled to Genoa in the fourteenth century, and another finds the family resettled in Aragon. Some have pointed to the frequency of biblical metaphor in his correspondence, while others more specifically point to the mysterious Hebrew letters *beth* and *hai* which preface correspondence to his son. They could stand for *Baruch hashem*, "Blessed be the name," which was customarily used as a greeting among Jews. Some have pointed to the disproportionate number of Jews and marranos, six in all, distributed among the crews of his three ships. For some the evidence is so abundant that there seems hardly any doubt that Columbus was a *marrano*.* But although one can accept that fact without much difficulty, the reason why so many have been so anxious to establish it is more open to question. It makes precious little difference what the original faith of Columbus was. For many, claiming Columbus as their own, or insisting that the interpreter—who was the first European to set foot in the New World—was Jewish, is a form of apologetics. It would be a harmless exercise of group pride were it not for the fact that such claims betray group insecurity and often conceal the fuller rendition of history because they pose the wrong historical question. Concealed by the Columbus question is the fact that Columbus's voyage would probably not have taken place with-

*See especially M. Kayserling, Samuel E. Morison, Cecil Roth and Salvador de Madariaga in the Bibliography at the end of this chapter.

out the influence and money of his marrano backers. The relationship of the second voyage to Jewish capital is more direct, since it is generally believed that it was financed from confiscated Jewish property, including the sale of precious religious objects. To put to rest the myth that Queen Isabel pawned her royal jewels to provide Columbus with the necessary money, the historian Herbert Adams observed that "not jewels but Jews were the real financial basis for the first expedition of Columbus."

The voyages of discovery that ultimately brought European "explorers" and settlement to all corners of the known world were an outgrowth of the commercial revolution, a period of business and trade expansion in which Jews played an important role. Having been excluded from the corporations comprising the social and commercial life of feudal Europe, Jews were able to go beyond the pervading localism and primary agricultural activity to interregional and even international trade. It is not surprising that Jews were prominent in developing basic instruments of banking and credit important for business life. The network of relatives and coreligionists, extended throughout the known world, was a formidable asset in carrying commerce forward. "They are like pegs and nails in a great bridge," noted one historian, "which though they are little valued in themselves are absolutely necessary to keep the whole frame together . . ."

Jews also contributed notably to the development and the transmission of the nautical technology that made the voyage of Columbus possible. They sometimes acted as bridges to carry these instruments, developed originally by the Greeks and further by the Arabs, to the Christian world. The astrolabe and the quadrant, sometimes called the *quadracus Judaicus*, are good examples of the transmission process. The crucial art of map making was heavily influenced by Jewish specialists. The most renowned of the "map Jews" were Abraham Cresques of Palma and his son Jehuda. The most comprehensive compilation of geographical data, the *Catalan Atlas*, was translated into Latin by the elder Cresques. Columbus carried on his first voyage the *Almanac Perpetuum*, an indispensable guide to the geography of the known world. It was compiled by the marrano Abraham Zacuto and translated from the Hebrew by his star pupil, Joseph Vecinho. Much of the data in these almanacs were gleaned from the memoirs of the Jewish *radanites*, world travelers and traders such as Benjamin of Tudela, Petachia of Regensburg, and Jacob Ben Nathaniel la Cohen. Thus Jews, among others, were in a position to contribute to the preconditions for voyages of discovery, of which the Columbus journey to the New World was merely one.

It is, however, in the remarkable group of immigrants from the Sephardic and Ashkenazic world that we find the most specific and direct contribution to the development of the distinctive American–Jewish relationship. The Colonial period is nearly equal in length to what followed; ample time to develop the tolerant precedents in the religious sphere that subsequently governed American behavior. The contrast between the treatment of Jews in the Old World and in the colonies startled a Hessian soldier, who wrote back to his kin in Germany that "the Jews have their own commerce and trade and are not identifiable because of their beards as is the case with the Jews who live among us." Other observers remarked on the frequency of intermarriage between Jews and gentiles. One historian places the rate at 10 percent. Still others wondered about the general acceptability of Jews and the fact that many were held in high esteem and frequently appointed to offices of high responsibility. But that general benevolence was far truer at the end of the Colonial period than it was at the beginning.

When the Jewish refugees arrived in September 1654, they were not received with open arms. They were, in fact, not "received" at all, since the power establishment did all it could to get them to move on. Part of that unfriendliness contains a special paradox which marks much of early American history. Although the search for a religious haven had brought many settlers to the New World, those settlers were not tolerant folk. They wanted religious liberty for themselves but not for others. Some, like Peter Stuyvesant, the governor of the colony, and his advisors, harbored a specific and quite common animus against Jews. They were anti-Semites and shared all the stereotypes generally believed about Jews: underhanded and overly shrewd in business dealings, separatist, money-hungry, and, of course, the omnipresent belief that Jews killed Christ. In his letter to the Amsterdam chamber of deputies of the Dutch West India Company, Stuyvesant complained not only of Jewish "usury and deceitful trading" but additionally requested that "the deceitful race—such hateful enemies and blasphemers of the name of Christ—be not allowed to further infect and trouble this new colony . . . " But despite the placing of commercial and religious restrictions on them, the Jews did not leave. Instead, they turned to the West India Company and to their coreligionists in Amsterdam for support, which was forthcoming. Gradually they gained the right to participate in the lucrative fur trade with the Indians in the Fort Orange area (present-day Albany). Eventually they were permitted to open retail and wholesale businesses, to practice crafts, and finally to stand "watch and ward" rather than paying an extra tax for not standing it. For a long time prayer services were conducted in private quarters but eventually the small Jewish community was permitted to purchase its own cemetery plot and practice other facets of its faith openly. Things improved more rapidly after England took over the colony in 1664 and renamed the now sizable town New York. The process of granting Jews full citizenship rights was begun. By the time the German mercenary noted how well Jews were treated in the colonies, they had gained almost the full complement of rights as citizens. The Revolution would further the process. How did a situation so rare that it existed nowhere else in the Western world come to prevail in America?

Only a small part of the religious and general toleration of Jews can be attributed to a specific Jewish struggle to win their rights. When Stuyvesant wanted to cast them out of New Amsterdam, the Jewish community, as a matter of course, appealed to the parent company in Amsterdam. There were some Jewish stockholders in that company who could be relied upon to take up the cause of their religious brethren. Indeed, they reminded the board of directors of the loyalty of the Jews to the Dutch cause in Brazil. There was proof in the loss not only of their fortunes but, in some cases, of their lives. The company reluctantly ordered Stuyvesant to permit the Jews to stay, provided that they would never become a liability to the company. The honoring of that solemn pledge is considered the beginning of the amazing Jewish self-help network which has ever since been a hallmark of the Jewish community.

Yet another part of the attitude of acceptance is related to the character of Sephardic Jewry, which, over the centuries, had learned to adopt practical strategies for living within Christian communities. Sephardic Jews were far less separatist than Ashkenazic Jews, somewhat less restricted by *halakah* (Jewish law), and certainly less dissident than other sects who also found haven in America. They did not shake or quake, they did not predict the end of the world, and, most important, they formed a relatively inconspicuous minority, of less than 3,000 by 1775. Indeed, Stuyvesant may have disliked Jews, but he despised Quakers and Catholics and had little use for the Congregationalists who had settled in the Massachusetts Bay colony. In the seething cauldron of religious animosity the situation of the Jews was anomalous. The existence of dissident Christian groups may actually have served as a deflector of animosity which might otherwise have been directed against Jews. Given a society in which religion was taken so seriously, it proved impossible for the larger, more powerful organized churches, the Episcopalians in New York or the Congregationalists in Massachusetts, to impose their stamp upon the whole by establishing a national church in America. Fortunately for minority religions like Judaism, Protestantism had a built-in penchant for fragmentation, which argued against centralist organization and in favor of denominationalism. The Congregationalists, who might have become *the* church, were strongly congregation centered; power resided in the local religious congregation. The Episcopalians were hierarchically organized but were linked in the public mind with the unpopular ruling caste of England. Neither church was acceptable to the bevy of religious sects that sprouted in the free soil of America. For those anxious to coerce religious uniformity, geography, the existence of vast empty spaces, posed a nearly insurmountable problem. A dissident sect could simply remove itself to free territory. All students of American history are familiar with the role of religious dissidence in founding the states of Rhode Island and Utah. The pluralism and plasticity of American culture gave Jews some breathing space. More important still for the growth of toleration may have been the impact of the free-reigning commercial spirit. Capitalism released a libertarian spirit in which religion became less important. The new priority was for showing profit on the ledger. Thus, when the Episcopal church of Virginia sought a charter for William and Mary College in 1691, it gave as its purpose the desire to save souls. The reply received from the Lords of the Treasury in London is instructive: "Souls, damn your souls; make tobacco." That was after all the first order of business and the reason why the colony of Jamestown was founded.

The prevalence of religious fanaticism could not long endure in such an atmosphere. Indeed, by the mid-eighteenth century, we hear complaints by ministers and other upholders of public order of the general waning of enthusiasm for religion and of downright sinful behavior among the young. Of course, even Stuyvesant had made such complaints; it may be that for the moral athlete, one could simply not be righteous and pious enough. What in fact may have happened is a general loss of the influence of the churches, not because people turned to atheism, but because in modernity the religious sensibility becomes internalized and privatized. Thinkers like Jefferson, who did so much to guarantee religious liberty in Virginia and in the young republic, considered themselves deists. That meant that they held a generalized abstracted belief in a supreme being or spirit but rejected the role of an institutional church as an exclusive conduit for the "word of the Lord." Such leaders were perceptive enough to realize that religious fanaticism was a luxury that the delicate fabric and security of colonial society could ill afford. It threatened chaos and even civil war by dividing the polity into "ins" and "outs." When the slightest trespass became a matter of sin, compromise—which was imperative in view of the variegated colonial society—became impossible and society was laid open to its internal and external enemies.

Finally, we need to say a word about the peculiar relationship of Jews to the American Puritans and to the Protestant reformation generally. Puritanism contains one of the keys to the comparative religious well-being Jews have experienced in America. When we call someone a Puritan today we mean to imply a certain restrictive attitude to human sexuality. There is little consensus among contemporary historians that Puritans in the Bay Colony were actually "puritan" in *that* sense. Court records which have come down to us indicate that they were actually a fairly earthy group. The impression that Puritans were otherwise probably stems from their extreme religious passion, which we naturally associate with sexual restriction and apprehension regarding "sin." The very evidence of such a direct influence in our language is but one sign that of all the fundamentalist Protestant sects which dot the American religious landscape, the influence of Puritanism on the national character was most powerful and sustained. It can be noted today not only in a continued passion for revealed religion among the "moral majority," but also in the attitude towards business success, towards work, and especially towards Jews, the "people of the book."

Much of the ambivalent attitude which American society traditionally has felt towards its Jewish community finds its roots in the posture of the colonial Puritans towards the "Israelites." The Puritans frankly admired the biblical variety of Jew, so much so that the Old Testament could serve as a kind of directory to their social and political organization as well as to their theology. The Puritans considered themselves the real Israelites and their Bay colony as the "New Jerusalem." The existence of real Hebrews in the colonies who little resembled the patriarchs in the Old Testament might serve as a disturbing fact. But since there were few Jews settled in Connecticut or Massachusetts, there was in fact little contact between the two groups. It would have been difficult for "outsiders" to live in the scattered Puritan settlements, since they were governed along theocratic lines by and for the members of the religious corporation. Yet the Puritans were in love with things Hebrew: the names of the children and their towns were drawn from the

Bible; they even had a desire to master Hebrew, and had Hebrew printer's letters cast in order to produce Biblical passages in the original Hebrew. Like many other fundamentalist sects, the Puritans were convinced that the American Indians were the ten lost tribes of Israel. They spent much energy trying to reconvert them. Those who traveled through the Bay Colony could note that its place names read like a Biblical atlas. The logo of Harvard, which was established to train ministers for the church, was written in Hebrew (as was that of Yale) and among the first theses delivered, titled in Latin, was "Hebrew Is the Mother Tongue." (Another was on the problem of whether Hebrew consonants and vowels were of equal age.) The *Bay Psalms Book*, the major prayer book in Puritan congregations, was a translation of the Hebrew *Book of Psalms*. Naturally, Puritans viewed the Jews they encountered in the colonies through the prism of the Old Testament. There must have been much disappointment when they discovered that contemporary Jews bore little resemblance to those described in the Scriptures. But primarily the Puritans were Christians, who believed that the Israelites had gone astray and were being punished for their sins. Above all else, they wanted to convert the Jews, since they believed that the second coming of Christ would not occur until such a conversion had taken place. He would not come until all the sheep which had strayed from the flock were together to receive the shepherd. It reinforced their sense that they were the real Hebrews, living by the terms of the covenant. When they succeeded in conversion, as with Judah Monis, the first Hebrew grammarian at Harvard, nothing exceeded their joy.

The love–hate tension could be felt in almost every Protestant denomination, but few were as Hebraic as the Puritans. It was that strain which worked itself deeply into the American national consciousness, where one can still observe its vitality. The proto-Zionism of some fundamentalist Protestant sects makes them militantly pro-Israel. Of course, there are also mainline Protestant groups gathered in the National Council of Churches who have been anything but pro-Israel. The real residual effect of Puritan Hebraism may involve something we might call the Herbergian phenomenon. Some time ago a religious sociologist, Will Herberg, wrote an insightful little book called *Protestant, Catholic, Jew* (1960), in which he noted the curious fact that whereas Jews formed (at the time) slightly more than 3 percent of the population, they were nevertheless considered and treated as though they were one of the three major religious groups in America. From that triangulation of the American religious enterprise, prestige and influence far beyond the Jewish proportion of the population accrued to Judaism. There seems little doubt that in some measure that division stems from the Protestant precedent of viewing the Hebraic content of their own religions as enormously important. That was especially prevalent in the Puritan church.

It was undoubtedly instrumental in establishing the theoretic and legal framework for religious liberty. It was a factor that enabled Jefferson and Madison to include religious liberty, first in the constitution of Virginia and then in the constitution of the United States. It is embodied there in two places: Article VI, Clause 3, which states, "No religious test shall be required as a qualification to any office or public trust under the United States," and the First Amendment, which forbids Congress to establish a church or to prohibit the free exercise of religion. Those legal provisions and the ideology behind them made America into the most secularized society. For Jews, that mandated separation of church and state was thought to be a boon, but it was also to become a problem—as we shall see in the final chapter.

To a man who does not have enough to eat, religious liberty is of little avail. How a group earns its bread is a crucial determinant not only of its condition but of its consciousness: how it thinks, and about what it thinks. In many cases, although strange to say not in the case of American Jewry, it can even tell the historian why a group behaves a certain way politically. In a word, a group's economic activity is a sure fingerprint to discover its identity. We shall see that just as individual identities develop within characteristic structures, so does the identity of the group. In some sense the economic activity of contemporary American Jewry strongly resembles that of the founding Sephardic group in the colonial economy.

The first such parallel we might call attention to is that, much like contemporary Jewry, the Jews of colonial times played an economic role out of all proportion to their small numbers. Contemporary American Jewry has played an important role in small business and in the professions, especially in medicine and law. Sometimes the two separate areas are combined, according to Nathan Glazer and Daniel Moynihan, in their classic work *Beyond the Melting Pot* (1963). They identify a new Jewish group they call "egghead millionaires" because they have made their fortunes by combining traditional business acumen with a professional skill like chemistry or engineering. That accounts for the many small Jewish firms which early could be found in the plastics manufacturing business or air conditioning. Similarly, colonial Jewry cast its lot with the nascent commercial and urban sector of colonial society when the overwhelming character of that economy and society was agricultural and rural. They lived and did business in the five cities—actually large towns—of the eastern seaboard, while the majority of Americans lived in the countryside. The urban/urbane character of American Jewry goes back to the early beginnings and so does their uncanny ability to choose that area of the economy which would thrive. By the end of the nineteenth century it would be commerce and industry that reigned supreme, and the nation would become urbanized. We see in both groups a talent for commercial pioneering. The writer Stephen Birmingham has made the development of Jewish commercial elites the theme of two popular books, *Our Crowd* (1967) and *The Grandees* (1971). Undoubtedly some author has by this time realized that the story of the third commercial elite, stemming from the migration of Eastern Jews, is no less remarkable. If that book is ever published, it will complete the popularization of the Jewish commercial success story, which began with the Jews of colonial America.

At the top of the pyramid of Jewish commercial success in the colonial world stood a small group of Jewish merchants involved in ocean and coastal commerce. Under the policy of mercantilism, such commerce was generally forbidden to all. The Navigation Laws, moreover, specifically prohibited Jews from such trading. Yet after the French and Indian War (1763) the British Board of Trade, for good reason, chose to close its eyes to the thriving "triangular" trade which had begun to develop. The family and "religio–ethnic" connection with the Caribbean sugar economy, from which a prominent group of Jewish settlers hailed, gave them a special connection. That was the primary reason why Newport, a major colonial sea port, also became the hub of a thriving Jewish community. I call that special connection between the Caribbean and mainland Jewish communities the *Caribbean nexus*. It refers specifically to the natural advantage the Jewish merchants of Newport and other communities had in conducting ocean commerce. The Caribbean mainland connection was not only the last leg of the "triangular" trade, which included the west coast of Africa and the infamous "middle passage" bringing slaves to the West Indies, it also gave Jewish merchants the commercial intelligence regarding market conditions, so that they could make informed business decisions. Furthermore, it served as a kind of natural market and, in some rare instances, as a source of needed risk capital.

The business career of Aron Lopez, probably the most successful of the "merchant princes," gives some idea of how far reaching the activities of the Jewish merchants were and how risky and challenging commerce was in those early days. Lopez emigrated from his island home in the Caribbean to the city of Newport while still a young man. Social connections gave him entree to the group of prosperous merchants who led the community. He married the daughter of one of these merchants, Jacob Rivera, whose father was a marrano who reconverted to Judaism and went through the painful surgical procedure of adult circumcision. Lopez received credit from his well-established father-in-law and other creditors in the merchant group. It enabled him to become involved in various business ventures: shipbuilding, merchandising, garment manufacturing, spermacetti candle manufacture, privateering, ocean and coastal shipping, slave trading, and even the manufacture of chocolate. He quickly earned a nationwide reputation for his business activity. By 1764 we find him deeply involved in the lucrative slave trade. His ledger books from the 1770s show that he was importing from 250 to 300 slaves per year, to be sold at a handsome profit in the South—Charleston, S.C.—and the West Indies. In both places there were family connections to handle the details. Yet the path to success was far from smooth, and several times Lopez found himself bankrupt and unable to pay his debts. Ocean commerce was a risky business not only because ships were lost at sea via the vicissitudes of nature but also because of societal dangers such as piracy and war. Even if one negotiated these shoals successfully, there was always a good possibility that customers, like the Jamaican planters who bought the goods that Lopez sold, would fail to pay their bills. Despite his reputation, the "merchant prince" experienced some difficulty in getting citizenship rights. That meant that he was unprotected even by the rudimentary commercial law existing at the time. The revolution caught Lopez in a squeeze, as it did many merchants involved in ocean commerce. His first loyalty, naturally, was to his business investment, which required the good will of those who controlled the seas. He did not sign the anti-British "nonimportation agreement" and this gained him the ill will of the colonial patriots. When the war came, he recklessly plunged into the whaling business, investing in the purchase and supply of some 20 ships. When the British seized 5 of his ships, Lopez again faced the bleak prospect of having to declare bankruptcy. His career serves as a good illustration that the commerce which drew the capital and energy of Jewish merchants and often proved to be a lucrative business was at the same time far from a secure livelihood.

What was required most of all was skill, daring, and vision, qualities which Aron Lopez and the Jewish merchants of Newport seemed to possess in good measure. Professor Jacob Marcus, who has done extensive research on colonial Jewry, has called them "courageous enterprisers," suggesting not only the risks they took but the pioneering role they played in establishing American commerce. Jews were among the earliest groups in New Amsterdam to realize the possibilities of the fur trade with the Indians. Furs eventually became so important in the specie-starved colony that they became a substitute for currency. The orange-and-blue seal of New York State still features an Indian holding a beaver pelt. Jewish settlers also introduced viniculture in Georgia, pioneered the indigo-dye industry, and were among the first in the Caribbean to trade in precious gems. Less commendable was their role in developing the tobacco trade with Europe.

Research into the similar role Jews play today in opening up new business areas downplays the heroic element of this role. Jews become courageous enterprisers not because they have a need to test their courage but because they gravitate towards the nonpreempted areas of the economy from which they are not excluded. The pioneering role played by Jewish entrepreneurs in establishing the three major television networks occurred when the industry was a relatively minor enterprise that welcomed capital and managerial talent from any quarter. In colonial times, Jews often brought with them "industrial secrets," which had been passed down from father to son for many generations. That explains the pioneering Jewish role in crafts like tanning, wig making, the setting, cutting and appraising of precious stones, watch making, soap making, and dozens of other arts and crafts. Jews had been involved in these areas for centuries. Two such secrets played a crucial role in developing the Jewish economy of Newport. One was the making of castile soap and the other was the development of a new kind of candle, made of the less expensive spermacetti oil rather than tallow. That development led to the establishment of the spermacetti trust in 1761 and was a spin-off of the Jewish involvement in the whaling industry. Today a cheaper means of making candles does not sound like much of a discovery, but in colonial times it represented real progress.

No matter how ingenious or courageous the businessman, however, the fortunes of war and the passage of time bring declines. The revolution wrought havoc with shipping, since

Britain continued to control the seas. The decline of Newport was inevitable, and with it the 60 to 70 prominent Jewish families, too, passed into the anonymity of time.

We must not let Jewish activity in Newport overshadow other commercial activities conducted by Jews during this time. Most facets of colonial economic life had some Jewish representation. Perhaps the best model to use in trying to picture the economic role of Jews then, a model which in some degree is still applicable today, is that of a bridge. Jews played the role of connecting, or bridging, the core economy—the factories in the towns and cities along the eastern seaboard—with the peripheral, which can be thought of in either geographic or social terms. Jewish fur traders connected with the Indian culture for an exchange of goods, they traded with the sizable community of freedmen in the antebellum South, and also sold second-hand clothing to the plantation owners for their slaves. Jewish merchants and peddlers sold their goods along the remotest frontiers of the country. They served as bridges by bringing the amenities of the established civilization—clothes, toiletries, needles, thread, and bolts of gingham—and also news of society and politics. They brought back specie with which to purchase more stock. Occasionally these links to the interior became the basis of a larger wholesale business. One of the first firms to ship goods into the new Ohio territory near Fort Chartres was a Jewish consortium of merchants.

The Jewish merchandising network included many steps. It went from manufacturer or importer to wholesaler–jobber to retail merchant and finally to peddler. It could sprout branches: undoubtedly the frequency with which Jews acted as purveyors and suttlers for the military was directly related to their position in merchandising. During the French and Indian War Jews played the same role on both sides of the conflict. The network could also lead to profitable real estate investment, since the opportunity to spy out likely prospects presented itself in the peddler's travels. Typical was the business career of Joseph Simon, who began as a humble Indian trader, became a peddler and merchant, and finally joined the consortium of Trent,

Levy, and Frank. When the French and Indian War broke out in 1754, Simon joined another merchant, Alexander Lowery, a gentile, as a purveyor for the Continental army. He also did some privateering. By the end of the war in 1763, Simon had become a man of considerable wealth.

Yet the attainment of great fortunes was not typical of colonial Jewry. For the most part they remained a middling group, belonging neither to the richest nor the poorest stratum of the population. That characteristic, first noted in the colonial period, holds true to this day. American Jews may not only be the subgroup most intensely committed to achieving and living an urban middle-class life, they may be the oldest group in America to do so.

Of course not all Jews were businessmen. A good many, we cannot say precisely how many, found their life's calling in the professions. It would have been highly uncharacteristic if there were no Jewish doctors. A certain percentage were employed to meet the requirements of religious ritual. Rabbis were almost unknown, but there were *shochetim* (ritual slaughterers) and *mohelim* (circumcisers). There may have been a few Jewish farmers as well. For the most part, however, Jews were prominent in establishing a modern capitalistic business economy. They were well known in trading and commerce and in establishing the institutions of a capitalist economy. Jews were involved in setting up the New York Board of Stockholders, which was the precursor of the New York Stock Exchange. From the beginning, too, there existed a small number of Jewish private bankers and factors. One can note that what business captured the interest of Jews was determined by the region and time in which they lived. In South Carolina the prosperous Jewish community was composed of planters as well as merchants and traders. There were also Jewish slave traders in the South. We have already noted early Jewish involvement with the indigo, vine, silk-growing and tobacco industries. As the revolution approached, we hear of the Harmon Hendricks family, involved in copper mining. Hendricks, some of whose descendants are still active in the Jewish community today, built a copper rolling mill in Belleville, New Jersey. Later, the names of Sutro, Guggenheim, and Lewisohn were added to the list of Jews who had made their fortune in mining.

The early restrictions, imposed by Peter Stuyvesant, on Jews in the practice of crafts and in their activities as merchants could not endure. Then, as today, an efficient economy could not be reconciled with discrimination and restriction. Talent, commercial energy, capital, and people willing to risk had to be taken where they were found. The truth of the ledger, the statement of profit and loss, proved a far greater liberator of the Jewish creative spirit than even the principles of middle-class democracy. That, too, seems to be a precedent first observed in the colonial period which remains true in the twentieth century.

Finally, we want to learn something of the early roots of American Jewish political culture. (That is a technical term, referring to a group's political personality, the political principles it holds dear, and the assumptions it brings into the political arena.) Jewish political culture is particularly intriguing because Jews behave like no other subgroup on the American political scene. If they voted their pocketbooks they would be overwhelmingly in the Republican column. But since 1928 Jews have been among the staunchest supporters of the Democratic party, especially the welfare-state aspect of the party's program. They are hyperactive in the political process as party workers, avid voters, and generous political "fat cats." One researcher has referred to them as the "merchandisers" and "packagers" of American politics, because of the disproportionate number of Jewish pundits, media specialists, voting analysts, pollsters, and campaign organizers. And, of course, until recently there has been a perceptible liberal bias and an optimism about the American political system in the Jewish political personality. In a sense, Jews have been the ideal human material to make democracy work, politically involved, superbly informed, and confident in the practicality of the democratic process. American Jewry has known how to use that process; that is one of the keys to how it has maintained its influence despite the fact that the Jewish proportion of the population has declined. The foundation of that affirmative approach to the American political system and the secular humanitarian assumptions that characterize American Jewish political culture were set in place during these beginning years. The American Revolution is a seminal event in American Jewish history. Jews maintained a low political profile everywhere in the Western world before the eighteenth century. They were simply not considered part of political society. Their zealous support of the patriotic cause demonstrated an uncharacteristic political boldness, especially when contrasted to the opposition or indifference of most of their fellow colonists. That posture really reflects their welcoming the emancipation transaction, which promised to secure them full rights as citizens. In American Jewish history the Revolution and the promulgation of the Constitution after the critical period play the same role as does the Enlightenment and the French Revolution in the history of the Jews of Europe. It was the harbinger of the emancipation. Viewed in retrospect, the faith they possessed in the American Revolution was not misplaced, for, unlike later revolutions in the nineteenth- and twentieth-centuries, which Jews also supported, it did not betray its promise. Moreover, rather than Jewish support generating a stigma of political radicalism which would be used against them, the victory of the patriots encouraged Jews to feel that they belonged. That sense of being "present at the creation" has ever since enhanced the Jewish feeling of security and well-being in American society.

The specific Jewish contribution to the Whig victory need not occupy much of our attention. Let it be said that the small Jewish community produced its share of military heroes and, because it was involved in business and commerce, it was also able to contribute disproportionately in the complex financing and supplying of the patriotic cause. The name of Chaim Salomon, known by every American school child as the "financier" of the patriots, deserves some attention because it gives us a clue to the public image of the Jews. Salomon was one of several "broker Jews" who accepted the risk of selling Continental notes and acting as a broker for credit. It is not difficult to imagine that the makers of myths and heroes arrived at an understanding to give every ethnic group in America a stake in the birth of the nation. It would act as a binding force and give the various subgroups making up the citizenry proof of their legitimacy. Thus Polish–Americans received as their heroes General Kosciousko and Pulaski; German–Americans, Von Steuben; French–Americans, Lafayette; and Jewish–Americans, Chaim Salomon. (A more likely hero might have been Mordecai Sheftal of Georgia.) There are two interesting facets to the popularity of the Salomon story. The first is that the small Jewish community should have been granted a hero at all, and the second is the kind of "hero of commerce" that Salomon was.

Chaim Salomon, whose biography is an almost prototypical immigrant rags-to-riches story, was, in fact, a man of great talent, courage, and passion. When he arrived in New York from his native Lissa, Poland, in 1775, he was already 35 years old and had had considerable small-business experience in Europe. But once here, he was compelled to start again as a humble peddler, selling notions to continental soldiers stationed along New York's northern frontier with Canada. His ardent support of the Whig side caused the British to arrest and imprison him when they occupied New York City. He was thought to be a spy, or at least an agitator for the patriot cause. The intercession of a Hessian officer who served as quartermaster in the city, and who may himself have been Jewish, freed him. Salomon was released in the hope that he would use his business talents for the British occupiers. It seems that for a time, that is precisely what he did. But his loyalty remained with the patriotic side. Secretly he continued to act as an agent for the patriotic cause, and when, in 1778, the situation in New York became truly precarious, he fled to Philadelphia, leaving his beloved wife and child behind in the city. Despite the war and his dire personal situation Salomon apparently had sufficient energy and freedom to attain some affluence and a reputation as a keen businessman. His ability to speak several languages and his good connections made him a natural for appointment as financial agent for the French consul–general. From there he became treasurer of the French army in the colonies. It was a position of the highest rank, since France had become a cobelligerent in the fight against Britain. At the same time he acted as a broker for continental bills of credit. More accurately he was employed by Robert Morris, superintendent of finance for the Continental Congress, to attain credit from friendly sources. Considering the bankrupt state of the continental treasure it was a thankless task. Salomon, probably the best known of these "bill brokers," may have discounted as much as $200,000 worth of continental notes, no small feat when the dim prospect of redeeming them is considered.

Salomon's personal generosity became apparent in 1782, when he extended credit to James Madison and Edmund Randolph of Virginia while both served as delegates to the Continental Congress. He refused to accept interest for the service: "I have for some time past been a pensioner in the favor of Haym Salomon, A Jew broker," wrote Madison to a friend, "the kindness of our little friend in Front Street, near the coffee house is a fund which will preserve me from extremities, but I never resort to it without great mortification, as he obstinately rejects all recompense." Salomon was also very generous to Jewish causes. He helped finance the construction of Philadelphia's first synagogue, Mikveh Israel. Withal, by today's standards Salomon was not a wealthy man at the time of his death. His estate is rumored to have contained a small fortune in unredeemed credit notes. The claim of his family for compensation was never recognized by the newly established federal government. Nor was Salomon the only Jew who lost money because of zeal for the patriotic cause. Included in that list would be Manuel Josephson, Mordecai Sheftal, Moses Hays, Isaac Moses, David Franks, and many lesser figures. It was probably the promotional activities of Salomon's son that made Salomon *the* Jewish hero of the patriotic cause.

The story of the Jewish "hero" Chaim Salomon deserves our special attention, not only because it is part of Jewish history but also because by looking at a group's "hero" the historian can learn a great deal about the image of the group. The nature of the hero linked to the Jewish community was not a man courageous and self-possessed on the field of battle, but a money lender, who, in Christian imagery, had to be "chased out of the Temple." That was precisely the connotation at the close of the nineteenth-century, when the populists, convinced that farmers were being squeezed by a deflationary cycle manipulated by Jewish bankers, conjured up such images. It has remained part of the anti-Semitic imagination ever since. Ultimately we must consider whether the hero represented by Chaim Salomon, that of a Jewish money lender, reinforced a negative Jewish stereotype. Whatever the case, the Chaim Salomon image tells us something about what Jews were thought to be. It has the ambivalence present in so much of the public imaginings regarding Jews. Salomon was a "hero" who financed the Revolution but could also be seen as "Shylock."

Finally, we must get back to searching out the roots of contemporary Jewish political culture in the American Revolution. It would have been highly unlikely for a disputatious people like the Jews to be of a unanimous opinion on anything, much less on a wrenching war—which was fought as much, according to the historian Carl Becker, about home rule as about who should rule at home. Jews were represented in the Tory or Loyalist camp as well as in that of the patriots. Particularly prominent were the David Frank family in Philadelphia and Isaac Hart of Newport. The Jewish community of Montreal remained largely loyal to the crown, and when Benjamin Seixas led the Jewish community of New York City away from the British occupation a goodly number of the congregants chose to remain behind. According to one diary, some of these, including women, were not at all shy about showering favors on Hessian mercenaries, some of whom were also Jewish. But most Jews were in favor of the break with Britain. They were more whiggish than other subcultures in the colonies.

One might reason that this was the case because, as Sephardic Jews stemming from the Iberian peninsula, they felt no particular loyalty to the mother country. But that would also have been true for the Swedish and French minorities. Moreover, those who took up arms against England were predominantly of English stock, who insisted that they were fighting for their "rights as Englishmen." Neither could the predominance of merchants among the Jews account for their Whig proclivities. Despite the restrictions of the Greenville and Townshend programs, not all merchants favored breaking ties with the mother country. Like Aaron Lopez, there were many who dreaded the costly disruption of commerce that a break in the ties with England would entail.

The uncharacteristic conspicuousness of Jews in supporting the American and French revolutions was directly related to the promise these revolutions held for suppressed groups like the Jews. It was the promise of the establishment of a modern secular nation state, without an established religion and with a full complement of political and civil rights for all citizens. It was the promise of a new society in which Jewish energies and talents would be allowed full play, a free society where religious preferences would be considered private matters. The documents embodying that hope were the Declaration of Independence, the American Constitution, and the French Declaration of the Rights of Man. What captured Jewish loyalty everywhere was the promise of the emancipation. The nation to extend it first, and one that never reneged, was the small, fragile, new republic in the New World. No one expressed the reason for Jewish support of the patriotic cause more eloquently than Benjamin Nones, a Jewish war hero, who was responding to a scurrilous attack on him in the Federalist *Gazette of the United States*, a newspaper with strong antidemocratic convictions:

> In the history of the Jews are contained the earliest warnings against kingly government, as anyone may know who has read the fable of Abimeleck or the exhortations of Samuel . . . I am a Jew, and if for no other reason I am a Republican . . . In the monarchies of Europe we are hunted from society, stigmatized as unworthy of common civility, thrust out as it were, from the converse of men, objects of mockery and insult . . . the butts of vulgar wit and low buffoonery. Among nations of Europe we are inhabitants everywhere but citizens nowhere *unless in Republics* . . . How then can a Jew but be a Republican?

Viewing the contrast between their condition in America and

that of their coreligionists in Europe, the majority of Jews in colonial America came to the same conclusion. So important were these principles that Jews overwhelmingly supported Jefferson, the physiocrat who saw America's future in agricultural terms, over Alexander Hamilton, whose financial program furthered the interest of the very areas of the economy with which Jews were associated—the cities and commerce. That priority of the ideological over the material has characterized Jewish political culture ever since. There is no other constituency in American politics with such a broad approach to politics. Jewish political culture has, beginning from the period of the Revolution, transcended narrow group interest. That is its most singular characteristic.

The revolution held out the hope to Jews of having community rather than being pariahs. That they had selected wisely became evident after the revolution, as state after state rewrote its constitution, liberalized the franchise, and removed religious tests for voting and holding office. As early as 1787 the Northwest Ordinance already contained a provision for religious liberty, free public education, and the prohibition of slavery. The new and reworked state charters followed suit, gradually extending the area of citizen's rights. One historian has noted that the American Constitution is similar in significance to the decree by which the Emperor Caracalla granted citizenship to all free men in the Roman Empire in 212 C.E. American Jewry became the first free and equal Jewry in the modern era, and, unlike the situation in Europe, that position was never destroyed. It is that fact which makes the American Jewish diaspora and the test of Jewish survival in it so startlingly different.

Bibliography

Birmingham, S. *The Grandees: America's Sephardic Elite.* New York: 1971.
Chyet, S. *Lopez of Newport: Colonial American Merchant.* Detroit: 1970.
De Madariaga, S. *Christopher Columbus* New York: 1940.
Grinstein, H. S., *The Rise of the Jewish Community of New York, 1654–1860.* Philadelphia: 1945.

Kayserling, M. *Christopher Columbus and the Participation of the Jews in the Spanish and Portuguese Discoveries* New York: 1968.

Levanon, Y. *The Jewish Travellers in the Twelfth Century.* Winnipeg: 1982.

Marcus, J. R., *The Colonial American Jew, 1492–1776*, 3 vols. Detroit: 1970.

Morison, S.E. *Admiral of the Ocean Seas: A Life of Christopher Columbus.* Boston: 1942.

Rosenbloom, J. R. *A Bibliographical Dictionary of Early American Jewry.* Lexington: 1960.

Roth, C. *Personalities and Events in Jewish History.* Philadelphia: 1953.

Wolf, E., and Whiteman, J. *The History of the Jews of Philadelphia from Colonial Times to the Age of Jackson.* Philadelphia: 1957.

CHAPTER II

The Success Story of
German Jews in America

THE second period of American Jewish history stretches from 1841 to about 1920 and was dominated by German Jews who settled in America. The arrival of approximately a quarter of a million Jewish immigrants before 1890 altered the character of the Sephardic Jewish community which had dominated the first period of American Jewish history. The religious ritual and the language became German Jewish. The immigrants infused not only energy and talent but an awareness of the challenge the emancipation process posed to the American Jewish community. Most important, the German Jewish migration assured the biological continuance of American Jewry, whose proportion of the general population had been declining.

But before we discover who these Jews were and why so many chose to uproot themselves and make their way to a new and unknown land, we need to scrutinize the periodization scheme first presented by Professor Jacob R. Marcus, one of the important founders of this discipline. Marcus sees the period of German Jewish dominance ending in 1920, when it is succeeded by an Americanization period marked by a fusion between Eastern and Central European Jewish cultures. That scheme unfortunately omits a period in which the descendants of Eastern European Jewry set the tone. Marcus undoubtedly extends the period of German Jewish dominance to a relatively late date despite the overwhelming numerical dominance of the new Eastern European immigrant, because the German Jewish stewards, men like Jacob Schiff and Louis Marshall and the organizations they founded, continued to exercise considerable, perhaps primary, influence in Jewish affairs. Their power was based not only on their great personal fortunes, which they generously used to subsidize Jewish affairs, but the fact that they possessed a greater at-homeness in America and a familiarity with its culture and values. That gave them a certain status among the "greener," more recent arrivals, who were not yet able to muster the confidence and financial resources to make their weight felt. Nevertheless, if the American Jewish Congress movement and the numerous philanthropic and social organizations are any indication, Eastern Jews were entering the arena by the turn of the century and there would be those who argue that the period of German Jewish dominance ends in 1890 or 1900 and that thereafter there existed two separate Jewish communities, linked by mutual need, to be sure, but also separated by the gulf of culture, class, and contrasting ways of coming to terms with their Jewishness. Practical considerations compel the historian to be precise in his periodization scheme, but in fact things are not really that neat in history. Things rarely simply end in a given year. There is, for example, an echo of the German Jewish migration of the nineteenth century in the 1930s, when Jewish refugees from Nazi Germany sought a haven in America. That migration lasted less than a decade and was of relatively small size. Its impact on America and American Jewry, however, was formidable, and requires us to make some observations about it.

To call these migrants German is technically a misnomer. In the early decades of the nineteenth century the majority came from what was called after 1871 the German reich. But that was merely one segment. There were others who came from Posen, Vienna, and other parts of the Austro–Hungarian empire, and also some who stemmed from Alsace. Actually, we are speaking about Jews who came from that part of Central Europe where Jewish communities took their cues from German culture. That meant that they spoke German as either a first or second language, admired and often studied German cultural heroes, such as Goethe or Heine, and generally looked hopefully on the prospect of continued emancipation. From the Jewish perspective it was a cultural energy field anchored in three cities—Berlin, Vienna, and Budapest—where there was a strong Jewish input into a developing cosmopolitan culture. It was these cities that would later produce major figures like Freud and Herzl. The remarkable effervescence of a Jewish culture in America with a distinct Germanic bent should come as no surprise to the reader. Portents of its brilliance were already in evidence in nineteenth-century Europe.

It is always difficult to determine why a group of people chooses to undergo the unsettling experience of uprooting and transplanting itself in an alien land. Immigration is not a comfortable process, especially for people well settled and advanced in years. Specialists in the field have come to speak of the "sacrifice" generation, which refers to the fact that the generation undergoing the actual process of transplantation never quite succeeds in living at ease in the new environment. In examining immigration motivation, historians speak of pushes—conditions that force certain groups to move from their native homes—and pulls—conditions that pull them to a new haven, like America. For the German Jewish immigrants these pushes are not difficult to identify. If one were compelled to focus on a single factor, it would be the loss of hope felt by many younger Jews at the turn of events. Those hopes were raised by the promise of emancipation, held out first in the American Revolution, then in the French Revolution. They were dashed by the defeat of Napolean in 1815. That defeat was followed by the Restoration, an attempt to get things back to the way they had been before the French Revolution had opened the floodgates to unwelcome change. It is, of course, impossible to set the clock back completely; but, as far as the Jews were concerned, the German principalities spared no effort to do so. Previously granted citizenship rights were withdrawn, special taxes were reimposed, membership in craft and merchant guilds was restricted, and in many cases even travel by Jews from town to town was hampered. The Jews were pushed deeper into their isolation; once again they were pariahs condemned to live in ghettos. Anti-Semitic riots occurred in cities with visible Jewish aggregations like Würzburg, Frankfurt, Hamburg, and many others. In August 1819, students chanting the ancient crusaders' cry of *"Hep, Hep"* sacked the Jewish quarter of Würzburg, one of the oldest Jewish communities in Germany. In the Bavarian Diet, cries of "Jews get out" could be heard. These anti-Semitic excesses were reinforced and perhaps triggered by a noticeable deterioration of the economic base on which Jews supported themselves in the smaller towns where many Jews lived. They were gradually compelled to leave these towns and to seek a livelihood in larger cities. The earliest group of German Jewish immigrants to America was drawn from this rural small-town population. Later, the failure of the revolution of 1848 extinguished the last hope for improvement. When Leo Kompert, the Viennese Jewish novelist and community leader, organized his "On to America" movement, many Jews were ready to join him. They were convinced that any place offered more hope than where they were. The second type of Jewish immigrant was a little better established, and made up a large part of this post-1840 immigration wave.

Such were the conditions pushing many Jews out of Germany. But why did men like Leo Kumpert and Leopold Zunz, a founder of the renowned *Wissenschaft* movement, turn to distant America for succor and a haven? There are several very good reasons, not the least important of which is that America seemed willing to welcome these immigrants. Mordecai Noah, a founder of Tammany Hall in New York and a major American Jewish political figure, responded positively to Zunz's request for information, although he was also candid in stating his preference for monied Jews. No such preference was expressed by the Reverend W. D. Robinson who, influenced by a literal reading of the Scriptures, viewed Jews (the children of Israel) as an enormous human asset for populating the empty spaces along the frontier. Jews would be settled along the banks of the Mississippi, as they once had been along the banks of the Jordan. Perhaps most important as a pulling force was the image of America as a land of openness and opportunity, especially strong among the underclass of Europe. From its inception, the dream of America had captured the imagination of Europe's poor and declassed, of which the Jews were one element. Not only Jews dreamed of coming to America: they were, in fact, only a small portion of a large wave of immigration from Central Europe. But a much greater proportion of Jews felt the urge to leave, a reminder of how hostile Gentile Europe had become to Jews.

That image of America, persistent today even in countries where it has been strenuously denied, grew naturally out of the knowledge that things were better for common people in the New World. There was the possibility of lifting oneself up by one's bootstraps. In case Europeans forgot about the opportunities in America, there was the "America letter" and the advertising for settlers by shipping and railroad companies and even by territorial legislatures anxious to increase their populations so that they might reach the statehood stage of their development. The "America letter" received by European relatives from the new immigrants drew a rosy picture of conditions in the New World. Many immigrants undoubtedly felt a need to exaggerate the bounty of the new land of their choice, if only to justify the decision they had made to uproot themselves. The resultant picture often bore only a remote connection with reality. Thousands of readers read these letters in the ethnic press. Not only did they raise the hope that the answer to their plight was emigration, but they often contained the necessary "how to" information: what to take along, how much money was required for passage, travel schedules, employment possibilities, points of danger—all of which insecure potential immigrants needed to know before they could embark on such a journey.

In the case of the Jewish immigration, the reasons given by historians do not ring true as far as personal motivation is concerned. They are too abstract, and human behavior is not based on abstractions. Religious persecution, often cited as a major reason for Jewish immigration, served primarily as a background factor. When questioned, immigrants spoke of a relative whom they could count on to see them through the process of resettling, a personal connection rather than abstractions like economic dislocation or religious persecution. It is the possibility of a job or of learning a trade, an unhappy love affair or the prospect of finding a suitable marriage partner, impending draft into the military service, or simply a desire for a new start, which are the human reasons behind emigration. They can remain forever latent if one does not find a relative or friend, willing or even unwilling, to temporarily act as a host until one can "get on one's feet."

What happened when the immigrants discovered the yawning gap between the idealized image of America that they had imagined and the reality? The ability to match the two is perhaps the core psychological problem in immigrant adjustment. The talent for doing so varied from immigrant to immigrant, depending on the emotional stamina each brought to the task. Abraham Kahan, who arrived in New York, from a small town in Bavaria in 1842, predictably found the big city a little overwhelming. "I enjoyed the first sight of the city," he wrote in his diary, "but as I went through the streets to look for my brother, I did not feel so very well. This confusion, this wild running around of all the people, the hundreds of chaises, carriages and carts, this noise can hardly be described . . . my head began to swim" New York City has not, after all, changed that much, but Kahan, or any immigrant coming from a rural area, might have experienced the same kind of emotional turmoil on first visiting a city in his native country. Finally, it was the strange behavior of the natives that troubled Kahan most: "The Americans are a peculiar people, they sit around in a tavern, dozens of them, they turn their backs to each other, no one says a word, is this the social custom of a republic, then I do not like it at all . . ." Yet another immigrant, who arrived in Chicago from the state of Hesse in 1875, singled out for special commendation the republic and republicanism:

> Perhaps even more exciting than religious freedom which I found when I came to this country, was my introduction to political freedom. I had been brought up in an atmosphere diametrically opposed to the true democratic principles . . . Here in America it actually was supposed to be. I plunged into politics with a zest and enthusiasm which has never wanted since . . . I

became a Republican from the first day I tasted the blessings of
democracy . . . I was impressed . . . with the fact that men and
especially women wore better garments here than they did in
Germany . . . I looked for the reason and found it in better wages
for all the workers. Workers here received double and three
times the wages they received in Europe for the same work.

Apparently impressions of the New World could be as varied as
the immigrants themselves, and how one found a suitable mid-
way point between fantasy and reality depended, one suspects,
on temperament and predisposition for contentment.

It is then not possible to draw a single typology of the German Jewish immigrant of the nineteenth century. There was
among them an infinite variety of types, and furthermore they
varied a great deal according to the time period of their immigration. Within certain limits, we can generalize that the first to
come were the poorest and least educated, and had the fewest
resources. They came primarily between 1820 and 1850. After
that we begin to note more established, but by no means
wealthy, Jews arriving. Beginning in the forties, too, a group of
rabbis made their way here to give spiritual sustenance to the
growing Jewish flock. Generally, with a few noteworthy exceptions, we can assume that the pioneers in the immigration process were those who had least to lose by uprooting themselves.
The more established they were, the more reluctant they were
to go through the resettlement process. We also know that
during the first phase the arrivals tended to be young single
males between fifteen and nineteen years of age. There were
also distinct regional variations. Many of the immigrants from
Bavaria were rustic *landsjuden,* small-town rural Jews. The
more cosmopolitan larger towns and cities usually did not furnish the human material prone to pioneer in a distant place.
(There were some distinct exceptions.) There was a world of
difference between an immigrant from a village in Bavaria and
one from a large city like Vienna or a middle-size town like
Kassel or Giessen.

What kind of Jews were they? According to Rudolf Glanz,
an authority on German Jews in America, they were for the

most part poorly trained Jewishly, which matched their poor secular education. We learn that from their letters home, some of which are available in archives. They were written in a form of Yiddish, actually a Judeo–German jargon related to the language spoken in the state of Saxony, which was later called *Deitschmerich*. The letters are full of errors in spelling and grammatical syntax both in German and *Deitschmerich*. They were letters from people unaccustomed to reading and writing. This fact will be important in our later discussion of the genesis of the Reform movement: its new adherents in America were not overly familiar with the Judaic tradition, some of which they proposed to abandon.

Yet, being poorly educated reflected lack of opportunity rather than lack of desire. In America Jews contributed disproportionately to the culture of the German-American community in whose cultural ambiance they frequently settled. Jews joined German literary societies, athletic and singing societies, and all kinds of other *"Vereins,"* which were characteristic of the German-American cultural landscape. Oswald Ottendorfer, after whom a branch library in New York City is named, became a virtual impresario of German culture in America while at the same time remaining a loyal Jew. He was also editor of the *New York Staatzeitung*, the major journal of German-Americans in the New York metropolitan area. Two other German-American newspapers in New York City were also published by Jews, *Der Morgenstern* and *Der Deutscher Courrier*. The newspaper *Der Anzeiger*, which served as the voice of Carl Schurz, a power in mid-nineteenth century American politics and the German-American community's leading spokesman, was owned in partnership with a German-American Jew. Before his unfortunate falling out with the Jewish leadership, Schurz was tireless in warning about the dangers of the new wave of anti-Semitism sweeping Germany and other countries. Like Francis Lieber, another leader of the German-American community, he was proud of the achievement of German Jews in America, whom he considered a subgroup of the German community.

Except for early decades of the twentieth century, the most

persistent problem of survival in America has been biological—producing enough Jewish offspring to carry on the distinctive Jewish culture. The problem has customarily been solved by importing Jews from abroad. Not only was the preexisting Sephardic Jewish community "saved" by the timely arrival of the German Jews, that new community was in its turn guaranteed continuance by the arrival of the Eastern Jews. It may well be that the pattern is continuing, at least in part. Jewish immigrants from Israel *(yordim)* and from the Soviet Union *(noshrim)* may be playing a similar role for contemporary American Jewry. The most direct impact made on American Jewry by the Jewish immigrants from Germany was demographic. By 1840 the number of Jews in America had increased to sixteen thousand, and twenty years later it reached a hundred and fifty thousand. There were, we estimate, perhaps as many as a quarter of a million Jews in America by the 1880s. More indicative of a renewed vitality was the rise in the number of congregations, from six in 1825 to seventy-seven in 1860. Whereas the increase in the number of American Jews was remarkable, however, it did not keep pace with the even greater increase of the general population. Proportionately, the American Jewish population was actually declining. That is a fact we want to keep in mind when we later examine the character of anti-Semitism in America. Until the arrival of millions of Eastern European Jewish immigrants, Jews were a relatively inconspicuous minority in America, barely a visible target for a special animus.

What of their relationship with the preexisting Sephardic community? To say the least, it was ambivalent. The rustic, ambitious Bavarian Jews had yet to make their mark, while the Sephardic Jews were already well established. Moreover, they stemmed from cultures—German and Iberian—that seemed to have in common only their distaste for Jews. In other respects—attitude toward work and commerce, religion, and concepts of masculinity—they were often at opposite poles. Among the Jews, these inherent differences were compounded by class antagonisms. The Sephardic Jews looked askance at these new arrivals who claimed to share a common faith, although they spoke a strange harsh language and prayed in an unfamiliar way.

Undoubtedly the more recently arrived German Jews resented the snobbishness of the Sephardic Jews. Ironically, it was a pattern not noticeably different than the one German Jews would later experience with the new arrivals from Eastern Europe. The latter resented the German Jews in much the same way, and for much the same reason, as the German Jewish immigrants resented the Sephardic immigrants. Yet in both cases, the intensity of the conflict must not be overstated. There was acrimony and bitterness, but the religious and human bond often built bridges anyway. More than one aspiring German Jewish immigrant lad made a "good" marriage to a Sephardic girl. Such conflict as there was tended to surface in the institution they shared, the religious congregation. It frequently came over the question of *minhag*, the order of prayer. It was a seemingly minor matter, but much of the social life of the nineteenth century was played out within the congregation, and even a question regarding the proper tune for a given prayer caused schisms within congregations.

We have suggested that if one were to characterize the German Jewish immigrants, a key to their behavior could be found in their inordinate ambition for a better position in life and for the material things such a position would bring. It was as if years of pent-up energy and talent were released in the free environment of America. Given the time they came and the energy they were willing to expend, their success was almost predictable. Perhaps to an even greater extent than their Sephardic predecessors, these Jews were "courageous enterprisers." That is, they sniffed out new opportunities for business, pioneered in them—often risking their meager fortunes, innovated in traditional callings such as merchandising, and tried again if they failed in their first ventures. Such pluck led early to their domination of both the men's and women's apparel business, manufacture as well as retailing. The pattern of domination of the garment trade, which served as an entrèe for Jews into the American business world, was similar to that occurring in other countries. In America, well-known trade names such as Hart, Schaffner and Marx, and Kuppenheimer and Sonnenborn, still serve as reminders of the Jewish initiative in the garment business. Similarly, when mass production of footwear began in the 1830s, a Jewish firm, Florsheim, was among the pioneers. The Great Lakes fishing industry was pioneered by two German Jews, Friedenthaler and Oestreicher, and the grain trade, which remains one of the nation's major export commodities, claimed the participation of Issac Friedenthaler, the "Grain King of California." Yet another German Jew, Nelson Morris, became involved in the meatpacking industry and innovated the shipping of live cattle to the European markets. In mining, there were the Lewisohns and the Guggenheims. These names barely scratch the surface of the different kinds of business ventures that claimed the energies and talents of German Jews.

In a society that permits some modicum of success, who achieves it and how, and what class or group they belong to, are naturally questions of abiding interest. There have been numerous theories on the success odyssey of German Jewry, and even a popular and successful book, *Our Crowd*, which deals with one phase of that story. But, in fact, it is difficult to pinpoint with any accuracy precisely why certain people or groups achieve what they do. There are, for example, humorous stories in which the success of German Jews is attributed to their typical German punctuality and other bourgeois virtues: thrift, hard work, integrity, and so on. Many groups share these characteristics, but in terms of good timing, few chose a more opportune moment to come to America than the Jews of Germany. They came when the frontier was open and the economy was expanding. America had need of precisely the kind of business verve possessed by these Jews. It was a good match, and soon enough the telltale signs that the German Jews were doing well in America could be observed. Between 1860 and 1870 the number of Jewish firms warranting a credit listing rose from 374 to 1,740. By 1890 there was an additional rise of 20 percent. A considerable portion of these businesses were capitalized at over $100,000, a respectable sum in those years. By 1900, New York City listed sixty Jewish millionaires, many of them still sporting heavy German accents.

We have noted that the German Jewish immigrants took advantage of the full spectrum of business opportunities offered by the expanding American economy. But the greatest proportion chose the traditional occupation of merchandising, selling retail. As in Europe, a career in merchandising frequently began with peddling, until sufficient capital could be amassed for owning a store. In America, peddling became a principal occupation of the new immigrants, because it offered many advantages for those who, for whatever reason, were on their own. It required relatively small amounts of capital to start, since peddling involved almost no overhead costs, such as rent or inventory. Usually the local Jewish resident merchant, desiring to increase his own sales volume, would willingly extend credit in the form of merchandise to a new arrival anxious and willing to work. The existence of a Jewish merchandising network, which extended from manufacture to wholesale to retail, gave the newcomer an "in" to small business. To be sure, he would have to start on its lowest rung, peddling, but most hoped that the peddling phase was merely a beginning and that greater things would follow. There were two other factors that aided the Jews of Central Europe in gaining the all-important first rung of small business. The first factor was the existence of an open market. In nineteenth-century America, with its moving frontier and its relatively undeveloped transportation grid, there existed a "merchandising vacuum," huge areas in the interior where there were no stores and no link to the factories that produced goods. In that area of the economy Jews often located themselves. The second factor was the early development of an intragroup system of credit, based on family ties, fraternal or social clubs, or even religious congregations or other social institutions, which extended to the immigrant anxious to go into business the initial "risk" capital required to start. That was a crucial factor, which more than anything else may account for the inordinate success of the immigrant generation in business.

We have seen how that extension of credit was virtually built into the calling of peddling. It is the reason why so many newcomers chose to start in it. Yet, in the absence of precise figures, we can only guess at the percentages involved. One researcher surveying the occupation of all adult Jewish males in the town of Easton, Pennsylvania has come up with the following estimates: 46 percent in 1840, 70 percent in 1845, 55 percent in 1850, 59 percent in 1855, 39 percent in 1860, and 12 percent in 1870. The variations in the figures from year to year may be explained by many things, including the vagaries of the business cycle, the approach of the Civil War, the fact that the territory may have been "filled in" by 1870. We have noted that peddling was an entry-level occupation, which means that by 1870, in the more established communities in the East, many of the immigrants might already have established themselves and the failures simply dropped out. The class of immigrants who arrived after the Civil War either went straight into storekeeping, without the preliminary step of peddling, or walked the roads of America with a pack of notions on their back further west, in less settled areas.

Rabbi Isaac Wise, the renowned founder of the Reform movement in America, commented bitterly on the Jewish "pack carrier . . . who indulges the thought that he will become a business man some day" while carrying from 100 to 150 pounds on his back. A portion, of course, did realize that dream, but there were also a good number who did not. "As often as not," according to Wise, "he bore his pack until his back broke under it and thereafter his food came from the toil of others, his wife, his children [and] kindly neighbors." We do not often hear of the failures, partly because the muse of history is partial to success. It is the successful, motivated by pride, who leave written records behind. From their memoirs we learn that a merchandizing career followed ascending sequential stages; as Wise saw it: "At first one is the slave of the basket of the pack, then the lackey of the horse in order to become finally the servant of the shop." There were also separate categories of peddling, with a different status assigned to each. The simple basket carrier was lowest in the pecking order, trunk and pack carriers came next, and finally "wagon barons" were highest of all. There were also specialists: some peddled only cosmetics and toiletries; others, sewing articles and yarn; a "jewelry count" was a peddler who sold only custom jewelry. Many peddlers never settled down to become resident merchants, choosing instead to become "customer peddlers," which meant that they had steady customers along appointed routes, and the routes themselves could be bought and sold.

Whatever the case, peddling was rarely an easy livelihood. In rural areas, potential customers were wary of strangers and generally unfriendly. "Winter has come," wrote one peddler in his diary.

> We were forced to stop Wednesday because of heavy snow. We sought to spend the night with a Mr. Spaulding, but his wife did not wish to take us in. She was afraid of strangers, she might not sleep well, we should go on our way, and outside there raged the worst blizzard I have ever seen. Oh God, I thought, is this the land of liberty and hospitality and tolerance? Why have I been led here?

Later the diarist, who was an observant Jew, made some general observations about the peddler's life: "Thousands of peddlers wander about America, young strong men, they waste in the summer's heat, they lose their health in the icy cold of winter. And they forget completely their creator. They no longer put on phylacteries, they pray neither on the working day nor on the Sabbath. In truth they have given up their religion for the pack which is on their back. In some cases, more than religion and the amenities of civilization were given up by the peddlers. Some became the victims of highwaymen, marauding Indians, or violence among their own kind.

Yet there were those who survived and prospered. What percentage we shall never know, but apparently the occurrence was common enough so that the "peddler-to-department-store-owner" legend became part of American Jewish history. Names like Adam Gimbel, Benjamin Bloomingdale, Benjamin Altman, Isador and Nathan Straus, Mark Jacobs, the Seligmann Brothers, Samuel Rosenwald, Arthur Friedlander, Gerson

Fox, Filene, Nieman-Marcus, and many others have become familiar to all America from the famous department stores they founded. Sometime the fortune was founded not on good luck in choosing the right territory or sales itmes but on an innovation in merchandizing. Thus two Jewish trouser manufactures, Levi and Straus, using an especially strong cottom denim (imported from Nimes in southeastern France), reinforced the seams with copper rivets to produce stong work pants, especially suitable on the mining frontier. Today "Levis" are popular worldwide. Merchandizing innovation such as installment buying, the mail-order catalogue, money-back guarantees, and, later, customer credit ratings were also introduced. But for the most part, the towns of the West in which Jews located their general stores were too small for such exotic features. It was often these stores, owned by Jewish merchants, that put the town on the map. That was true of such places as Rockovsky, Rittmayer, Kohn Brothers, Solomonville, and Helene (after Helene Goldberg). And because Jews were so early in the West and virtually the founders of these towns, they became the mayors, judges, and sometimes sheriffs. The role played by German Jewish immigrants in bringing the amenities of civilization to the frontier communities can hardly be overestimated.

Today the story of Jewish business pioneering in the West is less well known than the story of Jewish investment banking in America. That is so because over a decade ago Stephen Birmingham wrote a best-seller, *Our Crowd: The Great Jewish Families of New York*. (1967) Birmingham, a non-Jewish writer, possessed the professional eye to notice that the Jewish success story was dramatic enough fare to be interesting not only to Jews but to all Americans. What was required was that the story of the German Jewish banking families who formed a distinct stratum of the social elite be spiced up a little, popularized, so that it could be made interesting in its own right. It was probably that popularization—which meant distortion not so much of fact but of priorities, sequence, and tone—that nettled professional historians. In a popular history such as *Our Crowd* the facts may be true, but the composite portrait that emerges is not. Birmingham approached a rather staid group with a tradition of community service and philanthropy, much as a gossip columnist might. He focused on their eccentricities, their extramarital adventures, their conflicts, and, of course, the way they used their money. In reality, their peccadilloes were but an insignificant part of their story. The German Jewish bankers formed a truly remarkable commercial elite whose significance for the historian is that they were committed Jews who had power and were fairly comfortable with it. Historians rarely have the opportunity to observe Jews who have power and use it. Perhaps more can be learned from them than from any other single group. We can deduce certain conclusions if such a group abuses their power by overuse or otherwise fails to exercise it responsibly. Moreover, the success of these German Jewish bankers was only the visible tip of the iceberg. It was part of a broader success story of German Jewry in America. Nor is the fact that Jews entered banking significant in its own right, since there were bankers who stemmed from other ethnic groups. The significant departure is that Jewish bankers formed a self-conscious social and commercial set, which tried to exercise internal community leadership and to use its economic leverage to influence public policy, especially to ameliorate the condition of Jews abroad. How that set developed is an interesting story and warrants retelling.

The development of a Jewish banking group in America was in some measure a spin-off from the already established Jewish banking nexus in Europe, especially Germany. Its investments in the American economy began in the decade of the 1830s, during the era of canal building, and continued through the era of intensive railroad development. Some European banking houses, aware that there existed a great need for investment capital, sent agents to America. The Rothschilds of London were perhaps the first to do so, becoming the official financial agent of the State Department in 1835. Two years later the Paris Rothschilds sent August Belmont to America, and he opened an office at 78 Wall Street. That same year Philip Speyer, scion of a German Jewish banking family, also arrived in America to do business. His brother Gustavus joined him in 1845 to establish the firm of Philip Speyer and Company, devoted primarily to underwriting railroad bonds. Adolph Landenburg, son of another German Jewish banking family, established Ladenburg–Thalman and Company in 1880. The same pattern is discernable in the banking career of Lazarus Hallgarten, who arrived in 1849. The most important of these banker–immigrants was Jacob Schiff, who first arrived in 1867 armed with connections to the Warburg banking clan in Germany. He later became the director of Kuhn–Loeb and Company, the most prestigious and richest of the American Jewish banking houses. Without the timely arrival of these agents, Jewish American investment banking probably would not have developed. The agents not only possessed knowledge of the latest banking methods and access to huge sums of investment capital, but many also had a specific consciousness of being Jewish that served as the primary cement of this commercial banking elite. From the outset, "Our Crowd" was dependent on financial, human, and cultural resources which Jews had developed over generations in Europe.

The American dimension of the story stems from a second group of bankers, who had accumulated capital in America and were ready to enter the capital market. They were the most successful Jewish businessmen, some of whom had begun as humble peddlers and had gone on to earn their fortunes in merchandizing and other business ventures. The Seligmanns, Guggenheims, Heidelbachs, Straus—Goldmans, Kuhns, Loebs, Lehmans, Wertheims, and Baches had little help from European banks in accumulating their fortunes, but once established in banking they quickly established relations with them to do business overseas. What is unique about the establishment of these Jewish fortunes is that they are authentic illustrations of economic mobility in nineteenth-century America, which confirm the rags-to-riches legends. Recent research has shown that, in most cases, the fortunes amassed in the "great barbecue" period of post-Civil-War America were something less than Horatio Alger stories. They actually represent the further rise of people whose fathers were already in business and who stemmed from affluent middle-class backgrounds. They were from established Protestant denominations; they were already comfortable and became wealthy. Mobility such as that of the Seligmanns, who actually started as peddlers and culminated as bankers, was relatively rare among non-Jews. The real Horatio Alger story was hardly a myth for the new Jewish commercial elite. It is no coincidence that Horatio Alger, whose fictional stories created the rags-to-riches legend, was the tutor in Joseph Seligmann's household.

Most interesting for the Jewish historian, because it can tell us something about the position of Jews in the general society, is to discover the reason why a separate Jewish banking nexus developed in the first place. Individual motivations are so manifold that we can only present impressions of what occurred. We have seen that to some extent Jewish banking in America was merely an extension of a development that had already occurred in Europe. There, Jewish bankers, like the Rothschilds, Bleichroeder, and the Warburgs had made their mark. Part of the reason, then, lies deeply embedded in Western history and is too long a story to be told here. It is difficult to state categorically that these same reasons applied to the development of Jewish banking in America. We know that some of the more successful Jewish businessmen were able to envisage possibilities beyond mere merchandising. Once they saw the possibility, they were relatively quick to learn the requisite banking skills and to take advantage of the possibilities that the Jewish connection gave them. At the same time, Jewish banking was possible because Jews had amassed capital, without which there could be no banking. Banking itself was a measure of their success in other areas of the economy. That, in turn, was due to the comparative openness and rapid expansion of the American economy in the nineteenth century. It was an economy which, at least in commercial matters, did not permit itself the luxury of discriminating against Jews. Yet, at the same time, one subtle form of discrimination may have played a role in the establishment of separate Jewish banking houses. We have seen that some Jewish entrepreneurs were quite successful in accumulating capital in a capital-starved economy. Yet there is no record that the leading Yankee banking establishments ever welcomed such Jewish capitalists to sit on the boards of their banks. That entree was warranted by the amounts of capital Jewish capitalists were willing to invest; in fact, it should have been required for security's sake. Jewish capital was all dressed up and found nowhere to go, except to its own bankers. There the religious, family, and social bonds holding the "crowd" together also supplied familiarity and trust, which are necessary lubricants in the banking business. They substituted for the missing years of experience, which few among the Jewish bankers possessed when first starting out. An ethno religious link of shared ethical principles and cultural values was the real foundation of Jewish banking in America.

We are now better able to evaluate the leadership offered by this commercial elite of American Jewry. Of course, they had their eccentrics and those who trespassed against the rules of society. But profligacy is not really what made this group distinctive. For the most part, the German Jewish stewards were a sober and responsible patriciate. Most of its members established firm reputations for integrity and generosity which is rare in a group of *arrivistes* some of whom could still recall their own poverty. Their philanthropic giving was not bound by ethnic loyalties; they gave to non-Jewish as well as to Jewish causes. The most accurate part of Birmingham's description is the stress he gives to the well-known fact that there hardly exists a major cultural institution in the New York metropolitan area that has not been enriched by the generous giving of "Our Crowd."

Of course the German Jews differed in style and class from Eastern Jews, but not in their intense achievement orientation. There, the German Jews could serve as models for their East European compatriots. It comes out in the well-known story about two East-European *melamdim* (teachers), who are walking along Fifth Avenue viewing the newly built mansions of the Schiffs, Seligmanns, and Warburgs, when one turns to the other and declares: "If I were Schiff, I would be richer than Schiff!" His skeptical walking partner asks "How?" and the response comes back: "I would teach a little on the side." A common desire to achieve supplemented a common religious bond between the two groups. That is why, despite the fact that "uptowners" sometimes sensed that the new arrivals threatened their position, they nevertheless used their considerable political influence to fight against immigration restrictions and—in a desperate effort—to gain the diplomatic intercession of the American government to improve the security of Jews in Russia and Rumania.

The German Jewish stewards who came to lead the American Jewish community expressed their commitment to Judaism through service to the Jewish community as well as through *tsedakah* (ethical giving). Although the temptation was always there, few denied their loyalty to the faith of their fathers. If we want, for example, to discover what was most distinctively Jewish about these German Jewish bankers—an aspect of their lives Birmingham thought of little interest to the general reader, and therefore omitted—we need to know something about what they tried to do with their economic leverage to help Russian Jewry.

It is one of the least-known but most fascinating chapters of American Jewish history. A group of Jewish bankers, joined by many non-Jews, including the Morgan interests, attempted during the Russo–Japanese war—when the Russians found themselves financially strapped—to block the sale of Russian bond issues on the American market. Thereby they hoped to wring better treatment for the Russian Jews. Jacob Schiff, the organizer of the campaign, was sensitive to the fact that by using this strategy he ran the risk of reinforcing the anti-Semitic image, which pictured Jewish bankers manipulating the world money market from behind the scenes. But in the absence of political leverage with the Theodore Roosevelt administration, Schiff decided that the plan was worth a try. The attempts at more civil diplomatic intercession had had little effect in ameliorating the conditions of physical danger of Russian Jewry, manifest in such atrocities as the pogrom in Kishinev, Bessarabia, in April 1903. Worldwide protest against such government-sponsored depredations did not move the Kremlin. Perhaps the Russian authorities would be more sensitive to pressure on their depleted treasury. In 1904 Schiff contacted the well-known Jewish banking house of the Rothschilds in

London to inquire about the possibility of organizing a credit boycott against the tsarist regime:

> Assuredly when the Russian government again applies to the European money markets, as before long it must do, may we not hope that the Jewish bankers of influence will not again be satisfied with promises on the part of the Russian government . . . and not only decline cooperation but work with all their might against any Russian loan so long as existing conditions continue . . . it would indeed be an undignified spectacle if this turned out otherwise . . . if our influential coreligionists in Europe did not at least use the means of their command to make the Russian government feel that it cannot continue forever with immunity its shameful policy towards its Jewish subjects.

True to his word, Schiff organized a solid phalanx of bankers to block the extension of credit to the hard-pressed Russian government. The New York money market (which was gaining rapidly in importance) was, with the help of friendly bankers and insurance companies, totally denied to the Kremlin. When, as Schiff had forseen, the Russians did approach these bankers regarding floating a loan, he was prepared with his quid pro quo. The loan would be floated only when there were tangible signs that the Russians were abandoning their policy of singling out their Jewish subjects for a special animus. After Kishinev, however, Schiff was not optimistic that such a change in policy could easily be achieved. His anger at the Russian leadership was contained but burned fiercely. Kuhn–Loeb, his own banking firm, was used to pump vast sums of credit into the Japanese anti-Russian war effort. To keep the financially hard-pressed Japanese in the field, Schiff personally organized four loans between 1905 and 1906. Altogether, $180 million of Japan's $860 million bond issues were underwritten by the Schiff group, a sizable proportion for a comparatively small banking house. The honor and awards bestowed on Schiff by the Japanese and the inordinately high opinion that the Japanese had of Jews, which lasted through World War II, indicate that the financial policy played some role in setting the stage for the significant first defeat of a Caucasian nation by an Oriental one on the field of battle. That defeat led to a rearrangement of the European balance of power system, by means of which world peace was supposedly assured. The boycott of Russia was so effective that Count Serge Witte, who would eventually negotiate the peace treaty with Japan, informed his government in 1905 that "there was not the slightest hope of floating either a domestic or foreign loan. We could continue the war only by resorting to new issues of paper money, that is, by preparing the way for a complete financial and consequently economic collapse." It was that dire situation, undoubtedly aggravated by the credit boycott, which brought a reluctant Russia to the negotiating table at Portsmouth.

Yet, despite Schiff's strenuous effort and successful planning and implementation, the plan did not benefit the Russian Jews, who experienced new and often bloodier pogroms in 1905 and 1906. Schiff could not sustain beyond 1906 his campaign to deny to Russia America's money market, partly because the Russo–Japanese war had created a new situation in the Far East: now the national interest of the United States required a strong Russia to balance the ambitions of Japan in relation to the Open Door Policy in China. At the same time, France had become convinced that the danger to her national interests stemmed not from the Kremlin but from Berlin. But Schiff's attempt to use his financial leverage to influence world events in a Jewish interest is singular. He is representative of the remarkable group of stewards nurtured by the German Jewish migration. They were men who used their wealth and influence for what they thought served the Jewish interest at home as well as abroad. Not since they exercised leadership has American Jewry produced anything quite like them. They were people who believed that wealth carried responsibilities; they were willing to assume those responsibilities.

Finally, as was pointed out previously, the story of German Jewry in America does not really end in 1920 or 1890. There is a kind of historical coda in the new wave of Central European immigrants who came to America in the thirties. They came as a result of the anti-Jewish depredations in Nazi Germany, which showed signs of spreading after the *Anschluss* with Austria in March 1938. After *Kristallnacht*, the night of 9 November 1938, when a massive assault on Jewish property and lives occurred, few Jews could any longer imagine that these depredations were temporary. They began to seek a way out of Germany, which had been their homeland for a millennia. The more we learn about this last wave of immigrants, the more we realize that in many ways it is the most remarkable of all the immigration waves that have revitalized American Jewry.

To be sure, the immigrants of the thirties were not voluntary. Most did not dream the dream of the European underclass of the nineteenth century concerning the wonders of America. Established members of the middle class, they left their German homeland with great reluctance, and only at the historical juncture when there existed no other alternative. The fact that many of the emigrants were deeply attached to German culture and that they were relatively old to undertake the arduous task of transplantation (70 percent were over forty) made the adjustment process to America difficult. They had lost not only the homeland to which they felt they belonged, they were often declassed as well. The immigration was comparatively small. Of the approximately 525,000 Jews living in Germany in 1933, as many as 150,000 to 180,000 were able to leave before *Kristallnacht*. The majority of these, perhaps as many as 110,000 came to the United States; the remainder resettled in Britain, Palestine, and elsewhere. It was a migration extraordinarily rich in artistic, managerial, and scientific talent.

By 1935 over 1,100 non-Aryan members of the German university faculty had lost their positions. Most heavily hit were the faculties of mathematics and science. The story is told how in the world renowned Göttingen Institute of Mathematics, Professor David Hilbert, its mentor, received a call from the Nazi Minister of Education, Rust. It was an inquiry about how mathematics was faring without Jews. "But Herr Minister," the startled reply came back, "there is no mathematics left at Göttingen." The Germans were, of course, aware that they were decimating scientific teams that had taken years to build up.

But they believed Hitler, who said: "If the dismissal of Jewish scientists means the annihilation of contemporary German science then we shall do without science for a few years."

Germany's and Europe's loss became America's gain. In the group that came to America there were 2,352 physicians, 1,090 professors and educators, 811 lawyers, 682 journalists, and hundreds of first-class musicians, artists, actors, architects, scientists, and writers. Most Americans know only two or three names from this group: Albert Einstein, Henry Kissinger, and perhaps Otto Preminger. But they represent only the tip of the iceberg. The impact of the refugee intellectuals on gestalt psychology, psychoanalysis, psychotherapy, the new field of quantitative sociology, political science, history, art history, and musicology, as well as on mathematics and physics, was enormous. There are those who maintain that the great cultural and technological explosion of knowledge that occurred in America in the post-World-War-II period was based, in good measure, on intellectual capital imported from Germany and Europe in the thirties. A good portion of that precious cargo was carried in the heads of Jewish refugees.

One segment of that story is almost poetic in its symmetry and deserves special mention. The most interesting and perhaps most important of the refugee intellectuals were the theoretical physicists. The Nazis were particularly opposed to this field of knowledge: it attracted so many Jews that the Nazis were convinced that it was really a secret conspiracy against the Reich. It may have been a suspicion with uncanny prescience since it was, in fact, these particular physicists who were instrumental in ushering in the new atomic age. Had the war in Europe lasted longer, an atomic bomb developed with their scientific know-how would have caused the *Götterdämmerung* of the "Thousand Year Reich." That did not happen, but we do know today that once the bomb was in the arsenal of the allies, the possibility of a Nazi victory vanished. Thus, these physicists assured that there would be no Nazi world hegemony.

It is estimated that between 1933 and 1941 about a hundred physicists came to America. Most came from Germany, but there were also some from Austria, Hungary, Italy, and other parts of Europe. The most notable in the group were Leo Szilard, Eugene Wigner, Edward Teller, and Enrico Fermi. Their numbers were supplemented by the pure mathematicians who were easily able to cross over into the field of theoretic physics: e.g., Albert Einstein, John Von Neumann, and Richard Von Mises.

For sheer brilliance and versatility the most interesting of the group was Leo Szilard, who eventually turned his interest to biophysics and is today credited with setting the theoretic groundwork for the discovery of DNA. Szilard was particularly adept at seeing what had to be done and then, operating with extraordinary skill in the area where pure science and politics impinge, effecting it. It was Szilard who mobilized the American scientific community and set it on a war footing. As early as 1937, together with Arno Brusch, he approached Lewis Strauss, Hoover's former assistant and then an admiral in the U.S. Navy, to build "surge" generators—later known as cyclotrons—for atomic research. On 25 January, 1939 he alerted Strauss to the possibility that the sudden halting of uranium sales by Czechoslovakia might mean that Hitler was preparing to develop such a weapon and was threatening the Czech government. It was Szilard who prompted Einstein to write his famous letter of 2 August, 1939 to Roosevelt, in which he warned of the danger of Nazi Germany's developing an atomic bomb. That led Roosevelt to establish the Manhattan Project, which eventually produced the bomb. It was too late to be used against the Reich, but Hiroshima and Nagasaki were destroyed on 6 and 9 August 1945, respectively.

There has been official recognition of the role played by the refugee physicists in the Smythe report dealing with the development of the atomic bomb. "At the time American-born nuclear physicists were so unaccustomed to the idea of using their science for military purposes," the report reads, "that they hardly realized what needed to be done. Consequently, early efforts both at restricting publication and getting government support were stimulated largely by a group of foreign-born physicists centering on Leo Szilard and including E. Teller, E. Wigner, U. F. Weiskopf and E. Fermi."

For Jews victimized by the Holocaust there is something rehabilitating in the feeling that they were after all not totally vulnerable. Jews did have a certain kind of power, based on knowledge, which proved superior in the end. It was a disproportionate number of Jewish scientists, many of whom had felt the sting of Nazi anti-Semitism, who helped produce the atomic bomb, ushered in the new atomic era, and assured that Hitler could never win the war. What the researchers of the Smythe report did not know—because it pertained more to the American Jewish historical experience than to science—was that the Manhattan Project, the highly secret program that developed the bomb, was also the scene of a remarkable rejoining of two German Jewish immigration streams, the first of which had arrived in the nineteenth century and the second during the thirties. Robert Oppenheimer (a scientist) and Lewis Strauss (a manager) were descended from the first stream. Einstein, Wigner, and Szilard emanated from the same milieu a century later. One might say, at least in a historical sense, that German Jewry did balance the accounts with their former homeland.

The intellectual migration of the thirties was not only extraordinarily productive for human welfare generally, it also gave much to American Jewry. The German Jewish immigrants of the thirties seemed to have lost none of the talent for institution building so characteristic of their predecessors who had arrived in the nineteenth century. Yet paradoxically, despite shared talents and language, the two groups experienced considerable difficulty in relating to each other. That was partly due to the fact that by the thirties the former immigrants had been so acculturated that they no longer formed a self-conscious Jewish community. These new immigrants turned naturally to the sons and daughters of the later Eastern European migration with whom they too shared much in common. But here too relations were sometimes distorted by a residual animosity, which dated back to real and imagined grievances held by Eastern immigrants about their treatment at the hands of German Jews at the turn of the century. In the end, the German Jewish immigrants of the thirties found it practical to establish a full panoply of their own secular and religious agencies to serve their needs. They became organizationally self-sufficient. Included was a completed network of social-service organizations, old-age homes, nursing facilities, and credit unions, which aided many in starting their own businesses. In the judgment of many, *Aufbau* ("Rebuilding"), a weekly written in German, is the best ethnic newspaper in the Western Hemisphere. The need for fraternity with one's fellows is especially strong in an alien culture. Over thirty fraternal societies, similar in function to the *landsmannschaften* (voluntary membership associations), developed by Eastern Jews, were established. To fulfill religious needs, at least ten religious congregations were organized in New York City, and there were others in other major cities. Among the most noteworthy was the Breur group, originally part of the Jewish community of Frankfurt and reestablished in the "Fourth Reich," the name some had jestingly given to the Washington Heights section of Manhattan, where many of the refugees had settled. The ultra-Orthodoxy of the Breur group stands as living proof that German Jewry was not totally assimilationist. (Actually about 15 percent adhered to *agudat*, the Orthodox anti-Zionist branch of European Judaism, and many more to a neo-Orthodoxy similar to American Conservatism.) It also produced its own noteworthy religious leaders and thinkers. Best known is Leo Baeck who was religious leader of German Jewry and miraculously survived incarceration in Theresinenstadt. Rabbi Joachim Prinz earned a reputation here for his staunch advocacy of liberal Judaism and became president of the American Jewish Congress. Emil Fackenheim, a professor of philosophy at the University of Toronto and a renowned authority on Hegel, also exercises a profound influence on post-Holocaust Jewish theology.

The German Jewish immigrant community, now hardly distinguishable from other American Jews, has done something that many older Jewish communities have yet to do. It has established a special research institute to preserve the historical sources and write the history of German Jewry posthumously. The Leo Baeck Institute, partly supported by the West German government, conducts some of the best scholarly seminars in the academic community. Its *Yearbook* and other scholarly publications are eagerly awaited by the academic world and are known for their high quality.

In one area, the Jewish immigrants of the thirties were notably different from their predecessors. Through no choice of their own, they came at a bad time. Their progress is all the more remarkable because they arrived in the midst of the great depression of the thirties, when opportunities to earn a livelihood and to establish businesses were limited. Yet, from what emerges in statistics, the group was extraordinarily successful in all its endeavors, whether professional or commercial. There was much resistance to their coming, because it was felt that they would take jobs that belonged to native Americans. We know today that as early as 1942 they were, in fact, a group that generated employment; rather than taking jobs away from others, they made jobs. Their achievement in America is testimony to the human ability to endure and achieve even under the most trying circumstances.

There is a sad note in the immigration saga of the thirties, which stems from America's reluctance to welcome them. It adhered strictly to its restrictive immigration policy, making no allowances for the special plight of the refugees. When one stands back to consider what enormous spiritual and intellectual resources were contained in this Jewish community, when one ponders how many Einsteins and Szilards may have been destroyed in the Holocaust, the full tragedy of America's short-sighted refugee policy comes into sharp focus. It is a loss that might have been prevented, had decision makers been aware how especially rich in human resources the Jewish immigration from Germany has been in the nineteenth and twentieth centuries.

Bibliography

"American Jewish Business Enterprise: Special Bicentennial Issue." *American Jewish Historical Quarterly*, vol. 66 (September 1976).
Birmingham, S. *Our Crowd: The Great Jewish Families of New York* . New York: 1967.

Carosso, V. P. "A Financial Elite: New York's German Jewish Investment Bankers." *American Jewish Historical Quarterly*, vol. 66 (September 1976).

Glanz, R. *Jews in Relation to the Cultural Milieu of the Germans in America.* New York: 1947.

Grunfeld, V. V. *Prophets without Honor: A Background to Freud, Kafka, Einstein, and Their World.* Philadelphia: 1979.

Hirschler, E. E., ed. *Jews from Germany in the United States.* New York: 1945.

Korn, B. W. "German-Jewish Intellectual Influences on American Jewish Life, 1824–1972," Syracuse University, *The B. G. Rudolph Lectures in Judaic Studies,* 1972.

Mahoney, T. *The Great Merchants: The Stories of Twenty Famous Retail Operations and the People Who Made Them Great.* New York: 1955.

Strauss, H. A. "The Immigration and Acculturation of the German Jew in the United States of America," *Year Book XVI of the Leo Baeck Institute,* London: 1971.

Supple, B. E. "A Business Elite: German-Jewish Financiers in Nineteenth-Century New York," *The Business History Review,* 21, 1957.

Wischnitzer, M. *To Dwell in Safety: The Story of Jewish Migration since 1900.* Philadelphia: 1948.

CHAPTER III

Americanizing Judaism:
The Reform Movement

SOME readers have undoubtedly heard the story about the Jewish survivor of a shipwreck who is marooned on an island for many years before his rescue. To while away the lonely hours he builds an exact scale model of a typical American town. Everything is there: a firehouse, a school, the courthouse, a church. But there are two Jewish houses of worship. His rescuers are puzzled when he proudly shows them his handiwork and inquire why he has built two synagogues. The survivor responds: "Well, you see that second one across the street? That's the one I wouldn't be caught dead in."

Many American Jews smile knowingly at that response. They may have made the same statement about a second synagogue in their community. One of the facts of Jewish life is that the religious community is triangulated and often full of acrimonious conflict among the three branches. That is understandable when one deals with serious things like religion, and for Jews, especially, religion has traditionally been a serious matter. When things are accepted as a matter of faith rather than understanding, when one believes that the path being followed is the only true one, then the transactions between humans and their institutions tend to become rigid. As a rule, believers are not tolerant folk. That is reason enough for a historian to hesitate before plunging in to examine any religious movement. In a real sense, it is a battle that cannot be won. Therefore I will preface this discussion by reminding the reader that our interest here is to discover how the Reform movement in America originated, what problem it was addressing, why it advocated certain changes, and to what extent it succeeded. It is not intended to advocate or reject the Reform movement here, but rather to make sense of it.

Like all important movements in American Jewish history, the Reform movement possesses both European and American roots. The Union of American Hebrew Congregations—the umbrella organization of American Reform congregations, founded by Moritz Loth and a group of laymen under the leadership of Rabbi Isaac Meyer Wise in July 1873—was the capstone of a historical process whose roots reach back to the Enlightenment and to the Protestant Reformation. Isaac Harby, the leader of the Charleston Reform movement, who initiated Reform in America, actually cited the analogy with the Protestant Reformation and argued: "Why may not the virtuous example of a few Israelites, then, shake off the bigotry of ages from their countrymen". "When the Christian world sneezes, the Jewish world catches a cold," a Jewish proverb has it. Apparently what Harby had in mind was a kind of reformation against what he considered to be a religious system hopelessly outdated in the rapidly changing social environment of America. The word "Reform" itself defines Harby's intention.

The precise roots in the Enlightenment are less readily identifiable, because that entailed a change in the way people thought: from the mythic to the rational. It is precisely the same change that led to modern science. Thus, when Moses Mendelsohn translated the Pentateuch, the first five books of the Bible, from Hebrew to German in 1783, it became part of a chain of events that soon enough led to a questioning of the divine origins of Scripture. When the process was complete, the Bible was seen not as revealed truth given directly by God, but as the work of mortal men writing in different places and times. The new "scientific" reading showed that it was a historic document rather than a divine one. The Reform movement in Judaism, led by the *Verein für Kultur und Wissenschaft der Juden* (Association for Jewish Culture and Knowledge), founded in 1819 by fifty prominent Jewish intellectuals, gave priority to this new rational approach to their ancient faith.

It takes time for new ideas to trickle down to the people who must somehow make them usable in everyday life. The Jewish masses of Western Europe were barely affected by the Reform movement until the new secular nation state, also a product of the Enlightenment, compelled a confrontation. That occurred during the Napoleonic era. In 1806 Napoleon convened an assembly of Jewish notables, including both rabbis and laymen. A series of questions was placed before the group, designed to test the proposition whether Jews could indeed be loyal "citoyens" of the modern secular state—a position, incidentally, Jews had already assumed in America, the first child of the Enlightenment. In 1807 Napoleon ordered the convening of a Grand Sanhedrin, a governing body of Jews that had long ago fallen into disuse, to begin the process of secularization. Included would be such things as legalizing civil marriages, assigning permanent family names for all Jews living under French law, and even releasing Jewish soldiers from Jewish observance. It was the state, then, that actually triggered the process of bringing Jews into society as citizens. The Jewish side of the emancipation transaction would become clear only over time. But at the time, enlightened Jews welcomed the opportunity to become French citizens of "Mosaic persuasion." The Reform movement followed in tandem with these changes, and in one sense can be viewed as an attempt to fit Judaism into the new situation. The actual institutionalization occurred when Israel Jacobson established a model synagogue and school in the German town of Seesen in 1810. The changes he wrought would seem inconsequential today, but at the time they were earthshaking. There was an organ to accompany choral singing of prayers; there were sermons, which were not customary in Jewish liturgy; and the sermon and some prayers were presented in the vernacular—German. The basic pattern of the reform liturgy was beginning to emerge, and in some respects it resembled that practiced in Protestant churches. After the fall of Napoleon, even while some German principalities began to renege on the promise of emancipation, the signals sent out from Seesen and Cassel were picked up by Jewish groups in other German cities like Berlin. Finally, a full-fledged Reform temple was founded in the commercial and shipping center of Hamburg, which contained a sizable and prosperous Jewish community.

In America a parallel but quite distinct development was occurring in the largest and wealthiest Jewish congregation, Beth Elohim of Charleston, South Carolina. There, in 1824, a group of younger congregants, who had some familiarity with the developments in Germany, petitioned the *Kaal Kodesh*, the directorate of the congregation, for certain reforms, to counteract what they characterized as the "apathy and neglect" of the "present system of worship" stemming from "certain defects which are apparent . . ." They thought these could be corrected by implementing certain esthetic changes in the service and initiating "a more rational system of worshipping God." When the vestry rejected the memorial of the petitioners, twelve of them, led by playwright and pamphleter Isaac Harby, left the congregation and formed the "Reformed Society of Israelites." The revolt was not successful and the experiment withered on the vine. But the reformers did succeed in making their point. In 1836 the vestry of Beth Elohim invited Gustav Posnanski, from Hamburg, to the pulpit. After the old building burned down in 1840, Posnanski began to introduce a Reform liturgy, including the use of an organ, family pews rather than separation of the sexes, and a mixed choir. This time there was little protest from the traditionalists.

The developments in Beth Elohim were a visible manifestation of changes occurring in the practice of Judaism as a result of the impact of the social—and, even more important, the geographic—environment of America. In the free atmosphere of the new society, Judaism had never received corporate sanction from the state, which was, in fact, strictly separated from religion. There was no one who could order a Jew to belong to the Jewish community, which in many rural areas did not, in fact, exist. Even the fraternal, social, philanthropic, and educational activities formerly centered in the synagogue could not be compelled to be part of it and soon became separated.

Not only were there separate fraternal orders like B'nai B'rith (founded in 1843) and the Masons, a secular order favored by many Jews, but religious functionaries such as circumcisers *(mohelim)* and ritual slaughterers *(shochetim)* could not be prevented from going into business for themselves. In short, the congregation was becoming what it had never been in the old world, a purely religious institution—like the Protestant church.

The wide dispersion of the German Jews in America made it almost impossible to organize stable congregations, much less an authentically Jewish religious life based on the myriad rules of halakah (Jewish law). How could one not travel on the Sabbath if the nearest congregation was many miles away? How could one pray with a quorum if there were not ten adult male Jews in the vicinity? Where could one find a *shochet* to produce kosher meat? In short, the very circumstances of life in America, the great distances between places, the scarcity of Jews, and the nature of the merchandising trade, made it impossible to remain strictly observant. Accommodations often resembling those made by the Reform movement had to be made. Some felt great grief in doing so. "God in heaven . . . thou alone knowest my grief," wrote one peddler in his diary, "when on the Sabbath eve, I must return to my lodgings and on Saturday morning carry my pack on my back, profaning the holy days, God's gift to his people. I can't live as a Jew." Such cases were not exceptional. In the absence of Jewish congregations, Isaac Wise noted, Jews would worship in Christian churches, substituting Hebrew words at critical passages. There were "Episcopalian Jews in New York, Quaker Jews in Philadelphia, Huguenot Jews in Charleston, and so on, everywhere according to the prevailing sect." The shortage of eligible Jewish partners led to a high rate of intermarriage. "They came alone," noted an observer, "[and] found no one to pray with and no one to mate [with] . . ."

Naturally, Jews began to bend the rules. In New Orleans there were so many marriages between Jewish men and Christian women that the rule that Judaism passed down through the female line was abandoned. "No Israelite child," read the charter of one congregation in New Orleans, "shall be excluded either from the schools or the temple or from the burial grounds, on account of the religion of the mother." In congregations beyond the Mississippi, riding to synagogue in horse and carriage from outlying areas was taken for granted. The German Jewish immigrants who came in the earliest waves of immigration, moreover, did not boast a thorough grounding in Judaism. There was perhaps a greater predisposition by those poorly trained Jews to tamper with a tradition with which they were not overly familiar. By preselection, those most likely to immigrate—the young, reckless, and daring—were also the ones who welcomed change. Those most steeped in the religious tradition were by the same token least likely to emigrate to what was rumored to be a *tref medinah* (unkosher society). That, too, may have led to a further weakening of observance. Few trained rabbis were tempted to come to America, and those who acted as religious leaders were often untrained and uncertified. Although they sometimes affected the title of "Reverend," they frequently could act neither as teachers of the tradition nor its cultural mainstays. Finally, when a group of rabbis did arrive in the 1840s and 1850s—Leo Merzbacher (1841), Max Lilienthal (1845), Isaac Wise (1846), David Einhorn (1855), and Samuel Adler (1857)—they were more likely than not to act as catalysts for Reform, which had become difficult to implement in Europe.

In a real sense, the Reform movement in America cannot be considered apart from the intense Americanization process of the nineteenth century. It was the American environment itself that created the preconditions for change. It did so in two major respects. All religious establishments in America were organized on a voluntary basis. They were neither recognized nor supported by the state, and no one was compelled to belong to a religious community. Unlike Europe, there was no rabbinic establishment buttressed by law, which could resist the changes demanded from below. It was this support that eventually curbed the Reform impulse in Europe. But in the democratic and open society of America change was actually built into the system, and all religions were congregational and voluntary. That characteristic was apparent on the congregational level as well. There it was the trustees of the synagogue *(baalebatim)*, rather than the rabbi, who possessed the real power. This remains true to the present and is perhaps one of the major reasons why so many Jewish congregations "eat rabbis for breakfast." In the nineteenth century, every one of the stronger-willed rabbis eventually lost his pulpit: Isaac Leeser, Isaac Wise, David Einhorn, and others. Power came from below rather than from the top, and, as with Protestantism, fragmentation and splitting of congregations were inherent in the system. Denominationalism was the order of the day for those faiths not organized hierarchically like the Catholic.

But what did the reformers find so unsatisfactory? What changes did they want to make and why? There were actually two kinds of reforms demanded. The first concerned esthetics—how things looked and were done, mostly as regarded liturgy and form. The second concerned exegesis—a new theory and approach to the actual tenets of the faith. In the case of the former, the matter of esthetics and form, there was a concern for decorum, modernism, and the understanding of the individual worshiper. Much can be learned about these concerns from Harby's memorial to Beth Elohim in 1824. The petitioners complained that not only did the congregants race through the prayers as quickly as possible, each *davening* (praying) at his own pace, and raising a cacophony of unholy wailing, but few understood the actual meaning of the prayers which they had learned by rote. "It is not everyone who has the means, and many have not the time, to acquire a knowledge of the Hebrew language, and consequently become enlightened in the principles of Judaism." For the petitioners the meaningless service was a sham. "Your memorialists would further submit . . . whether, in the history of the civilized world, there can be found a single parallel of a people addressing the CREATOR in a language not understood BY THAT PEOPLE." The memorialists had forgotten the case of Catholic laity, who no longer understood Latin; but we should note one of the principal characteristics of reformers, their keen interest in what was being done in other religious communities. Why not follow the practice of the "Catholic, French and German Protestant churches," the memorialists suggested. Let the *hazan* (Cantor) "repeat in English such parts of the Hebrew prayers as may be deemed necessary." That would not only bring "decency and decorum," but it would allow worshipers to understand what they were saying. Moreover, they felt that the service was too long and suggested that it be shortened to include only the most solemn parts, those to be read in English. They were convinced that financial transactions such as the auctioning of *Aliyot* (ascending the platform to read from the *Torah*) was unseemly. They suggested in its place the paying of yearly dues or a tithing system, such as was the practice in Protestant churches. Separation of women by a *mechitzah* (curtain, railing or other object separating men from women) was considered particularly onerous and not in keeping with "modern" practices. Reformers preferred family pews with mixed seating, again as was practiced in the churches. Some were convinced that a mixed choir and an organ would help beautify and solemnize the services, as would choral responsive reading. Dignity was so important that some reformers, convinced that the presence of great numbers of restless children compromised that dignity, earnestly recommended that children below the age of five be excluded from the service. Eventually various suggestions for improvement emanated from many different congregations. At the outer extreme were suggestions like changing the Sabbath from Saturday to Sunday, worshiping with bare rather than covered heads, and eliminating medieval rite's d'e passage like the *bar mitzvah*. The influence of the Protestant model was pervasive.

Yet the reformers insisted that their purpose was to strengthen Judaism. The Charleston petitioners stated that they "wished not to ABANDON the institutions of Moses, but TO UNDERSTAND AND OBSERVE THEM . . . we wish to worship GOD, not as SLAVES, but as enlightened descendants of that chosen race." The problem was that what was thought to be esthetic, modern, and enlightened seemed to derive directly from the Protestant model. It was natural that it should be so. The pervading secularism of the American governing polity was itself derivative of the Protestant Reformation. The two were intertwined in American culture. Jewish children learned Protestant hymns in public schools on Thanksgiving Day, and it is likely that at Christmas time they were also taught where their forefathers had erred in not accepting the true Messiah. Yet a group desirous above all of attaining middle-class respectability and of being accepted by society naturally looked to the majority culture for their model of what was respectable, and were inclined to rebuild ther religious culture to resemble it as far as possible. Thus, if the congregants no longer understood Hebrew, their suggestion was not to teach the language of their faith but to convert to the vernacular. That was, after all, the language used by Protestants in their services. The Charleston reformers turned to leading non-Jews like the aging Jefferson for approval of their program, and later Isaac Wise was gratified that "the most cultured non-Jews" of Albany were present when he inaugurated his reform congregation *Anshe Emeth.*

Yet clearly it would require more than tampering with external appearances to make Judaism "modern" and "rational," so that it could blend into the American scene and allow its adherents to participate fully in the American society. There were tenets in the Judaic faith that separated Jews from others and deliberately so. Judaism was never a faith to which one adhered only on the Sabbath. Not only was Judaism an entire separate religious civilization, a point that would be made later by Mordecai Kaplan, it was basically holistic. It offered rules and regulations, from dress to diet, to govern virtually every moment of the waking day. Restructuring these basic principles required more than merely tampering with esthetics.

The restructuring of principles proceeded more slowly. It was not fully formalized until Rabbi Kaufman Kohler, the theoretician of the early Reform movement, brought together nineteen liberal rabbis in Pittsburgh in November 1885 to create the Reform platform. It formalized many of the long-held tenets of the Reform movement. The "scientific" criticism of the Bible was accepted: the Bible would be considered a historic rather than a divine document, a record of the "conse-

cration of the Jewish people to its mission as priest of God."
That was an entirely new approach to the vexing problem
posed by the notion of covenantal chosenness so often mis-
understood by the Gentile world. Jews were not special or
superior in their relationship to the Almighty, they were chosen only in the sense of having a special obligation, a priestly
mission to the nations. It was important to anchor Judaism in
rationalism. The Pittsburgh platform declared: "We recognize
in Judaism a progressive religion, ever striving to be in accord
with the postulates of reason." So pervasive was the impact of
rationalism on the Reform movement that not until generations
later would some concession be made to the notion that faith
involved a different type of understanding, which was deracinated by reason. They were two different categories of intelligence, and they sought to gain understanding in two different realms. There was an extrarational component involved in
faith that did not yield to reason. An excessively rational approach to faith would necessarily be unable to cope with the
mystery and magic of religious belief.

What to do with the myriad rules and regulations that bound
Jews to their faith and served to separate them from others?
Reformers desired to do away with these rules. It was a matter
of scraping away the "tattered encasing," imposed by generations of rabbinic interpretations, from what was eternal and
indestructible in Judaism.

> Today we accept as binding only the moral laws and maintain
> only such ceremonies as elevate and sanctify our lives, but reject
> all such as are not adapted to the views and habits of modern
> civilization. We hold that all such Mosaic and Rabbinical laws as
> regulate diet, priestly purity and dress originated in ages and
> under influence of ideas altogether foreign to our present mental
> and spiritual state. They fail to impress the modern Jew with a
> spirit of priestly holiness; their observance in our days is apt
> rather to obstruct than to further modern spiritual elevation.

Although the Charleston petition did not state how "modern"
spiritual elevation differed from that of the ancient, the new
elements desired clearly entailed finding a rationale. No

modern people would long feel itself bound by a "rabbinic crudescence" that piled regulation upon regulation until it was impossible for Jews to live in the modern world and become emancipated. Extremists like Kohler felt that they had to be swept away.

A major problem, for example, was the question of the nature of the exile. Jewish tradition viewed it as a kind of divine punishment from which they would be absolved when the Messiah appeared. But that notion viewed Jews as a people rather than merely a religion. If one belonged to a separate people temporarily in exile, then how could one accept the emancipation, that offered Jews the privilege of becoming citizens of the modern secular state? Implicit in the traditional assumption was the problem of dual loyalties.

The exile had to be converted from a curse into a blessing and from a temporary condition into a permanent one. That was achieved by reformers by defining Judaism purely in denominational terms. "We consider ourselves no longer a nation," stated the Pittsburgh platform, "but a religious community, and therefore expect neither a return to Palestine, nor the restoration of any laws concerning the Jewish state." Gustav Posnanski put it more simply: "This country is our Palestine, this city our Jerusalem, this house of God our temple." The exile was, in fact, God's will for His people, who would serve as priestly missionaries unto the nations. But by insisting that the exile was permanent and defining Judaism in one-dimensional religious terms, the Reform movement set itself on a collision course with other Jews, primarily those of Eastern Europe, whose ideology, Zionism, would insist that precisely the reverse was the nature of Judaism. The Jews were one people and their homeland was Palestine. It would be Zionism that served as the centerpiece for a new kind of civil religion for American Jewry in the twentieth century.

But in the final quarter of the nineteenth century, the Reform movement entered its period of triumphalism. Its institutional structure was completed in 1889 with the creation of the Central Conference of American Rabbis. Earlier it had established its rabbinic training academy, the Hebrew Union College, in

Cincinnati, a city of the West far removed from European influence.

It remains for us to consider some of the implications of the Reform movement in America. It was the first organized attempt by American Jewry to deal with the problems posed by the Americanization process. It did so by modifying Judaism so that it could operate in America. It is to the credit of the early Reformers that they understood that America posed special problems for Judaism, and that they had to be confronted. But the appropriateness of their solutions have never been finally determinable.

Those who see Reform as a dangerous development, which created merely a pale imitation of a liberal Protestant sect—a back door out of Judaism—can see nothing familiarly Jewish in nineteenth-century Reform. They argue that in making Judaism rational, Reformers threw out the baby with the bathwater. Their purpose was not to strengthen Judaism but to make it convenient for those Jews anxious to enter fully into the secular society. Its effect was to conceal momentarily the self-abnegating effects of the act of assimilation.

There are those who argue just as vehemently that the Reform movement saved Judaism in America by bravely confronting the problems posed by an intensely secular society, which was at the same time free and open. It offered Jews a survival strategy, allowing them to maintain a connection with their faith while becoming acceptable Americans. It served as a break on what might have become a headlong flight out of a Judaic belief system so all-encompassing that a rupture under the intense pressure of American society was preordained. American Jews of the nineteenth century, they point out, were already making many of the moves in their personal lives that Reform later sanctioned. They point to the fact that the Reform movement is dynamic and self-correcting. Its position on women in the synagogue was generations ahead of other branches, which are just today catching up with it. It remains in the forefront, making the necessary changes without which no institution can survive. If the Pittsburgh platform went too far in rationalizing Judaism, then future conferences such as the one held in Columbus in 1937 corrected the effort. That conference declared that Zionism and Reform were not incompatible. Today the rabbis trained at Hebrew Union College have spent a year in Israel and speak Hebrew. In some respects they have become indistinguishable from Conservative rabbis.

The argument of Reform advocates continues: It is that ability to change which has permitted the Reform movement to survive the challenge posed by the Eastern Jewish immigrants and their descendants, who for various reasons were far more imbued with the concept of Jewish peoplehood. Most candidates for Reform pulpits today are the descendants of East European immigrants. In the twenty years after World War II, the number of Reform congregations more than doubled, and Hebrew Union College is turning away almost as many applicants as it accepts. These signs of vitality would not have been possible had the Reform movement sought to compromise Judaism, as its opponents argue.

Readers may judge for themselves who has the better of the argument.

Bibliography

Ahlstrom, S. E. *A Religious History of the American People* New Haven: 1972.

"The Centennial of Reform Judaism in America." *American Jewish Historical Quarterly*, vol. 63 (December 1973).

Fein, L., et al. *Reform Is a Verb*. New York: 1972.

Heller, J. G. *Isaac M. Wise: His Life, Work and Thought*. New York: 1901.

Jick, L. A. *The Americanization of the Synagogue, 1820–1870* Hanover: 1976.

Lenn, T. I. *Rabbi and Synagogue in Reform Judaism*. New York: 1972.

Philipson, D. *My Life as an American Jew: An Autobiography*. Cincinnati: 1941.

Plaut, G. *The Growth of Reform Judaism: American and European Sources until 1948*. New York: 1965.

Wise, I. M. *Reminiscences*. New York: 1901.

Chapter IV

The Ghetto as Bridge
between Past and Future

NEW YORK'S Lower East Side and the dozens of similar enclaves in American cities deserve our special attention, because there the Eastern Jewish immigrants developed a unique transitional culture, whose residual effects still nourish what passes for a distinctive Jewish culture today. Nostalgia for that culture partly accounts for the popularity of books like Irving Howe's *World of Our Fathers* (1976) and films like "Hester Street." But the task of the historian examining that culture is more challenging, because over the years it has been impacted by an idyllic haze that conceals the full truth. Moreover, the Lower East Side and the dozens of smaller ghettos it has come to symbolize represent more than congested geographic locations where thousands of immigrant Jews settled and lived out their lives. We are examining a peculiar culture composed of elements of the Old World, amalgamated with elements of the new. The Jews lived delicately suspended between the two, trying to achieve some kind of balance, only to discover that even in this special incubator acculturation was such a dynamic process that ultimately such a balance served as only a temporary survival strategy. It permitted immigrants to better cope with the shock of transplantation by entering the new culture at their own pace; ultimately they would be overwhelmed. Despite our great idealization of that culture from hindsight, it was never destined to be a permanent community. A perceptive observer might, in fact, be able to measure the process of acculturation by the progressive dissolution of the elements of that culture: the general decline of population density after 1910, the declining attendance at performances of the Yiddish theater, declining circulation of the Yiddish press, and declines in the rank and file of the United Hebrew Trades; these changes were symptomatic of the decline of a transitional community.

The New York ghetto, located on the East Side of Manhattan below Fourteenth Street, where the island bulges towards Brooklyn, contained some of the oldest housing in the city. However, it was not the quality of the housing but the number of people who tried to squeeze into it that determined the principal characteristic of the ghetto: its congestion, its sheer mass of humanity, which made its crowded streets appear to be in a perpetual state of near riot. Some viewed that bustling street action through a romantic haze, but for those compelled to live in these crowded dumbbell flats, where beds were occupied by different tenants night and day and families were forced to take in a boarder to help with the rent, it was the source of constant nervous anxiety. At the turn of the century, some blocks in the ghetto surpassed cities like Calcutta in congestion. But even the extreme congestion was transitory. After New York City developed its transportation grid, it was possible for the Eastern immigrants to escape to new neighborhoods—Williamsburg, Brownsville, Harlem, and the East Bronx—where they soon developed satellite ghettos.

At least part of the reason for the geographic location of the ghetto was its proximity to the garment industry, which was at that time located below Fourteenth Street and controlled by a kindred group of German Jewish entrepreneurs. It would be an error to think that Eastern Jewish immigrants were born with a natural penchant for sitting bent over a sewing machine. In fact, only 10 percent of the East European immigrant labor force were trained tailors. Many of the immigrants who found employment in the garment industry actually learned the trade here and were dubbed "Columbus tailors." Aside from the approximately 60 percent of the Jewish labor force employed in the garment industry, 5.9 percent found work in the construction industry. Among these were included the famous "*paintners*," about whom there is so much jesting among Jews. There were, in addition, numerous other crafts and skills, cigar makers, iron workers, tinsmiths, roofers, a growing number of white collar workers, and, of course, the omnipresent salesmen and drummers. There were also a goodly number who, at the

earliest convenience, reverted to the traditional Jewish preference for self-employment in small business. Predictably, merchandizing, grocery and candy stores, haberdasheries, pushcart
peddling, and customer–peddling were popular. About 23.5
percent of the ghetto's breadwinners earned their living in this
way. In the almost all-Jewish Eighth Assembly district, fondly
nicknamed *Der Ate*, there were 144 groceries, 131 butcher shops
(where, we shall note later, the purchaser could not always be
certain that the meat purchased was indeed kosher), 62 candy
stores (which became social hubs for a youthful street-corner
society), 36 bakeries, and 2,440 peddlers. About 1.4 percent of
the labor force earned a meager living servicing the religious
requirements of the community. They were rabbis, teachers,
cantors, ritual slaughterers, and sextons. The ghetto also had its
share of people who appeared to have no visible means of support. Some were poets or pundits or simply bohemians, who
gathered around the cafeterias of East Broadway and apparently sustained themselves by all-night discussions over innumerable glasses of hot tea. They preferred to dwell on the
problems of governing the world rather than on those of governing themselves. Then, of course, there was a minuscule
proportion who made their living through crime.

Until recently there has been little mention of crime and vice
in the ghetto. This has been understandable, since insecure
immigrant groups are especially reluctant to wash their dirty
linen in public, and Jews in particular have had difficulty in
confronting this reality. That was already apparent in Eastern
Europe, where crime had also made its debut among Jews. It is
summed up in the famous story of the desperately poor Jew
who decides to turn to a career in crime. He plans to rob the
wealthy Reb Sender who is approaching the *shtetl* in his coach.
He holds a knife to Reb Sender's throat and threatens to kill
him if he doesn't hand over his money. But Reb Sender knows
his Jewish highwayman. "You can't kill me with that knife," he
argues. The puzzled Jewish robber asks "Why not?" Reb Sender replies: "Your knife is undoubtedly *milchig* (dairy), while,
on the other hand, I am *fleischig* (meat)." According to the story,
the Jewish robber was last seen fleeing into the forest, loudly
imploring God to forgive him for his sin—not of committing

robbery and possible murder, but of mixing *milchig* and *fleischig*. How could a people so imbued with adhering to its laws participate in crime?

Jews took great pride in their civic virtue and were outraged when their reputation for being relatively free of the plague of violent criminality was challenged. That is what Police Commissioner Theodore Bingham discovered when, in September 1908, he accused New York Jewry of generating over half of the city's crime. The cries for the benighted commissioner's political scalp that arose from the Jewish community were long and loud, and the commissioner was compelled to apologize. In recent times, the idea that social pathology existed in the Jewish ghetto was concealed by the frequently heard comparison between the Black ghetto, "theirs," and the Jewish ghetto, "ours." Anxious to "prove" how much more honest the Jewish poor were, many memorialists simply overlooked the existence of crime in the ghetto. It was not totally their fault. The accusation regarding Jewish vice, especially prostitution, often originated with Progressive reformers who were apprehensive about the assimilability of the "new" immigrants and were, moreover, less open and perhaps less honest about human sexuality. Like most Victorians, they externalized their sense of guilt about sex by projecting its presumed evil properties to the nearest dependent minority. If one wants to discover what these Progressives were anxious about, one need only read what failings they were accusing others of having.

Often what the grandfathers ignore, the grandchildren seek out. Today historians seem to positively delight in dwelling on Jewish crime in the ghetto, and there is some danger that we may exaggerate in the other direction, just as former generations underplayed its existence.*

*The new interest stems from Arthur Goren's classic work, *New York Jews and the Quest for Community* (1970) which contained a remarkable chapter entitled "Crime in the Jewish Quarter." That was followed by an interesting article in *Judaism*, "The Jewish Gangster: Crime as 'Unser Shtik'," by David Singer (1974). The author, who today serves as the editor of the *American Jewish Yearbook*, pointed to the general misinformation about this area of the American Jewish experience and suggested that the time had arrived for more research on the problem. Today two doctoral dissertations are in progress on the subject of Jewish crime.

Although it is important not to read the Jewish experience on the Lower East Side entirely in terms of crime and vice, it also should not be swept under the rug. In 1960, Daniel Bell, in a chapter entitled "Crime as an American Way of Life" in his book, *The End of Ideology*, suggested that in America crime is much more than symptomatic of social disruption. It serves as an important clue to the crucial mobility question in American society. If that is true, then we need to know more about this aspect of Jewish social behavior. However, uncovering the facts is no simple task. We know that there was Jewish crime and vice on the Lower East Side and in the many other enclaves where Jews settled, but because Bingham's indictment was followed by a war of statistics, the waters are now so muddied that it is difficult to determine its extent and nature. The Lexow and Mazet investigation of the 1890s and the several investigations by immigration commissions are not much help because they are not completely value-free. The same is true of the reportage of a Progressive journalist like George Kibee Turner, who spoke of Jewish *cadets*, pimps, and procurers who loitered about the dance halls of the ghetto to lure lonely Jewish girls into prostitution. He has his own problems with prostitution and assigns mysterious and excessive sexual prowess to these pimps. But there are sufficient accounts, from Jewish and non-Jewish sources, to indicate the reality of prostitution and other forms of vice in the ghetto. "On sunshiney days," reads one such account, "the whores sat on chairs along the sidewalks. They sprawled indolently, their legs taking up half the pavement. People stumbled over a gauntlet of whores' meaty legs. The girls gossiped and chirped like a jungle of parrots. Some knitted shawls and stockings . . . others chewed Russian sunflower seeds." One Yiddish daily began to publish lists of Jewish prostitutes to "shame" them into giving up "the life." But such pressure did little good. The president of the Allen Street Synagogue complained that the Jewish prostitutes "annoyed the congregation. They . . . call to the people that are passing by . . . It is a very bad thing for the men and children going to the church to have to pass through all the things in all the houses."

What can current observers make of the prevalence of prostitution? Many religious Jews argued that such vices were caused by the wholesale abandonment of faith and were products of the American environment exclusively. But vice and crime among Jews, although undoubtedly abetted by the transplantation process, was also well known in Jewish communities in Odessa, Warsaw, and elsewhere. If it was a symptom of the deterioration of Jewish life, then that process had already begun in Europe. In the new environment, vice may be considered a particularly onerous form of mobility, as much as an act of desperation. Generations later, few would bother to inquire about the source of a family's wealth.

Prostitution was not the only vice in the ghetto. Jewish youngsters in the ghetto were as familiar with the names of Jewish gangsters who ran the extortion, protection, and gambling rackets—Kid Twist, Yuski Nigger (King of the Horse Poisoners), Dopey Benny, Kid Dropper, Gyp the Blood—as they were with Jewish prize fighters sporting Irish names. Yet, during the immigrant generation, there is some reason to believe that most Jewish crime was of a different type. Jews were more prone to commit crimes like embezzlement, failure to pay wages, business fraud, and breaking of Sunday ordinances— that is to say, bookkeeping crimes—than crimes of violence. According to Police Commissioner McAdoo, the ghetto was a relatively tranquil place. The Jews he observed were "not apt, unless under great pressure, to resort to force or to commit crimes of violence . . . Among themselves disputes are mostly confined to wordy arguments. They argue with great vigor and earnestness but the argument ends as it begins." A police report comments that Jews are "prominent in their commission of forgery, violation of corporation ordinances, as disorderly persons (failure to support wife and family), both grades of larceny, and the higher grade of assault." They were "notably little addicted to intoxicants" and furnished only "a very small proportion of vagrants." Yet, two decades later, when American-born Jewish criminals appeared on the scene, this picture had changed considerably. Then we hear of professional murder organizations like Murder, Inc., in New York City and the

Purple Gang in Detroit. The sadism of Bugsy Siegel was well known to the police. "For two bucks that Bugsy–Meyer (Lansky's) mob would break the arm of a man they'd never seen. They'd kill for less than fifty," observed one detective. "Bugsy seemed to like to do the job himself . . . it gave him a sense of power. He got kicks out of seeing his victims suffering, groaning and dying." "With the rest of us it was booze, gambling, whores, like that," testified Lucky Luciano, "but Lepke took the bread out of the workers' mouths." Jewish criminals had become no less vicious than others. They were no longer the element that supplied moxie to organized crime while others supplied muscle. By the 1920s, too, the contempt for Jewish criminals in the community had also been altered. They were sometimes considered minor folk heroes among Jews, as criminals often were among the general population.

Readers should not be surprised at these revelations. Undoubtedly the actual number of Jews who turned to crime was disproportionately small, despite the fact that all the conditions to spawn crime—grinding poverty, social dislocation attendant on the immigration experience, generational and cultural conflict—were present in ample measure in the tightly packed ghettoes. What is surprising is that there was not more crime and that the Jewish inhabitants of the ghetto sought to stamp it out without turning to the authorities. This was, indeed, a different kind of ethnic community.

The Jews as a community only barely understood the underlying causes for what they were convinced was a shameful and un-Jewish phenomenon. To be sure, they complained long and loud about the difficulty of training their children to uphold the Jewish tradition in the new environment. They must have understood that their Judaism had already become a broken vessel in Eastern Europe, but the manifestations of that fragmentation were not yet totally clear to them. America had merely accelerated the process by offering temptations like working overtime on the Sabbath, and other exciting forms of secular social diversion, which further fragmented an already beleaguered religious culture. The religious community could no longer muster the organizational energy and skill to furnish

the total environmental context required for the sustained func-
tioning of the Orthodox Jewish enterprise. There were many
congregations in which to pray, but, with few exceptions, they
were transient and local, and thus could rarely be enlisted for
tasks of social betterment. Despite the proliferation of these
shuls and *shtiblach* the crucial job of establishing schools for the
young was sadly neglected and even *mikvahs* (ritual baths) were
in short supply. The *rebbes* who acted as teachers for the children were hardly adequate for the task of passing on the tradition. Being themselves marginal to the new life, they offered no
models for the children of the ghetto and certainly no competition for the excitement of its teeming streets, which increasingly drew Jewish children. One of the secrets of Jewish survival lie in the unbroken cycle of generations whose rupture now
seemed inevitable. A gap developed between the European-born
"green," older generation, and the traditional values it upheld,
and the street-bred Americanized younger generation, whose
survival depended in some measure upon understanding the
values and modus operandi of the new environment. The flats
were small and cramped, and much living was done in the
street. Parents worked hard and were unable to supervise their
children. Moreover, despite the much-touted success stories
that initially had drawn the immigrants to the "goldeneh
medinah," many, especially in the early stages of the transplantation process, actually experienced a decline in status. Where
they had been craftsmen in the Old World, they were now
merely hands in shops. The very symbols of *kavod* (honor) had
changed. Wealth and patrimony, to be sure, had counted for
something in the Old World, but they were not the only ways
to achieve status. In Eastern Europe, arranged marriages between the daughter of an established household and a poor
scholar were commonplace, but in America the earning of
money became the exclusive path to honor. Frequently the low-
status wagon driver of the Old World could load a similar
wagon with produce and earn a better living by peddling his
wares in the streets of the ghetto than the *melamed* (the Old-
World scholar–teacher), who was unhappily compelled to in-
struct rebellious children on the subtleties of the Judaic tradi-

tion—which, in the New World, had little meaning for them. It was a world turned upside down. Not only did the old values not apply, they seemed positively to interfere with raising one's social and economic status. Honor went to the "allrightnicks," those who discarded the trappings of their old system quickly and became Americanized, and no one measured the pace of becoming acculturated, *(oisgegrint)*, more harshly than did the children.

The drive to earn a living and then a better living—the dream of leaving the ghetto, perhaps for a satellite enclave in Brooklyn or the Bronx—was pursued by the ghetto inhabitants with such relentless zeal that it inspired much commentary by the observers of ghetto life. It placed family life under enormous stress. Contrary to the popular notion regarding the strength and cohesiveness of Jewish family life, the Jewish immigrants of the Lower East Side experienced considerable family disruption, which was reflected outwardly in the highest divorce rate in the city. Undoubtedly, too, that disruption was related to ghetto crime, especially desertion of the family by the breadwinner. The defeated man who, in desperation, deserted the family hearth; variability of rate of acculturation between husband and wife; the earlier-arrived husband, compelled to live for years as a bachelor, only to find when his wife stepped off the gangplank that he no longer knew her, or wanted to; the omnipresent boarder in the flat; all contributed to malaise in the family. Fathers who could no longer command their sons to follow in a tradition of whose value they were themselves no longer certain, and sons nurtured in America who would not obey in any case, since they were more attuned to what the New World required—these ruptures were often real, not merely the source for melodrama in the Yiddish theater or the countless plots of the shundromanen ("trashy novels"), to which many ghetto inhabitants had become addicted.

One would imagine that life lived with such stress and under such poor physical conditions would break down the health of the immigrants. That was not the case. There are some indications that illness related to stress—various psychosomatic disorders, ulcers, hypertension, and neurasthenia—were well represented among Jewish immigrants. But the perennial complaints of immigration officials regarding the generally low physical state of the new arrivals: their poor musculature, small stature, and sallow complexions—observations often made by Jewish labor organizers as well—was not reflected in the mortality tables. According to one report, the almost all-Jewish Tenth Ward had the lowest mortality rate in the city (lower than the comparable Italian ghetto and even the native-born population). Tuberculosis, the bane of the poor living in congested areas at the turn of the century, was less prevalent among Jews than among other ghetto inhabitants.

How can we account for the relative good health of Jews living in such miserable circumstances? Puzzling over that fact, contemporary observers attributed it to the sobriety of the Jews and their generally temperate and moderate life-style. Alcoholism was then (although not today) virtually unknown among the Jews. They were addicted to only one drink, seltzer, and drowned their sorrows in alcohol only on Purim, when it was permitted. A more likely reason was that Jews also simply maintained a better diet. Even the poorest among them ate well, at least on the Sabbath, and as a group they were notorious for their concentration on nutrition in their religious laws. But even here one can have some doubts, since the sketchy reports that we possess show that the Sabbath was honored more in the breach than in the observance and that *kashrut* (observance of Jewish dietary laws) may have willingly or unwillingly gone unobserved. The new-found fondness for the *shwitz*, (Turkish bath) may have gone far to maintain personal cleanliness as well as to relieve stress, but that would hardly account for the longevity of the Jews in the ghetto. More likely, the small edge the Jews had in retaining their health amounted to a generally superior knowledge of preventive health care (gleaned from the Yiddish press, which featured columns on health avidly read), and to the fact that the local pharmacist, one of the popular first avocations of Jews, was often able to give good medical advice. Medicine was an honored profession among Jews; as a result, the ghetto early possessed a medical-care network composed of pharmacists, private doctors (who made house calls), and hospitals with outpatient clinics, which served the needs of the ghetto dwellers for health care. Finally, it should be noted that the original observations of government officials concerning the poor physical state of the Jewish immigrants is to be accepted with some care. The observations were made by native-born government officials, who naturally assumed that good health had something to do with height and complexion—that is, height and complexion like their own.

Yet, in retrospect, the objectives of Jewish immigrant ambition were modest. The desideratum was not to become a millionaire—whose richly appointed mansions on Fifth Avenue were, however, admired—but merely a modest rise in station, which would permit the family to leave the ghetto; if not the parents, then at least the children. The twin conduits for such a rise were small business and education, or, more precisely, certification. Contrary to popular belief, which assigns a major role to education in the amazing mobility of the Jewish immigrant generation, small business may actually have played the more important role. Unbridled ambition could create problems as well as prospects. No small portion of the crucible of the sweatshop experienced by so many Jewish immigrants can be attributed to the headlong rush of Jewish workers to become subcontractors. We shall discuss this in more detail in terms of the Jewish labor movement (Chapter VI). It is sufficient here to note that, after 1900, many of the new arrivals worked for bosses and paid rent to landlords, who may have arrived as Jewish immigrants but a decade before, and established themselves since then.

The craze for education may well have been a separate *meshugas* (craziness), apart from the notion that it held out the promise of a rosier future. For many who dragged their weary bodies to night school, or to the many free lectures in the ghetto, it did no such thing, since the professions and the lower rungs of the civil service were for many reasons beyond the Jewish ken and thus played but a minor part in their aspirations. It might be best to view the desire to be in business and the craze for education as part of a general release of energy that for generations had had to be suppressed in the Old World and was now released with the force of a tensed steel coil in the free environment of the New World. It was as if Jews were making up for centuries of time lost in Eastern Europe. Then, too, the educated man, the Talmudist or doctor, had traditionally earned enormous, often uncritical, respect in the Jewish community. It was but a small jump to bestow the same respect on someone who had "education" in secular subjects. That was, in any case, the direction in which most Jews were moving. This may partly explain why a disproportionate number of immigrants achieved professional status so early: it had a psychic as well as monetary reward. In the decade after 1897, the number of Jewish doctors doubled, the number of lawyers increased almost as fast, and the same rapid increase held true for accountants. That was merely the tip of the iceberg, beneath which could be found an enormous increase in the number of immigrants enrolled in one kind of school or another. A survey of seventy-seven institutions of higher learning in the New York metropolitan area, taken in 1908 when Jews formed roughly 2 percent of the population, indicates that they then supplied 8.5 percent of the student body. By 1888 each succeeding class of the City College of New York (formerly a sleepy academic playground for the established Protestant middle class, but soon to be dubbed the College of the Circumcised Citizens of New York) was at least 25 percent Jewish. With that change, it became a vibrant "Proletariat Ivy League" with a nation-wide reputation.

Nor was the desire for education confined to any particular class of the Jewish population. Night schools in the ghetto were packed to the brim, as were the dozens of free lectures presented every night to an education-starved Jewish audience. It was observed that Jewish parents, having themselves only the barest rudiments of education, brought their children to school as if it were a holy temple, and the Irish schoolmarm, herself often boasting only the outward signs of an "educated person," its high priestess. The truancy rate was remarkably low in Jewish neighborhoods, the surviving records inform us, and whereas many young Jews were compelled to curtail their education prematurely because of the need for additional breadwinners in the family, the drop-out rate for Jews was considerably below that of other groups—Poles, Italians, and Ukrainians. That may be more a sign of the high priority given to education among Jews than to their relative prosperity.

They did well in school. "They are mentally alert," one exasperated teacher noted, "colorful, intelligent, the backbone of my class, but they can be an insufferable nuisance because of their constant desire to distinguish themselves." Jacob Riis, who did not always muster much enthusiasm about the ascetic ways of the Jews, nevertheless admired "the ease and rapidity with which they learn." Yet the Board of Education, perhaps unaccustomed to having its product taken so seriously, warned in 1908 about the negative side of this enthusiasm: "Overintellectuality, overdevelopment of mind at expense of body, impatience at slow progress, supersensitivity, little interest in physical sport . . ." And if poorly trained professional educators sometimes found their Jewish students exasperating in their eagerness, local librarians might feel gratification at the avidity with which their shelves were emptied by Jewish readers in the ghetto. The old records show that libraries in Jewish neighborhoods were so packed that often lines of anxious readers formed outside the library's doors. What did Jewish readers prefer in books? The records show that ghetto libraries ranked first in the city in the circulation of books on history and science. That preference seemed to symbolize the very tension of the acculturation process and the unique transitional culture developed by Jewish immigrants on the Lower East Side. Everything in the New World seemed to be undergoing an accelerated process of change, but there was still something recognizable that remained of the older tradition. Jews were still the "people of the book," even while the theme of the book was no longer the same.

Bibliography

American Jewish History, December, 1981. Vol. LXXI. Issue: "Centennial of Eastern European Jewish Immigration, 1881–1981."

Bell, D. *The End of Ideology* New York: 1962. (See Chapter 7. "Crime as an American Way of Life: A Queer Ladder of Social Mobility."

Berrol, S. C. *Immigrants at School*, doctoral dissertation, City University of New York, 1967.

Cahan, A. *The Rise of David Levinsky*. New York: 1917.

Gold, M. *Jews Without Money* New York: 1930.

Goren, A. *New York Jews and the Quest for Community* New York: 1970.

Gurock, J. *When Harlem Was Jewish, 1870–1930* New York: 1979.

Hapgood, H. *The Spirit of the Ghetto*. New York: 1965.

Howe, I. *World of Our Fathers*. New York: 1976.

Karp. A. J., ed. *The Jewish Experience in America*. Waltham: 1969.

Kessner, T. *The Golden Door*. New York: 1977.

Lindenthal, J. J. "Abi Gezunt: Health and the Eastern European Jewish Immigrant," *American Jewish History*, June, 1981, Vol. 70.

Metzker, I., ed. *A Bintel Brief*. New York: 1972.

Rischin, M. *The Promised City*. New York: 1962.

Sanders, R. *The Downtown Jews*. New York: 1977.

Chapter V

The Yiddish Theater and the
Genesis of Cultural Consumerism

"WHEN I hear the word culture," the Nazi ideologue Alfred Rosenberg is purported to have said, "I reach for my gun." Nazi cosmology did not have much use for cultural refinement. Civilizations that paid too much attention to such things were thought to be effete and vulnerable. Preoccupation with culture compromised the ability to wage the Darwinian struggle for survival, which was the driving force of history. In an indirect way the Nazis' murderous hatred of Jews was linked to that concept. Jews as culture carriers were compromising the fighting spirit of a renascent Reich. There was a paradox in all this, which could not have escaped the most fanatical Nazi. The people who have survived perhaps longer than any other civilization, the Jews, placed ideas, literature, and the theater arts high on their list of priorities.

That was as much true of the Jews of Eastern Europe who settled in the ghettos of the cities of the Eastern Seaboard as it had been of the Jews of Germany. Food for the mind and spirit was as important as nourishment for the body. No matter how poor, the family could scrape together enough money to purchase a book, attend a theater performance, and sometimes even to buy a second-hand piano. We want to examine the unique cultural effervescence developed by the Eastern Jews in America generated by these extraordinary priorities. No other immigrant group in America developed anything quite like it: Although these other groups also developed their own theater, literature, and press, it was not nearly as extensive and broad as, nor did it possess the sustained vibrancy of, the Yiddish-speaking culture.

Before continuing, the term "culture" should be defined for purposes of the discussion. That can be complicated, because, in one sense, anything a given community does—from its bread baking to its courting—can be considered its culture. That is not what we are speaking about here. As we are employing the term "culture," it has a highly specific meaning: a contrived and artificial series of activities—theater and fine arts, dance, literature, and music—by means of which a people states its values, thinks about its condition, examines its history and its heroes, and identifies itself to the world and itself. American Jewry, as it developed at the close of the nineteenth century and the early decades of the twentieth century, is singular because of the richness of its culture. Although not confined to the Yiddish theater, that richness was especially apparent there.

The distinctive culture developed by the Eastern immigrants on the Lower East Side was composed of many strands. There were from the outset writers and poets who did not form a self-conscious group. Because they earned their bread by working and wrote about their crucible, they were sometimes called "sweatshop" poets, and judged by contemporary standards, their work, primitive and full of raw emotion, might be considered amateurish. Yet their work served a cultural purpose. "The poems and stories helped them to understand their new environment," writes one critic, "and most of all themselves . . . they thought in literature the same thing they wanted in a newspaper: a way of becoming somewhat less a 'green horn,' a way of escaping a little from their loneliness." The poet Chaim Grade and the writer Isaac Bahevis Singer, who recently won the Nobel Prize for literature, are modern sophisticated echoes of this movement. The early poets and writers gained almost no recognition in the general world of literature, but they were very popular and close to their Jewish audiences, whose experiences they depicted in the Yiddish press. Abraham Reisin became a kind of folk hero, and a hundred thousand fans and admirers paid their last respects by visiting Sholom Aleichem's Bronx apartment when he died in 1916. The writers and poets did not long remain alone in the cultural enterprise. Almost from the beginning they were joined by a group of social philosophers, political thinkers, and commentators, typically of socialist persuasion. There was also a school of painting centered around the Educational Alliance, which, while not precisely devoted to the exploration of Jewish themes, was populated by immigrant Jewish painters like Chaim Gross, Raphael and Moses Soyer, Max Weber, and Jacques Lipshitz. And there was the Yiddish theater, on which we will focus in this chapter.

Perhaps the most interesting facet of Yiddish culture in America was the development of a separate Jewish intellectual establishment, which generated ideas and analyses largely unknown in the American world of ideas. Ideologies and prescriptions for the cure of societal ills were traditionally taken seriously in the Jewish community, as were their propounders. The man who spoke well and could explain complex ideological systems, the intellectual who could claim some smattering of education, was highly esteemed, perhaps uncritically so. It may well be that these intellectuals, whether they became newspaper editors, journalists, labor organizers, or people who waxed eloquent in the all-night discussions in the cafeterias on East Broadway, were simply endowed with the prestige assigned formerly to the rabbi–teacher. They were the latters' secular equivalents and substitutes. Their ideas about socialism, anarchism, or simply the best way to organize society—in a word, the prescriptive literature they produced—appeared in the Yiddish press and small irregularly published journals. It was from these humble beginnings that the Yiddish press, a press like no other, originated. If one wanted to tune in on a vibrant discussion of the questions of the day, or learn something about American government, or the problems facing Jews in Russia or Rumania, or even learn how best to handle a health problem, one could do so by reading the Yiddish press and journals. The Jewish intellectual establishment that developed in New York and other major metropolitan centers differed substantially from the standard American procedure for generating ideas. Rather than being connected with a university, it was independent, or was sponsored by a political faction or organization like the Jewish labor movement or a religious branch. Eventually, a nexus of thinkers of all persuasions developed, earning a precarious livelihood by packaging and merchandizing ideas through transient minor publications. Its resonance is still felt in the Jewish community today. Listen to Irving Howe describing contemporary New York intellectuals:

> They appear to have a common history, prolonged now for more than thirty years, a common political outlook, even if marked by ceaseless internecine quarrels, a common style of thought and perhaps composition, a common focus of intellectual interest, and once you get past politeness—which becomes these days, easier and easier—a common ethnic origin. They are, or until recently have been, anti-communist, they are, or until some time ago were, radicals, they have a fondness for ideological speculation; they write literary criticism with a strong social emphasis, they revel in polemic, they strive self-consciously to be "brilliant" and by birth or osmosis, they are Jews.

That neatly portrays New York intellectuals. Howe sees them as Jewish types rather than genetically Jewish, and, in fact, like all who assume an intellectual posture vis-a-vis society, they are as much alienated from American society as they are from their Jewish roots. In fact, I have called it Yiddish or Jewish culture, rather than Judaic, to circumvent a problem posed by these culture carriers, whether they be writers or playwrights. This culture was Jewish in the ethnic rather than the religious sense. It was Jewish because the artists and writers who produced it were Jewish, used a Jewish metaphor, and wrote for Jewish audiences in the language used by Jews. The creators in many cases were alienated from or ambivalent about the religious roots of Jewish peoplehood, and so too was much of their audience. Although frequently resorting to religious fables, customs, and even prayers, Jewish culture was basically secular.

On what basis did this enthusiasm for elevation through culture grow? One might imagine that a group so preoccupied with earning its bread and adjusting to a new environment would not have the time to write its *tsoris* (troubles) down and act them out on the stage. We must be aware that, like so many other things in American Jewish history—its religious branches, the extraordinary German Jewish banking establishment, and the Jewish labor movement—the Yiddish culture of the American ghetto was heavily derivative. It borrowed form, subject, and, of course, the artists themselves from European Jewry. The blossoming of a Yiddish culture on the Lower East Side was in good measure a spin-off of the vibrant Yiddish culture of Eastern Europe. Then what did America, or more specifically the ghetto, contribute? It gathered together in one place, a large cosmopolitan city, a potential audience large enough to support such a culture. The aggregation of Jews in New York City at the turn of the century was already the largest in the world. Moreover, it was an audience unlike that which could be found in other Jewish population centers, such as Warsaw or Vilna. New York Jewry was a collectivity composed of all the various regions and centers of Eastern Europe: the Russian Pale, Galicia, Lithuania, Rumania, Hungary, and others. Paradoxically, a unified expression of all the components of European Jewry was possible only in New York. The audience itself was unique in another respect. It had become largely proletarianized in the transplantation process and possessed only a rudimentary education. Yet, it was a peculiar type of underclass, for Jewish workers aspired to higher things, they wanted a culture like that usually associated with the middle class. Perhaps the most remarkable facet of the Yiddish culture generated in America was its consumers. They were people who toiled bone-wearying hours in the shops and then mustered the energy to drag themselves to the libraries, lectures, innumerable discussion groups, and theater to get culture and education. Few other groups in America, native or immigrant, has had such an appetite, such a desire to elevate itself.

The second factor that contributed to the generation of a distinctive Yiddish culture in America was that the immigration and transplantation experience possessed an epic quality. It had heroic, tragic, and sometimes merely puzzling aspects that could serve as the plots for a thousand stories and dramas. In a real sense, the immigrant generation required a literature and a theater to explain its experience to itself. That is, in fact, what the writers and playwrights really did. The urban environment of America merely presented the required conditions—freedom of expression, a new urban experience, and an outlet for the latent talent of its writers, artists, and playwrights—in which the culture could develop.

The Yiddish theater was an important component of that culture and deserves a more detailed examination. To find its roots we must go back to Eastern Europe. The Jewish religious tradition had customarily featured a kind of primitive dramatic skit in its Purim plays. There were also itinerant musicians, tales of wondrous chassidic *rebbes*, and traveling troupes of performers. By the mid-nineteenth century these separate strands of what might compose a theater culture began to come together under the impact of improved transportation, which permitted groups of players like the Brody singers to travel safely from place to place to perform. At the same time, the secularizing influence of the *haskala* (definable here as simply a Jewish version of the enlightenment) encouraged potential Jewish creative spirits to view themselves self-consciously as a group apart, while at the same time preparing the Jewish audience to receive its message. It was these circumstances that led playwrights like Israel Grodner and Abraham Goldfaden to organize theater and write for it. From the beginning, it was a secular theater, and it probably could not have succeeded, even in a limited way, if the potential audiences had not become similarly secularized. Performances and skits developed first in the active Jewish cafe life of Jassy, Rumania, where Abraham Goldfaden, the father of Yiddish theater, held sway. The fare was rudimentary: light musical numbers and short skits on historical themes in Jewish history—Judah Macabe and Bar Kochba. It was Zelig Mogilevsky, an actor who appeared in Rumania under the stage name of Sigmund Mogulesco, who brought the first Jewish acting company to New York in 1882. It took hold in the public mind only after many trials. In 1886 a troupe headed by Boris Thomashevsky established itself as the National Theater. When talented playwrights like Jacob Gordin and "stars" like Jacob Adler joined the enterprise, its success was assured. By

1900 there were three major theater troupes, and numerous smaller endeavors in other Jewish population centers. By 1918 New York City alone boasted twenty Yiddish theaters of varying size and importance. In addition, theater groups had developed in Philadelphia, Boston, and Chicago. There were also about seventy to eighty Yiddish actors and a dozen playwrights. According to one critic, the Yiddish theater surpassed in quality, impact, and popularity the legitimate Broadway stage.

What kind of theater was it that won the plaudits on non-Jewish critics? The answer depends on what period is being examined. The earliest productions were little more than improvizations based on plot outlines, with actors making up the dialogue as they went along. It was a superb training ground for actors, but drove playwrights like Jacob Gordin to distraction. The immigrant community could boast of few heroes, military or athletic, who might be idealized by the populace. The star of the Jewish stage was the closest they came to hero worship. The minutest detail of the stars' personal lives, including their gastronomical and sexual prowess, were known, discussed, and admired by their fans. It may well be that the prototype of the groupie, the adoring fan, first appeared in the Jewish ghetto, in relation to stars of the Yiddish theater. Stars like Boris Thomaschefsky and Jacob Adler strode around the Lower East Side with their courts, followed everywhere by adoring fans. To this adulation the stars responded with haughtiness and contempt. By the standards of the ghetto inhabitants, they had reached the pinnacle of success and therefore earned the right to take themselves seriously. At the outset, they were paid a share of the box office receipts, and later, when the theater was more established, a fixed salary. The stars' roles were not as specialized as they are today, since actors also played some part in production and direction. But the star system worked well only for the stars: choristers were among the first group to petition the United Hebrew Trades for a union charter. If the system sounds familiar to the reader, it is because it is reminiscent of the culture of show business even today. In fact, research on the relationship between the show-business culture of Hollywood and its link to the Yiddish version of "show biz"

might yield some interesting findings. It may be that the uner-
ring instinct of the Hollywood dream-factory technicians for
placing their offerings precisely where popular sentiment is—
perhaps the key to Hollywood's influence—was first honed in
the Yiddish theater.

The popularity of the theater among the Jewish working-
class audience was based in good part on the fact that the plays
did not demand literacy or abstraction from the audience. They
were pitched, especially on weekends when the ever-popular
shunde ("trashy") plays were featured, on the lowest level; they
were designed for quick release of emotions. Once could have a
good cry, followed by a quick laugh. Today we would probably consider much of the fare to be melodrama or soap opera,
although in later years some plays, which were adapted from
major playwrights like Strindberg, rose above that level. For
the most part, the themes of the plays sought to portray the
lives of ordinary Jews caught up in the problems of living in the
new social milieu: disoriented immigrants who chose the wrong
path, generational conflict, wayward sons clashing with pious
fathers, daughters gone bad or daughters in conflict with cruel
stepmothers, deserted wives, and so on. The themes were
based on "realism with a little extra." But although the plots
were realistic in the sense that the audience could recognize the
possibility of the life presented, the acting was exaggerated and
unabashedly corny. Yet critics have observed that the acting,
overstated as it was, was probably among the finest that could
be found on the American stage; many budding thespians came
to Second Avenue to learn how it was done. The secret of
success of the Yiddish stage was that it remained unerringly a
popular art, in which the immigrant audience could recognize
itself. One observer noted that, more than anything else, it
resembled Italian opera without singing. That format remained
constant even when the dramatists adapted plays from Shake-
speare, Strindberg, or Ibsen. The plot was then changed to suit
the sensibilities of a Jewish audience. If a play seemed flat and
tedious or did not generate enough emotion, the directors and
actors were unmerciful in employing special devices guaranteed
to heighten the involvement of a Jewish audience. The chanting
of the Kaddish, the prayer for the dead, was a sure-fire device

to bring crying and moaning from the audience. It could redeem the worst *shmate* (literally, "rag," the skeptical theater-
goer's term for a poor formula play; sometimes also called a
Horowitzism, after a playwright who seemed to be able to write
them on an assembly-line basis). In sum, the Yiddish theater
was one of primary emotions, and it was precisely that character that made it popular among immigrant audiences.

The most remarkable element in the world of the Yiddish
theater may not have been the dramatic fare at all but the
audiences that patronized the theater. Their involvement was
fervent and total. Often they would become so involved in the
happenings on the stage that they would intrude themselves
into the performance, yelling out advice, and venting their anger at the villain or their sympathy for the victim. Overcome by
Jacob Adler's performance in "The Jewish King Lear," a man
rose from his seat and ran down the aisle shouting: "To hell
with your stingy daughter, Yankl! She has a stone not a heart.
Spit on her Yankl, and come home with me. My Yidene
[Jewish wife] will feed you. Come Yankl, may she choke, that
rotten daughter of yours."

Hutchins Hapgood (9), an intrepid observer of Jewish life
in the ghetto, describes the theater audience this way:

Poor workingmen and women with their babies of all ages fill the
theater. Great enthusiasm is manifested, sincere laughter and
tears accompany the sincere acting on the stage. Peddlers of soda
water, candy, of fantastic gewgaws of many kinds mix freely
with the audience between the acts. Conversation during the
play is received with strenuous hisses, but the falling of the
curtain is the signal for groups to get together and gossip about
the play or the affairs of the week . . . On the stage curtain are
advertisements of the wares of Hester Street or portraits of star
actors . . . On the programs or circulars distributed in the audience are sometimes amusing announcements of coming attrac-
tions or lyric praise of the stars . . .

These theater-goers were not members of the genteel, decorous
bourgeoisie, concerned about decorum, but rather an audience
of plebian character, unabashed in their emotion and caring
little to conceal their feelings. "It was an unruly theater," ob-

serves Irving Howe. "People munched fruit, cracked peanuts, greeted *landslayt.*" The lack of decorum while the play was in progress, the loud audience reaction at strategic turns in the plot, disturbed some of the more serious theatergoers. As in the synagogue, when worshipers talked during a solemn prayer or the rabbi's sermon, there were loud shouts for order, which were echoed and reechoed by others until they themselves became a source of greater disorder. The purchase of tickets and attendance at the performance was not recommended for those with delicate nerves or excessive sensitivity.

Though the tickets cost anywhere from twenty-five cents to a dollar, not cheap for the stretched budgets of the immigrant workers, great numbers were purchased and used. In 1910, it was estimated that twenty-five thousand tickets a week were sold. Not all who attended were regular theater buffs. Many were lured to the theater by the clever marketing strategies of the producers, who soon learned to establish links to the larger membership organizations *(landsmannschaften)*, fraternal clubs, and locals of the labor unions, which would be sold the house or a section of it at a discount rate for a "benefit" performance. Usually done during a weekday night or matinee performance, the "benefits" guaranteed the producers a full house and the organizations were at the same time sponsoring an activity and (by selling the tickets at a higher price) able to keep their coffers filled. It was mutually advantageous.

Despite their enthusiasm, the untutored audiences were not uncritical of their theater experience, nor were they necessarily satisfied with what they saw. As a rule, the lower the common denominator of the play, the more *shunde*, the more popular and profitable it tended to be. Nevertheless, the unspoken rules for what could be portrayed on stage were strictly adhered to. Scenes of explicit sexuality were shunned, and the family was considered sacrosanct. Yet there could be sexual innuendo and sometimes an earthy vulgarity, so that the religious segment of the ghetto did not attend the Yiddish theater, considering it sacrilegious. Even for recently secularized Jews, religious sensibilities could pose a problem for producers. Hapgood observed Jewish audiences openly hissing the actors who lit cigarettes on the stage on Friday night, even while the protesters themselves were in the theater rather than in the synagogue or in their homes observing the Sabbath. It was a confused and confusing audience. Another group rarely to be seen in the Yiddish theater were the "uptown" Jews who had come from Germany in the nineteenth century and had reached middle-class respectability. They were offended by the Yiddish jargon, for which they had great contempt, and embarrassed by the raw emotionalism of the Eastern Jewish audiences. Yet upper-class reformers like Lincoln Steffens greatly enjoyed the theater, especially the emotionalism, which was rarely on display in their own cool Anglo-Saxon world.

Finally, the Yiddish press, especially Cahan of the *Forward*, often criticized the fare of the Yiddish theater. There may have been two reasons for this: a genuine distress at what they considered the low level of the art and a pique at the strong competitive influence the Yiddish theater posed for the minds and hearts of the ghetto inhabitants. Next to the press itself, which not only serialized the latest *novels* but served as a conduit for the literary and intellectual offerings of Yiddish culture, the theater was probably the most successful single cultural agent in the ghetto. It was an essential element in the remarkable transitional culture generated by Eastern Jewish immigrants in America.

Bibliography

Cahan, I. *The Education of Abraham Cahan*, ed. Leon Stein. Philadelphia: 1969.

Hapgood, H. *The Spirit of the Ghetto*. New York: 1965.

Howe, I. *Decline of the New* New York: 1970—Chapter: "The New York Intellectuals."

Howe, I. "The East European Jews and American Culture." *Jewish Life in America: Historical Perspectives*, ed. Gladys Rosen. New York: 1978.

Howe, I., and E. Greenburg. *Voices from the Yiddish*. Ann Arbor: 1972.

Lifson, D. *The Yiddish Theater in America*. New York: 1965.

Madison, C. A. *Jewish Publishing in America* New York: 1976.

Waxman, M. *A History of Jewish Literature*. New York: 1960.

CHAPTER VI

Matching Power and Responsibility:
The Jewish Labor Movement

I F anyone were to ask me what I thought was the most important single network of organizations developed by American Jewry, I would have to answer, those associated with the
American Jewish labor movement, especially the United Hebrew Trades. The reason why I assign them such importance is
that the Jewish labor movement was singular in developing
power in the economic sphere. Other organizations, those
grouped around the Zionist ideology or religious or fraternal
activity, developed indirect power based on persuasion or influence in Washington. They used words, arguments, and
sometimes threats, but only the Jewish labor movement could
exercise direct power by means of the collective action of its
rank and file. The ability to exercise direct power is of crucial
importance, because how a group handles power—whether it
over- or under-uses it, and whether it matches its use with
responsibility—tells us much more about its real character than
does its rhetoric. With Jews, drunk as they are with the use of
language, it seems more important to watch what they do than
to hear what they say. Unfortunately, there is little opportunity
to do that in the American Jewish experience, because examples
of Jews exercising real power are so rare: Jewish power is usually the power of words rather than of action. The Jewish labor
movement is an exception.

There is another reason why an examination of the Jewish
labor movement gives the historian important insights into the
character of American Jewry. It broadens our gauge. We have

no other examples of how Jews behave when they are not a segment of a middle-class group—merchants, small industrialists, or professionals. The existence of a group gathered in one place who—in the way they earned their bread, if not in their aspiration level—belonged to the working rather than to the middle class, gives us a basis of comparison available nowhere else in American Jewish history. One soon learns that Jewish workers and their organizations were no less remarkable than Jewish businessmen.

The first problem for the historian is to determine what is Jewish about the Jewish labor movement other than that it involved Jews: Did it carry a particularly Jewish message? Was it motivated by a Jewish ethos? Even though the movement operated in a virtually all-Jewish context—both "bosses" and workers were Jewish—these are difficult questions to answer. Although the struggle to organize and win better working conditions was waged within the community rather than against an outside force, the movement itself, in its propounding of a universalist socialist ethos and in its insistence on considering itself part of the general working-class movement rather than a particularistic Jewish one, tended to deny its Jewish content.

On its face, the development of labor unions among Jews should not puzzle us. They were, after all, workers, and workers often organize. What is less clear is why Jewish workers insisted on forming separate locals rather than joining those already in existence. Yet, even that does not seem so strange among newly arrived immigrant groups. In the nineteenth century, German-Americans did so; it was, in fact, a remnant of the German Workers Federation that gave the United Hebrew Trades its start. The basis for such unions was in the common historic experience and condition of the rank and file. The reason for forming a Jewish labor movement is first and foremost related to the proletarianization of immigrants, 60 percent of whom became workers. Of course, many had also toiled for a living in Eastern Europe, but there was a difference in their condition in America. With the exception of cities like Lodz, sometimes called the Manchester of the East, and a few other nascent industrial centers, Jews in Eastern Europe were rarely simply factory hands. In the preindustrial condition of that area, they could be artisans and craftsmen, which allowed for a combination of business and craft skills. They were independent tailors, cobblers, tinsmiths, butchers, and bakers. When they arrived on American shores they discovered that many of these crafts had either never developed or had been displaced. There were factories that made shoes, clothes, and even bread. Like Talmudist–scholars, crafts workers too were prone to suffer a precipitious decline in status. It was this loss of status attendant on their proletarianization that served as a basic precondition for the development of the Jewish labor movement. Like the Jewish banking nexus and the Yiddish culture developing on the East Side, the Jewish labor movement drew heavily from its European predecessor for its philosophy and organizational principles. The prototype was the Jewish labor movement developing at the same time in Eastern Europe, where it was known as the *Bund*. We shall note that this heavy dependence on the European precedent gave the Jewish labor movement a distinct alien flavor, which was soon noted by the general American labor movement.

A distinct and separate Jewish labor movement might never have developed had it not been for the leadership of a group of socialist-oriented Jewish intellectuals, who sensed the existence of a large Jewish work force in the city was an opportunity for putting their ideology into practice. In the final decades of the nineteenth century, that ideology was fairly amorphous: it contained sundry elements of anarchism and socialism of both the "scientific" and utopian variety. The common denominator for all varieties was an empathy for the "masses," especially the worker. Socialists believed that the worker was the source of all value and would, if history followed the immutable laws which governed its development; ultimately dominate the social order. The historical task of men like Abraham Cahan, Morris Hillkowitz (Hillquit), Joseph Barondess, Louis Miller, and others, was in a sense to rush history on its way by making the Jewish worker class-conscious. Often that was a far more difficult challenge than they had bargained for. Their early approach was frankly instrumentalist, that is, they viewed the organization of

Jewish workers as an instrument to hasten the coming of the new socialist order. That would solve not only the workers' problem, which the intellectuals believed was primarily one of exploitation—of not receiving a just share of the value they produced—but many other problems, such as anti-Semitism, as well. The role of these socialist-oriented intellectuals—one might call them opinion leaders because their prestige and writing skill allowed them to project their ideas on the community—sharply differentiated the Jewish labor movement from general American organized labor. The American Federation of Labor, which incidentally was also led by two Jews, Samuel Gompers and Leo Strasser, considered the instrumentalist approach of the socialists to be a cynical exploitation of the workers for political ends. They had no overall view of societal development, distrusted systemic ideologies purporting to favor the worker, and preferred to work in the economic rather than the political arena. Rather than rejecting the capitalist system, they were convinced that they could gain a fair share for workers by using the power of organization to win an ever-increasing share of the profits for them. Agitation for shorter hours and higher pay, labeled "bread-and-butter" unionism, placed such unions in direct conflict with the socialist-oriented trade unions. The latter were, in effect, organized from the top down by socialist intellectuals, whereas the A.F.L. was organized from the bottom up; its basic power was held by the strong independent craft unions at its base.

No discussion of the Jewish labor movement can long proceed without examining the garment industry, in which the majority of Jewish workers found employment. It was the poor working conditions of this industry that, perhaps more than anything else, gave the impetus for organizing Jewish unions. The major problem was the fragmented nature of the industry. At the turn of the century, it was composed, in part, of small contractors who competed fiercely for work that was subcontracted to them from the entrepreneurs who cut the garment according to pattern. Because of the proliferation of these contractors, the profit margin was extremely narrow, and workers in these small sweat shops were required to work long hours at breakneck speed to earn a meager living. The continuous influx of new immigrants into the work force kept the price of labor down. The boss could always recruit new workers at the *chazer-mark*, (literally the pig market) an area on the Lower East Side where workers, who had to own their own *katerinkas* (sewing machines), collected to sell their labor. To compound the difficulty, the flow of work in the garment industry was erratic. Hectic periods of activity would be followed by slack seasons of enforced idleness for workers. Indicative of this is a report of the Industrial Commission describing the "sweating system":

> The contractor . . . would go to the manufacturer. Finding there was but little work to be had, he would offer to take the coats cheaper than the price theretofore paid. When he came home, he would tell his men that there was not much work and he was obliged to take it cheaper, and since he did not want to reduce their wages . . . all they would have to do is to make another coat in the task* . . . The wages were always reduced on the theory that they were not reduced at all but the amount of labor increased. In this way intense speed was developed . . . The hours began to be increased, in order to complete the task in a day.

The working conditions produced by such a system were so miserable that it was small wonder that workers involved in the "sweating system" were ready to listen to the preachments of their socialist leaders honoring labor. Recently minted Jewish workers would probably have been prepared to believe anything that redeemed the value of labor and their own lowly status. The hard, tedious, insecure work was compounded by their isolation. The immigration process had destroyed the social and fraternal network that had nurtured them in the old world. Unions allowed the worker to once again find the company of fellow Jews of similar station, who faced similar problems and spoke the same language. The union hall began to play the same function that the *beth hamidrosh* (house of worship) had played in the *shtetl* (small town) in Eastern Europe. Instead

*The allotted number of units to be produced by the worker for each workday—H.L.F.

of the revered *rebbe*, there was now the socialist intellectual labor organizer; instead of *Torah*, there was the doctrine of socialism; and instead of *mitzvot* (good deeds), there was struggle to improve the conditions of the underclass. Sometimes the transfer from the old to the new belief was so naive as to appear comical. A formerly religious Jew, a recently converted socialist or "free thinker," wrote to the letters to the editor column (called *bintel brief* "bundle of letters") that he had become infatuated with his boss's daughter. He was sadly aware that she was the offspring of an exploiter of the worker, but he could not help himself. Was this love permissible? One had to know the new halakah (rules of behavior followed by religious Jews), or how could one live? True, the doctrine had changed and with it the rules. But surely there was a socialist halakah too. Jews, whether free thinkers or observant, remained what they had always been, zealous believers. It was almost as if they simply transferred their religious passions to a secular system.

We have mentioned the poor working conditions which served to promote union organization and the remarkable group of leaders who made the Jewish worker aware of them. We need to know something about the Jewish workers who would be corralled into these locals. It was not an ordinary group. Rather than being the largely displaced peasants of the "new" immigration from southern and eastern Europe (which composed the labor force in the factories and mills), the Jewish worker was often a displaced craftsman, petty merchant or scholar who retained basically middle class aspirations. He frequently desired to rise above his class rather than with it. In his *Loose Leaves From a Busy Life*, (1934) Morris Hillquit, who was an organizer of Jewish locals, complained of the difficulty of getting Jewish workers to act collectively. They appeared to accept the message of socialism with enthusiasm, but their goals remained highly individual and lived in tandem with a good deal of the old belief system. They enjoyed hearing a good cantor at religious services, said the prayer *(Kaddish)* for their departed ones, and at the same time read a socialist newspaper. Consistency was not their strong point. Hillquit believed that Jewish workers' sluggishness was caused by their low physical condition. But we have seen that the general health of Jewish immigrants was in some respects superior to comparable immigrant groups. The Jewish workers were apparently "workaholics." The "avenging nemesis" which Jacob Riis thought pursued Jewish workers was in reality an aspiration for a better life. Sending a child to college or buying a piano or bringing over a relative as they had been brought over, buying a house in Brooklyn or renting an apartment in the Bronx, things associated in their minds with a middle-class life-style, made inordinate demands on their meager incomes. It was the same ambition which made so many Jewish workers aspire to subcontracting, the proliferation of which, we have seen, was one of the mainstays of the sweatshop system.

There were other problems that made the organization of Jewish workers problematic. The same radical intellectuals who informed them of their grievances were also heavily committed to an ideology of a grand design not matched by their operational and organizational skills. The rank and file also became imbued with these ideas, which promised a "new day." When strikes did not bring in their wake a noticeable improvement, they could be followed by disillusion and despair. After investing so much, the locals tended to burn themselves out, and the painful task of organization had to be begun again from scratch. Moreover, ideology tended to lead to splits and fragmentation and made settling for half-a-loaf difficult. Justice and righteousness cannot, after all, be compromised, certainly not among Jewish believers. The hidebound socialist labor leaders, furnished with absolute conviction on how the problem of work and society would ultimately be solved, brooked no interference. The notion that all bosses were implacable enemies was matched by a peculiar stubbornness in the shop owners, who were frequently but a few years and dollars removed from having been workers themselves. They tended to view unions as not only a threat but somehow unfair in a free society where everyone could be a boss by following their route.

The dispersion of the garment industry into many little shops all over the city made organization and unified action difficult to achieve. The problem of collective action was compounded by the fact that the industry was divided into several levels of skills. A highly skilled cutter jealously guarded his prerogatives and could not be easily convinced to risk his position for lowly finishers and operators. Often, too, these stratifications were overlayed with ethnic differences. Cutters from Posen did not take easily to tailors from Galicia, despite the Judaism they held in common. Sometimes the smaller shops were composed of *landsleit* (people from the same region in Europe) and family. In such cases, agonizing choices had to be made between bad conditions and loyalty to one's own. Finally, the question of bad working conditions deserves reexamination, for the workers' view of conditions depended on their frame of reference. A small shop, where there prevailed a kind of *heimich* (domestic) atmosphere and a boss who understood the requirements of a religious Jew to turn to the east wall and pray, and to leave early to prepare for the Sabbath or holy days, was for religious workers preferable to a larger, more impersonal factory, where physical conditions were better. Moreover, even after toiling a fourteen-hour day during the season, many workers, especially if they were green, compared their lot to the way things were in the old country, where they had often experienced years of unemployment, and they were thankful to be gainfully employed. Five dollars per week could seem like a small fortune to those who had rarely seen cash at all in their original situation. They worked close to where they live; or, after 1910, convenient public transportation could speedily bring them to the shop. These compensations could loom large in workers' minds. The immigration experience was a wrenching one, which for many proved revolution enough for one lifetime. Jewish workers were ready for their personal thermidor, anxious above all to get their lives back on an even keel and get on with the business of living. There were, then, sufficient reasons why Hillquit and others found Jewish workers so difficult to organize.

But organize they did, and, in part, success was finally made possible by technological developments within the garment industry itself—the "inside factory," which unified all the steps of production of a garment under one roof rather than by subcontracting of bundles to the sweatshops for sewing and finishing. The "inside factory" never totally eliminated subcontracting, but the center of economic gravity of the industry was now a factory loft. Nor did it necessarily improve the condition of all the workers, although the physical facilities were better. The factory loft in which all operations were concentrated made possible a greater division of labor. Each worker was now responsible for a specific operation, but in the case of the less skilled, the wage scale may have actually declined whereas the specialists—cutters, pattern makers, and managers responsible for the entire operation—were able to demand higher pay commensurate with their new responsibilities. For union organization the development of larger shops was a boon, since it consolidated the labor force and thus enhanced the possibility of collective action.

Let us now return momentarily to the genesis of the Jewish labor movement to see what can be learned. Jewish locals had appeared and disappeared from the labor scene with some regularity since the mid-nineteenth century. These locals, we have seen, had difficulty sustaining themselves, and the several strikes in which they participated left little in the way of organization or experience. Thus, when the Socialist Labor Party, to which many of the socialist-oriented Jewish intellectuals belonged, surveyed the field in 1888 they found only two Jewish locals: typesetters and choristers. Three years earlier, Abraham Cahan and Bernard Weinstein had founded the Russian Jewish Workers Association. It organized an Anti-Sweating League whose goal it was to improve conditions in the garment industry. The Association began the precedent of publishing its own newspaper, the *Yiddishe Folkzeitung*. (Much of the Yiddish press was thereafter linked to the growth of the Jewish labor movement.) In 1886, in recognition that it was operating on the American scene rather than merely being a bit of Russia displaced to America, the Association dropped the word "Russian" from its title. But few unions joined the organization, while Jewish socialists and anarchists conducted an unseemly conflict over the nonexistent spoils. Two years later, in 1888, the Socialist Party, now able to work through its separate Jewish branch, established the United Hebrew Trades (UHT). It was an umbrella organization for the Jewish locals, based on the German-American model. The leaders of the UHT, Jacob Magidow, Morris Hillquit, Abraham Cahan, Bernard Weinsein, and Louis Miller, would become well-known names in many Jewish households. But the idea of building unions on the basis of ethnic identity did not sit well with mainline labor organizations. Samuel Gompers, for example, opposed such separatist organizations; moreover, he disapproved of its socialist orientation, which he was convinced was alien to the American scene. Nevertheless, he gave initial support to the organization drive since he was aware that given organized labor's opposition to unrestricted immigration, the AFL had little chance to organize Jewish workers.

Despite valiant efforts by the organizers (few of whom joined the workers in the shops), their socialist rhetoric did not attract the potential Jewish rank and file. Not until the knee-pants makers, supported by the UHT, went on strike and won, did the UHT gain recognition. It taught the organizers an important lesson—"nothing succeeds like success." The few Jewish locals now flocked to the UHT for affiliation. Among the first was a local representing actors and choristers. The choristers had a bitter grievance. Conditions for the lesser lights in the Yiddish theater were in dismal contrast to those of the well-paid "stars," and producers were not above importing choristers from Philadelphia to act as strike-breakers. The delegates appeared at the disorderly, sparsely furnished office of the UHT dressed in formal evening clothes, and insisted upon being addressed in German. One can imagine the chagrin of the socialist-minded labor organizers when they witnessed this first sampling of the Jewish workers for whom they had such grandiose plans, but it was a beginning. The shirtwaist makers, a local with a more radical tradition, and the cap makers followed in affiliation, and by 1890 the UHT could claim 40 locals under its banner. Included were seltzer bottlers, rag pickers, newsboys, and bootblacks.

Almost as soon as it had established itself, the UHT was

wracked by conflict, not with employers, but among the socialist organizers who led the movement. The issues and the organizational ramifications of this conflict would take us far
afield, since they concerned basic principles of the burgeoning
socialist movement of which the UHT was a part. Simply
stated, it amounted to a conflict over what role the Jewish locals
were to play in the general socialist schema for America. Were
they to be instruments of the Socialist Labor Party, under
whose auspices the UHT had been organized? Should they be a
power base in the internal struggle within the socialist segment
of the labor movement, or were they to remain autonomous, an
integral, if aberrant, part of the general labor movement headed
by the AFL? Daniel De Leon, a nominal Sephardic Jew, originally from Curaçao, pushed for the long-range view. The locals
should remain firmly bound to the Socialist Labor Party, to be
used by it for the general enhancement of American socialism.
The protracted conflict nearly tore the budding Jewish labor
movement apart. Hillquit and Meyer London, soon to serve the
Lower East Side in Congress, assumed the moderate, less dog-
matic position of the Eugene V. Debs faction of the Socialist
Party. They retreated from the instrumentalist revolutionary
approach of the De Leon faction. The struggle was actually a
precursor of the bitter conflict between Social Democrats and
Communists that plagued the movement in the twenties and
thirties. In the first two decades of the twentieth century, the
moderates withstood the onslaught of the extreme left and
gradually built the Jewish labor movement on a triad of organizations: the UHT, which served as a container for the Jewish
locals; the *Jewish Daily Forward*, which served as its press organ;
and the Workmen's Circle, which in 1892 had become its fraternal order and welfare agency. It was a solid foundation for the
first all-Jewish power base in organized labor.

The travails of the movement, however, were not yet over.
There remained the basic goal of improving the lot of Jewish
workers. The primary instrument for achieving this objective
was the strike, and within the first decade of the century,
strikes—some won and some lost—continued to be a fact of life
for the locals. In 1910, the ultimate strike broke out, when some

major garment unions, in an effort to gain the right of collective bargaining and improvement in working conditions, called the workers out of the shops. As the strike grew more bitter, week after week, it was clear that this was to be a test of strength between labor and management. Neither side was willing to compromise, but after four months cooler heads prevailed, and a call for mediation was issued. Out of the "great upheaval," as the incident is known today, came the "Protocol for Peace," negotiated with the help of Louis D. Brandeis. The protocol gave the unions the recognition they desired, as well as a sanitary commission to regulate health conditions. Although it was considered a hallmark in labor–management negotiations, the permanent peace in the industry held out by the protocol proved to be chimerical, and strikes continued to occur. However, the protocol did illustrate that reasonableness could prevail, especially when workers and management spoke the same language and possessed similar cultural backgrounds. Brandeis was later to comment that he had never participated in negotiations like this, where each side was as likely to quote Isaiah as it was to quote a legal clause. The humanitarian idealism demonstrated by the labor leaders left a lasting impression on Brandeis, reawakened his Jewish consciousness, and played a significant role in bringing him into the Zionist fold in 1914, when he became head of the Provisional Executive Committee for General Zionist Affairs (1914)* and the Federation of American Zionists. Just as strikes were perennial and complicated by the fragmentation of the garment industry, so too were internecine quarrels among the union leadership. During the 1920s and 1930s, another onslaught from the communist left had to be withstood. At the same time, the Jewish unions never gained much of a voice in the inner circles of American organized labor. When the government finally took a hand in regulating working conditions, it was as much prompted by the tragic Triangle shirtwaist fire (March 25, 1911), which broke out in a supposedly modern "inside factory" loft, as it was by the unions' struggle for it.

*See chapter IX.

Finally, we ought to note that the Jewish labor movement was like other facets of Jewish immigrant life—a temporary phenomenon of a transitional culture. Despite their strong advocacy of socialism, most Jewish workers sojourned among the working class for only one generation. He was neither the son of a worker nor would he raise a son who was. The amazing thing is that even though it was only a one- or two-generation phenomenon, the Jewish labor movement had an impact on American and Jewish life that can hardly be over-estimated. Its successes and failures directly affected the quality of life of thousands of first-generation Jewish immigrants. In the final analysis, its role in restoring their sense of self-esteem and giving them some mooring in the new environment was perhaps more important than the economic improvements it was able to wring for them from a reluctant employer class.

The group of socialist organizers in whose imagination the Jewish labor movement was born deserves special attention. We have seen that American Jewish history has no dearth of cohorts who are remembered for their achievements: the courageous Sephardic enterprisers and merchants of the colonial period, the German Jewish peddlers who made their way into the interior of the country to fill a merchandising vacuum, the remarkable group of German Jewish bankers who furnished the nation with risk capital during the nineteenth century. To this list we must now add what in some respects is the most remarkable group of all, one which made its mark in a notably different way: the leaders who organized the Jewish labor movement matched the former elites in their courage and ability to grow—and, perhaps most important, in their vision.

They began their enterprise imbued with an idea, not for self-improvement, but for the betterment of an entire class of Jews who they felt were exploited. True, they were sometimes so convinced of the inevitability of fulfillment of their vision that they were impractical in solving the day-to-day problems of workers. But their experience in the real world of labor served to make them more flexible. They had to deal with real power, where dogmatism and rigidity during negotiations could have dire consequences for the workers. The grandiose abstract principles of socialism under such circumstances had to be tempered, but their noble goals and humanitarianism were retained to serve as an underlying motivation to gain improvement. In a word, they became practical men of humanitarian vision, and, like so many priesthoods of nascent religions, they were incorruptible.

In later years, they would come to the bargaining table with more accurate ideas of what was ailing the industry and better plans for amelioration than the employers. It was not uncommon for the more established unions to furnish capital to businesses in need. At the same time, the International Ladies Garment Workers and the Almagamated Clothing Workers became experimental laboratories for social-welfare programs for their rank and file. After achieving collective bargaining rights, they were among the first unions to negotiate for pensions, sick benefits, and paid vacations. On their own, they established comprehensive medical care programs, educational benefits, housing cooperatives, home care for the aged, and cooperative loan associations. Welfare programs first pioneered by the Jewish unions found their way into the New Deal welfare state, especially its labor and social-security laws. They had their genesis in these unions because union leaders believed in an ethos that demanded a more just order for workers. That was perhaps the major contribution of the Jewish labor movement to American society.

A judgment of what the Jewish labor movement contributed to the enhancement of American Judaism is more difficult to make. In principle the movement shunned particularism. Its leaders spoke in the universalistic terms of socialism. The notion of building a specifically Jewish labor movement did not sit easily with some, and had already caused endless problems in the socialist movement in Europe. Nor did they have much use for the purely religious aspects of Judaism. As socialists they tended to see religion as a reactionary force. Yet the militant antireligious posture espoused by many Jewish socialists during their "sectarian" phase of development, which led to such things as Yom Kippur balls, eventually gave way to a mild secularism tolerant of the dual worlds—the secular and the religious—in which much of the rank and file lived. Cahan's responses to the perplexed, born of their joint loyalty to Judaism and to socialism, indicate that he increasingly accepted a normative position on Judaism. What was good was what most Jews practiced, even if it was full of contradictions. Socialism might be scientific but human beings were not. With time, even the nationalist position embodied in Zionism— which in socialist thought was considered a bourgeois throwback—was tempered. Eventually the Jewish labor movement established links to the Zionist socialist labor movement (*histadrut*) and played an important role in pressing for the establishment of the state. The point is that the leadership was able to abandon positions that did not fit.

If the Jewish labor movement shunned Judaism, it paradoxically contributed notably to Jewishness, which necessarily serves as its underpinning. Jewish unions made for a sense of Jewish peoplehood. It brought Jews together in a common enterprise and served as a major support of the vibrant Yiddish culture on the Lower East Side. The Yiddish press, theater, and *landsmannschaften*, (membership associations) affiliated with the unions proved the most enduring institutions of that culture. For thousands of Jews it was the Jewish presence they experienced most directly. The conclusion that the American Jewish enterprise was enriched by the presence of the movement can hardly be avoided.

Bibliography

"American Jews and the Labor Movement." *American Jewish Historical Quarterly*, vol. 65 (March 1976).
Cole, S. *The Unionization of Teachers: A Case Study of the United Federation of Teachers*. New York: 1969.
Dubinsky, D., and A. H. Raskin. *David Dubinsky: A Life with Labor*. New York: 1977.
Dubofsky, M. *When Workers Organize: New York City in the Progressive Era*. Amherst: 1968.
Epstein, M. *Jewish Labor in the U.S.A.*, 2 vols. New York: 1950–1953.

Hillquit, M. *Loose Leaves from a Busy Life.* New York: 1934.

Hurwitz, M. *The Workmen's Circle.* New York: 1936.

Pratt, N. F. *Morris Hillquit.* Westport: 1979.

Tcherikower, E., et al. *The Early Jewish Labor Movement*, trans. and rev. Aaron Antonovsky. New York: 1961.

Yellowitz, I. "Jewish Immigrants and the American Labor Movement, 1900–1920" *American Jewish History*, vol. 71 December 1981.

CHAPTER VII /

Is American Jewry
Really Organized?

I T is impossible to think about American Jewish organizational life without smiling to oneself. Its proliferation has
been the source of much of the special mocking humor which is
so much a part of the Jewish style. There is the story of the
hard-pressed Jewish speaker debating the relative merits of his
religion with a minister of another faith. In desperation he
mentions that Judaism is the one true faith, and the proof is that
it assures immortality in this world as well as the next. Startled,
the minister asks, "How so?" and the Jewish speaker responds:
"Jewish organizations never die."

One cannot really make light of Jewish organizations, because their superabundance remains one of the most remarkable
characteristics of Jewish life in America. The Jewish organizational structure is probably the richest of any American ethnic
group. As early as 1918, the Jewish Communal Register listed
3,637 organizations in the metropolitan area, one for every 410
Jews. One recent study of the Jewish community in Boston
indicates that the majority of Jews belong to at least one Jewish
organization and many belong to two or three. The same is true
of Providence. American Jewry has established every possible
kind of organization. Daniel Elazar, the noted specialist on this
aspect of the Jewish experience, lists dozens of different types:
religious, educational, cultural, community service, community relations, defense, Zionist, government-like, fraternal,
professional, political, philanthropic, local, regional, national,
formal, and informal—from cousins' clubs to federations, there

is no end to them. They are so numerous that not even the *American Jewish Year Book's* annual listing can keep track of them. Every social segment, every ideology, even every transient mood has developed an organizational expression. But what such an extensive corporate structure signifies is difficult to determine. American Jewry may well be the most organized group in the world; it possesses the most far-flung "secular church," but that does not mean that Jews are united. It may, in fact, be the surest sign that American Jewry is a variegated tribe indeed. Nor can we be certain that even by the most primitive measure—"Is it good for the Jews?"—these numerous organizations, with the duplication of function they entail, are an asset to the Jewish community.

Isaac Mayer Wise, the founder of the American Reform movement, recognized that Jews are joiners. He sensed that the disputatiousness that characterized much of congregational life was attributable to boredom and frustration. In the nineteenth century, Jews let off steam in their organizations that could not safely be vented in the hostile outside world. Yet that tells us virtually nothing about the reasons for the superabundance of Jewish organizations. Wise may have been on to something when he attributed it to the Jewish character. But rather than sensing only a low tolerance for frustration, he might also have noted an extraordinary need for *Gesellschaft*, a need to break through the isolation of modern life to establish ties with people of like status and sensibility. A good many of the organizations fulfilled a fraternal function even when their focus was on other objectives. We have seen that that was as true of the locals of the United Hebrew Trades as it was of the far-flung chapters of B'nai B'rith. It is almost as if Jews, especially energetic and talented Jewish women, instinctively realized that the privatism of modern life could also serve as a kind of trap. They used the Jewish organizations (as much as they were used by them) as a communal arena, a polis, in which the human need to "make" politics, to go beyond merely the concern for self, could be fulfilled. A great deal of that energy was expended in the organization. Some have pointed to the fact that the existence of a separate Jewish organizational world simply reflected the fact that, with the exception of orders like the Masons, most Christian or secular organizations were either formally or informally closed to them. It was precisely that restriction which led to the founding of the major American Jewish fraternal order in 1843, B'nai B'rith. But that still does not explain the extraordinary number of Jewish organizations and the fact that when organizations like the Elks or the Citizens' Union beckoned Jews to enter, there was no rush to do so, and Jewish organizations did not decline in numbers.

A brief glimpse into the first two decades of the twentieth century, a period which saw the founding of the major Jewish organizations, presents us with still another reason for the elaborate organizational network with which the Jewish community is furnished. The primary objective of their establishment was not to fulfill a domestic need but to nurture Jewish communities abroad. The commitment to Jews overseas is the most constant preoccupation in American Jewish history. It goes beyond concern to the very manner in which modern American Jews identify with their Jewishness.

The American Jewish Committee (AJC), founded in 1906 primarily by a group of concerned "uptown" Jews, was a response to the Kishinev pogrom and the general persecution in tsarist Russia, issues about which the Eastern immigrants, crowded into ghettoes in major cities, were continually exercised. In her history of the American Jewish Committee (*Not Free To Desist* (1972), Professor Naomi Cohen points out that "organization was in the air," and had the patrician stewards not founded a major organization to address itself to the problem, the frustration of Eastern immigrant Jews would have expressed itself in less acceptable ways. They decided on a more active leadership role not only out of genuine concern with the fate of Russian Jewry, but also out of fear that more rambunctious, often socialist-oriented, immigrants would employ radical methods of protest rather than respectable behind-the-scenes activity—which they were convinced was more effective in the long run. The AJC preferred the traditional *shtadlanut* (court Jew) strategy employed by Jewish communities during the middle ages. Rather than mass organization and activity, influential Jews like Jacob Schiff and Oscar Straus would use their influence on power holders to ameliorate the condition of the Jews. Yet, although that approach remained true in theory, in practice the leaders of the Committee were ready to use every weapon at hand, including the burgeoning Jewish political leverage and the threat of mass action. That flexibility and practical operationalism was evident in the remarkable campaign to abrogate the Commercial Treaty of 1832 (see Chapter XII). There they conceived of virtually every tactic of popular pressure on decision makers subsequently used to influence policy by American Jewry and other special-interest groups.

The successful abrogation struggle did not noticeably improve the condition of Russian Jewry, nor could it permanently head off the increasingly insistent voices from the ghetto calling for democracy in Jewish life and a new kind of leadership. With the arrival of masses of Eastern Jews, something had changed in the American Jewish community. Its portent was the cry for democracy, a new theme for American Jews in speaking about Jewish affairs. The first major organization of American Jews, the Board of Delegates of American Israelites, established after the Mortara kidnapping case in 1859, was based on congregational representation. Simon Wolf, who represented the Jewish interest in Washington during the second half of the nineteenth century, was an official of B'nai B'rith utilizing the approach of the court Jew. Neither did the several rabbinic associations speak of democracy. Yet, it was quite natural that democracy would serve as a rallying concept for the Eastern immigrants; their yearning for it had been one reason for their immigration.

The desire for democracy led naturally to the movement for the American Jewish Congress, whose primary concern at the outset was to gain some Jewish input at the negotiations at war's end in Versailles. Between 1918 and 1940, the intense concern for democracy in Jewish organizational life led to the startling spectacle, still unprecedented among the many other ethnic groups in America, of three internal elections in which thousands of Jews voted through their organizations. The Congress was supposed to dissolve itself after achieving its mission at Versailles and did, in fact, do so in 1921. But Stephen Wise, its founding light, immediately reestablished it, and it still exists and has maintained its strong Zionist orientation, at the same time becoming the "lawyer of the Jewish community." Its strong link to Jewish interests abroad was underlined in 1936 when the World Jewish Congress—the first of the multinational organizations founded at the initiative of an American Jewish organization—was formed under the aegis of the A J Cong. Technically the A J Cong. is not part of the Zionist Federation of America, renamed Zionist Organization of America in 1918. Although this grouping has periodically experienced some difficulty in keeping large units like Hadassah and Mizrachi under its umbrella, it continues to be the most powerful constellation of organizations in America. All American Zionist organizations, regardless of their place on the political spectrum, play a dual role in that they are at the same time Zionist and American. Their primary goal is the welfare of the *yishuv* (Jewish community in Israel) which means today that they are preoccupied with the welfare and security of a foreign sovereignty. But they also fulfill all the functions—fraternal, philanthropic, defense, and even cultural and political— normally associated with non-Zionist agencies. At the outset, for example, they played an active role in the campaign to democratize Jewish life. The uptown stewards were, after all, largely anti-Zionist. Today it is not uncommon to find that in addition to their primary Zionist-oriented activities, Zionist agencies maintain a full cultural and social welfare program on the domestic scene.

The American Jewish Joint Distribution Committee, established in 1914 from a group of preexisting overseas relief agencies, continues that basic mission. It is strictly a philanthropic service agency and has kept apart from the turbulent political currents sweeping through the American Jewish community. In one sense, the many Jewish agencies which are involved in collecting and distributing philanthropy are an institutionalization of the *mitzvah* (a holy deed obligatory for all observant Jews) of *tsedakah* (in the contemporary sense, ethical giving).

Philanthropy is thus especially important in the Jewish community. Some commentators believe that by careful observation of the extent of philanthropic giving and the flow of the philanthropic dollar, not only the vitality but the sources of power in American Jewry can be measured. Organized philanthropy became well established in the community by the second half of the nineteenth century. In 1869 a group of organizations involved in charity in Philadelphia organized themselves into the Society of United Hebrew Charities. It was the beginning of a movement to federate locally agencies involved in local charity. Such federation was encouraged by "big givers" such as Jacob Schiff, who was interested in making the charitable dollar go as far as possible. These organizations followed the Protestant model of organized philanthropy. In 1896, the Federation of Jewish Charities in Boston conducted a federated fund-raising campaign with considerable success. The early path of these federated charities was rocky, filled with conflict and bitter feelings, but out of it ultimately grew the federation movement, which today is perhaps the single most powerful organizational effort within the American Jewish community—not by dint of its numbers, but by its control of the funds without which the Jewish community could not operate.

Spurred by the crisis situation faced by Eastern European Jewish communities devastated by World War I, the JDC followed the federation pattern and undertook a massive and organized effort to stave off starvation. Its work was highly praised by Herbert Hoover, who had organized a similar relief effort undertaken by the American government. Thereafter, the tradition of service under centralized auspices continued; in the thirties it was extended to the Zionist cause. Today, one of the fastest-growing organizations in American Jewry is Woman's American ORT (Organization for Rehabilitation through Training), a purely service-oriented agency providing vocational training for Jews in need the world over. Charitable service as exemplified in ORT has traditionally been a mainstay of Jewish community living, especially for American Jews, where the weakening of purely religious forms of commitment has heightened the importance of *ahavat Yisrael* (love of Israel) through the strengthening of ties to *k'lal Yisrael* (the universal community of Jewry).

We have seen that there are numerous kinds of Jewish organizations. The Kehillah experiment in New York, between 1908 and 1921, is atypical, but it warrants our special attention not only because it is one of the most fascinating episodes in the organizational history of American Jewry but also because one of the best studies in American Jewish history puts all the available information at our fingertips (Arthur Goren, *New York Jews and the Quest for Community* (1970). In addition, the Kehillah experiment was a unique effort—some might say a last desperate effort—to reestablish some general form of governance among Jews living in a free society based on voluntarism. It did not work, and we know today that the basic concept was rooted in a misunderstanding of the realities of community life in a free secular society. Yet even in failure, the episode has much to teach us about the nature, structure and concerns of Jewish communal life.

The original Kehillah was the Jewish community's governmental body in Poland during the sixteenth and seventeenth centuries, when Jewish self-government was almost complete. Echoes of the Kehillah were still evident in Poland in the early twentieth century. The circumstances that led to the establishment of the New York Kehillah concerned allegations of crime among Jews in the ghetto. In September 1908, then Police Commissioner of New York Theodore Bingham wrote in an article in the prestigious *North American Review* that Jews were responsible for over 50 percent of crime in the metropolitan area. The public tumult that greeted Bingham's report reinforced the feeling among the leaders of uptown Jewry that something had to be done to bridle both the "demagogic" leaders in the ghetto and the downtown immigrant community.

The guiding spirit behind the organization of the Kehillah was Judah P. Magnes, the remarkable 31-year-old associate rabbi of the flagship Reform temple Emanu-El. Magnes was no ordinary member of the uptown "Our Crowd" set. He was an ardent Zionist who played a prominent role in helping to establish the Federation of American Zionists and who possessed a special sympathy for the kind of Judaism practiced by the newly arrived immigrants from Eastern Europe. The Kehillah became an extension of Magnes's energetic personality, and when his interest waned, so too did the Kehillah.

Fully established in 1909, the Kehillah was organized into bureaus, each one focusing on a special area of activity: education, philanthropy, morals, religion (especially *kashrut*— religious dietary laws), and labor and industry. Its activities in professionalizing Jewish education, directed by the noted Baltimore educator Samson Benderly, soon earned the plaudits of the larger community. But it was the attempt of the Kehillah to control vice and crime in the ghetto that was most remarkable. Here a kind of secret service was established to ferret out wrongdoing, and, if all else failed, report it to the municipal authorities. Special steps were taken to bring order into the chaotic *kashrut* and *shechita* activities (authentication of kosher foods and ritual slaughter) required by the Orthodox. Also notable was the Kehillah's attempt to serve as an employment exchange and to settle peacefully the bitter labor disputes then dividing the Jewish community. In regulation of kosher food and in the labor sector, the Kehillah was often successful.

However, the Kehillah could not long withstand the strong centrifugal pulls separating the community it sought to govern. After seven years it began to lose vitality. Even at the zenith of its influence, the Kehillah attracted only 15 percent of the Jewish organizations. Conspicuously absent was the socialist-oriented Jewish labor movement. Its newspaper organ usually opposed the activities of the Kehillah. Those organizations that did participate often did so for opportunistic reasons. The American Jewish Committee, anxious to expand its popular base while retaining its oligarchic hold, enlisted the Kehilla's executive committee as its New York branch. When socialist-oriented groups did attend the annual convention, where the agenda of the organization was hammered out, they formed an alliance with the uptowners to check the influence of the Zionists. Nahum Syrkin, the founder of the Labor–Zionist movement, took note of the unholy linkage between Hester and Wall streets. The Zionist organizations were no more altruistic. They sought to use the Kehillah to further their own objectives, one of which was to detach the Kehillah from its uptown moorings. It was the flow of funds from uptown sources that allowed the wheels of the Kehillah to turn. No group would support the Kehillah for its own sake and the sake of New York Jewry. Subject to such particularist forces, it could not thrive and accomplish its mission. Given the turbulence of Jewish communal life during this period, that may have been a forlorn hope at the outset.

Nonetheless, the Kehillah was a high water mark in the several attempts to unify and govern American Jewry on a voluntary basis. Subsequent attempts to do so through the American Jewish Congress movement and the American Jewish Conference, organized in 1943, were no more successful. We need not go far afield to discover the reason for the inability of American Jewry to find a basis for unified action: there were no roots in a common historical experience, no sense of shared enterprise, not even agreement on what being Jewish meant. The very vitality of Jewish organizational life, reflecting as it did the diversity of the community, augered against unity. Each separate group and its organizations—the American Jewish Committee, the various Zionists' organizations, the Orthodox community, and the socialists—wanted to impose its stamp on the whole. None was prepared to surrender any organizational integrity to serve the interest of the whole community. Furthermore, each organization itself represented subgroups in perpetual conflict, especially the Orthodox and the Zionists. Rather than mediating these inter- and intra-group conflicts, the existence of the Kehillah tended to exacerbate them. The Kehillah became caught in the crossfire and, much like the United Nations, became a victim rather than an arbiter of conflict.

During its existence, which did last about 13 years, the Kehillah spurred some important changes in Jewish organizational life. Noteworthy is the habit of professionalism, which today is pervasive in Jewish organizational activities. Paradoxically, even professionalism is a mixed blessing; it means that the community pays professionals to do what volunteers are no longer willing and able to do.

The problems of unity and coherence, so manifest in the Kehillah, are perennial for American Jewry. American and world Jewry have paid dearly for their absence. This became especially apparent during the years of the Holocaust, when the weakness of the community was compounded by its inability to speak to the Roosevelt administration with one voice. Jewish organizations differed on everything, from the nature of the Nazi threat to the efficacy of an anti-Nazi boycott. The delicate bridges that had been built between uptown and downtown Jewry collapsed in the face of the crisis, and each group sent its delegations to the Oval Office to plead separately for the rescue of its particular clients. So exasperating did the situation become that Roosevelt once suggested that the Jews elect a pope. The State Department, which was interested in blocking the arrival of Jewish refugees to American shores, was fully aware of the divisions; no doubt it welcomed them. "The Jewish organizations are all divided amidst controversies . . . there is no cohesion nor any sympathetic collaboration . . . rather rivalry, jealousy and antagonism," one State Department official confided in his diary in 1944 when twelve thousand Jews a day were being gassed in Auschwitz.

The ineffective performance of American Jewry during the Holocaust brought the question of American Jewish governance to the fore, and the perennial crisis in the Middle East has kept it there. We have seen that it is possible to question whether the rich organizational structure of American Jewry is a symptom of unity and strength. The Holocaust years raised the question whether there is such a thing as an American Jewish community. Some would say that there are many separate Jewish communities in America, or that there is merely a kind of Jewish presence. The question of the existence of a Jewish polity is a crucial one because, in a real sense, the survival of some Jewish communities abroad depends on how well American Jewish power can be brought to bear on policy making. That, in turn, depends in some measure on how strong is the organizational structure of American Jewry.

The researcher who has most interested himself in this question of American Jewish governance is Professor Daniel Elazar. His thinking is set forth in his well-known book, *Community and Polity: The Organizational Dynamics of American Jewry* (1975). Elazar maintains that although there is frequent overlapping of role and function and much conflict, there *is* an organized Jewish community in America whose polity faithfully reflects that of the American host culture. Its power is widely diffused between different economic, social, and even regional centers. Like the American polity itself, power within the Jewish community is divided; it is federal rather than centralized. Moreover, Jewish governance is based on voluntarism; the choice of belonging and degree of commitment is a free one. It is this voluntary character that most sharply differentiates it from organized Jewish communities which find their historical roots in the pre-emancipation period. There is, for example, no formal corporate structure, no single organization sanctioned by government to speak for Jewry. Instead, there are many organizations, all speaking in a cacophony. Power itself is forever shifting from one center to another. In America there is no chief rabbi who can speak for the community. Strict separation of church and state means that Jewish clergy, schools, and communal programs are supported through voluntary contributions rather than by the state. Since there is no way to compel a Jewish citizen to belong to and support the Jewish community, the base of popular support is a shifting one. To avoid the danger of erosion of popular support, Jewish citizens must be constantly convinced of the need to extend such support. The absence of financial support from government means that fund raising is one of the most crucial activities of organized Jewry. It is one measure of the viability of organizations and the principal reason why the federations have developed into the most powerful agencies within the community. It also means that a democratic governance in which each member of the community has equal weight is not possible. Wealthy Jews who use their wealth to support Jewish organizations and causes can amplify their influence by giving. To some extent the monied piper calls the tune, although today many other influences determine where resources will be invested.

At the base of Jewish organizational life is the religious congregation. Certain primordial requirements at birth, confirmation, marriage, and death, which continue to win adherence, though secularism holds sway, give the religious congregation a degree of stability not present in other Jewish agencies. Despite the existence of various congregational assemblies linked to the three branches of Judaism, the individual congregation is basically autonomous. Compliance with the various religious assemblies is widespread but voluntary. The congregation is the basic building block of Jewish life in America and on the grass roots level it is governed by the trustees of the congregation. It is they who govern in congregational matters, not the rabbi, whose influence, depending on his stature, is indirect and confined in theory to the spiritual realm. That model is at sharp variance with Catholic and Protestant churches, and together with the different role the rabbi plays in a Jewish congregation when compared with Christian spiritual leaders, often makes it difficult for non-Jews to understand the dynamics of organized Jewish religious life.

Elazar suggests that the numerous organizations with their overlapping functions actually represent a brilliant accommodation to the American scene, where flexibility is imperative. A rigid organizational hierarchy in such a dynamic society would long ago have cracked under pressure. As it stands, there is something for everyone in the organized Jewish community, whose governance is democratic, its power diffuse and flowing up from the ranks. Without an organizational straitjacket the Jewish community is able to change with changing conditions. That ability is one of the factors in its survival.

Finally, we must return to the crucial question posed at the outset: Is there such a thing as an American Jewish community? The answer depends on what one means by "community" and what one thinks "community" does. If one uses Webster's dictionary definition, which speaks of a society of people having "common rights, privileges, common interests, civil, political and ecclesiastical," then clearly the idea that American Jewry, through much of its recent history, has formed such a community is a product of a fevered imagination. There have been few of the "common" interests mentioned in Webster. We have seen that American Jewry for much of its history was riven by conflict and rarely able to speak with a single coherent voice. It may be more accurate to speak of a multiplicity of small Jewish communities sometimes able to act together on a limited number of issues. It was natural that such should be the case, since none of the building blocks making for commonality were present in the Jewish experience. American Jews originated in different geographic areas, had no common language, took different approaches to the tenets of Judaism, held widely divergent political views, and stemmed from different economic classes. Moreover, in the free atmosphere of America, power—the defining element in any governmental relationship—was missing. There was little possibility of making these diverse groupings, whose relationship was one of conflict, comply with the decision of the would-be governors. Without sanction, leaders could not lead, because followers would not follow. There was, in fact, no one who could speak for the Jewish community, and in the absence of such an authoritative voice organizations or popular leaders could preempt that position. But they could not really speak with authority and were inevitably challenged by other "leaders," newer voices. Since everything depended on voluntary adherence, weapons such as a delivered Jewish vote could not be brought to bear.

That does not mean that Jews have no measure of influence in America. All groups do, and Jews probably possess more than their declining numbers warrant. We will learn elsewhere how American Jewry has been able to amplify its voice by other means. The power of the organizations to influence public policy may actually be declining even while the influence of individual Jews, not necessarily linked to a Jewish community interest, is stronger than ever. The relentless process of secularization and atomization inherent in all modern societies progressively diminishes the number who voluntarily give their allegiance to Jewish organizations. The quality of Jewish commitment to the "secular church" is also declining, and American Judaism's most viable elements—its youth and its professionals—are not drawn to Jewish organizational life. Viewed from without, the organizational structure of American Jewry appears brilliant and powerful, but survivalists may be aware that there is less there than meets the eye. Jewish influence and survival in America are linked to the mysterious forces that bind Jews together and convince them to identify themselves as Jews. With the occasional exception of the religious congregation, few secular Jewish organizations have evolved successful programs to enhance that identification. What a paradox! Their continuance as well as the survival of American Jewry are dependent upon it.

In Jewish history there always seems to be a glimmer of hope amidst the prevailing gloom. Many of our observations regarding American Jewish disunity and incoherence pertain to the pre-Holocaust period. In the last decades the acculturation process itself has supplied a possible basis for more unified action. American Jews have in common their Americanness. Their children have been processed through the public-school system; there is more uniformity in their general middle-class status; avidly held religious differences give way to a tempered religiosity, which occupies a place of lesser importance in determining behavior and life goals; and they share a common concern for the welfare of Israel. In a word, the former sources of division among Jews have also declined in importance. Jews speak the same language in more than one sense. Americanization has created new, more urgent problems concerning group survival, but it has also solved some of the older ones that plagued the forebears of American Jewry.

Survival anxiety is endemic among Jews, and may in fact be the surest sign of vitality. At least, Jews remain concerned enough to worry about their continuance. The problem is how to transmit a strong sense of identity to the next generation. It is obvious that without such identification even the most elaborate organizational structure can be of no avail. There are forces at work in modern society that militate against such group identification. Not even the Jewish family, which has traditionally served as the principal conduit for the transmission of the distinctive Judaic culture, has been able to withstand its corrosive effects. Jewish survivalists are increasingly aware that at some future juncture there may simply be an insufficient number of committed American Jews available to carry the Jewish enterprise forward. As with other subgroups in America, the religio–culture can no longer be imbibed with one's mothers' milk. The totalistic environment, which brought Jews to their Jewishness by exclusive exposure, no longer exists. The startling fact is that a modern American Jew must be taught the culture, after being converted at some point in mid-life. To do that, new programs and instruments are required. It may be that, at some future point, this will become the major objective of all Jewish organizations: they will become Judaizing agencies. That does not mean that secular Jewish agencies will overnight become transmission agencies for a religious sensibility; but secularism need not have the antireligious component it has traditionally possessed among American Jews. At the grass-roots level, American Jews have demonstrated a genius for such unlikely amalgamations as secularism and Judaism. One is reminded of the newly minted socialist "free-thinker," who continued to attend services faithfully every Sabbath, not because he wished to pray to a God in whom he no longer believed, but to speak to his neighbor and to listen to cantorial music. The secular world provided no space for such activities. Thousands of secular-minded Jews today live harmoniously with such contradictory elements in their lives.

There exists in American Jewry today a triumphant Orthodox community which considers itself the guardian of the on-going religious tradition. It presses for Torah centeredness and compliance with *halakah*. In a pluralistic free society there will undoubtedly rise other principles around which American Jews can organize themselves. One such may be the remarkable Jewish performance in the various professions: science, law, medicine. It is not too far a leap of the imagination to conceive that the remarkable Jewish achievement in these areas is not simply attributable to sociological processes but is somehow related to the values, even echoes of values, inherent in Judaic culture. Generations of adherence to principles of universalist egalitarianism has prevented Jews from openly recognizing and acknowledging their extraordinary achievement. They possess all the hallmarks of a patrician elite not unlike the Quakers. Jews continue to maintain their primary associations with other Jews outside the synagogue to a far greater extent than other groups. They do so not because they are despised by the host culture. They are actually beckoned to enter and do so whole-heartedly. That is one aspect of the burgeoning intermarriage rate that is seldom examined. There is in the non-Jewish world a growing recognition of Jewish elan, which is reflected in the desirability of Jewish mates. There is a conventional wisdom among students of Jewish culture that nothing can receive full recognition until it has the stamp of approval of the Christian world. If that world has recognized American Jewish elan, can the Jewish world be far behind? From that point it is but a small jump to understanding Jewish achievement in all areas of modern endeavor—even deracinated Jewish audiences proudly toll the number of Jewish writers, scientists, virtuosos, Nobel laureates—that are somehow related to a rich culture preserved by a long historical tradition. When that realization occurs there will be many Jews who will want to learn it and be a part of it.

Bibliography

Baron, S. W. *The Jewish Community: Its History and Structure to the American Revolution*, 3 vols. Philadelphia: 1942.

Bauer, Y. *My Brother's Keeper* Philadelphia: 1974.

Cohen, N. *Not Free To Desist*. Philadelphia: 1972.

Elazar, D. *Community and Polity: The Organizational Dynamics of American Jewry*. Philadelphia: 1975.

Feingold, H. L. "Jewish Life in the United States: Perspectives From History" in *Jewish Life in the United States* ed. J. B. Gittler. New York: 1981.

Feingold, H. L. *A Jewish Survival Enigma: The Strange Case of the American Jewish Committee*, New York, 1981.

A Midrash on American Jewish History

Goldin, M. *Why They Give: American Jews and Their Philanthropies.* New York: 1976.

Goldstein, S. and Goldscheider, C., *Jewish Americans: Three Generations in a Jewish Community* Englewood Cliffs: 1968.

Goren, A. *New York Jews and the Quest for Community.* New York: 1970.

Karp, A. J. *To Give Life: The UJA in the Shaping of the American Jewish Community.* New York: 1981.

The Golden Heritage: A History of the Federation of Jewish Philanthropies of New York from 1917 to 1967 New York, 1969.

Chapter VIII

A Problematic Synthesis:
The Conservative Movement

M ANY are undoubtedly familiar with the story of the Jewish college student who arrives home one day and announces proudly to his parents that he has become an atheist. The father is properly shocked but the mother, undaunted, immediately responds: "Yes, yes, of course, but what kind are you? Orthodox, Conservative, or Reform?" There is always some wisdom to be garnered from such stories. This one may be pointing to the fact that the fastest growing branch of Judaism is atheism. Or it may be humorously recognizing that on the grass-roots level disbelief is commonplace but has no bearing on belonging to the Jewish religious community. One can be Jewish and atheistic at the same time. Perhaps it means to say that Judaism goes on and that the current secular rages are merely so many fads without much staying power. Whatever the case, whether one has accepted atheism or Zen Buddhism, according to Jewish law one remains a Jew, which means that one persists in being a member of a much divided tribe. It is therefore necessary to know what kind of Jew our recently converted atheist is. Those involved with their Judaism may smile knowingly at the mother's reply. Not only have children from Jewish homes been returning for generations to announce their conversion to the latest heterodoxy, but they are familiar with the tensions in belief which emancipation and modernity have left in their wake. It is more difficult to believe implicitly today because modernity has fractured all belief systems. In the synagogues as well as churches there are thousands of active loyal members who in the inner recesses of their minds question the existence of a caring God. That is what modern secular rationality does. Jews who tend to accept secularism with a zeal reminiscent of their former enthusiasm for monotheism are particularly subject to doubt. Yet they accommodate to that secularism as Jews—used here in the peoplehood sense—which means that American Judaism is evolving into a kind of ethnic religion, where concern and commitment to the Jewish people is primary. The branch of religious Judaism that most accurately reflects not only the modern tensions of faith but also the sacrilizing of the Jewish people is Conservatism. In a sense, it is out of the very tension inherent in the accommodation, out of the desire to accept some elements of modernity and yet to maintain a link to the classical premodern Jewish tradition, that the Conservative synthesis has developed. The tension inherent in that situation is the reason why the Conservative movement seems to be perpetually flirting with disaster, while at the same time representing the most acceptable solution to living a Jewish life in America.

Like the other branches of the religion, the Conservative movement finds its theoretic origins in the Judaic culture of Central Europe, although its institutional development took place here. One of its earliest expressions can be traced to the Franfurt conference, where Zacharia Frankel, founder of the Breslau Seminary, and a group of followers, unhappy with the ultrarationalist direction taken by the Reform movement, called for a return to "positive historical Judaism," which would recognize the need for change while emphasizing the organic continuity of Judaism. Other reactions against the sharp break of the Reformers and in favor of a revitalizing of classical Judaism where soon heard in other Jewish communities in Western Europe.

In America, too, the Conservative movement was not at first a self-conscious effort to establish yet another Jewish denomination, but rather a reaction against the sharp break with traditional Judaism represented by the Reform movement. It was not a contrived strategy to find a middle ground between orthodox fundamentalism and Reform rationalism. For many decades it was a movement without a name or a position. It remained within the traditionalist fold. That nonschismatic approach is exemplified by the early career of Isaac Leeser, who took up the cudgels for traditional Judaism in nineteenth-century America. Leeser arrived from Germany in 1824 and became the spiritual leader of Mikveh Israel, the largest congregation in Philadelphia. Like Isaac Wise, the founder of the Reform movement, he was an energetic and gifted organizer. His interests ranged from the establishment of Jewish hospitals and the organization, first of Sunday schools, then, of Maimonides College (the first rabbinic academy in America, which lasted about seven years), to writing a Hebrew English prayerbook and translating the Bible. He was particularly perturbed about the activities of Christian missionaries among Jews and struggled to alert Jews about their real goals. Throughout his life he fervently worked toward achieving a unified structure for nascent American Jewry. It was for that reason that he attempted for years to work together with moderate Reform leaders like Isaac Wise. Only when it was apparent that the more radical Reformers like David Einhorn and Kaufman Kohler were determined to radically refashion American Judaism did Leeser compose long polemics defending the traditionalist position for publication in the *Occident* and the *Jewish Advocate*, papers which he founded. In the nineteenth century and in the first decade of the twentieth, the amorphous Conservative movement did not consider itself a rival to the traditionalist Orthodox position but rather an extension of it. The same was true of Leeser's successor at Mikveh Israel, Sabato Morais, who arrived in America in 1851 from Italy by way of London, and of Alexander Kohut, formerly a leader of the Conservative movement in Hungary, and other religious leaders such as Marcus Jastrow, Henry Pereira Mendes, and Samuel Meyer Isaacs. Nevertheless, a year after the Reform convention (held in Pittsburgh in 1885), signaled the advent of a radical Reform direction, Morais and others established the Jewish Theological Seminary to train rabbis. But it did not fare well.

Despite the fact that those who adhered to positive historical

Judaism had little self-consciousness as a movement and did not
view themselves as a separate sect, events conspired to lay the
foundation for the triangulation of the American Jewish religious scene. The most important we have already noted, that
is, the highly rationalistic Pittsburgh Platform, which threw
down the gauntlet to more traditional-minded Jews, who simply could not accept avowals that Jews were no longer a nation
but simply a "religious community" and that dietary laws and
much of the rest of the religious law or *halakah* were "foreign to
our present mental and spiritual state." The situation might
simply have remained static had the Reformers not flaunted
their lack of observance of traditional dietary laws at the *"tref*
(nonkosher) banquet." This incident occurred in 1883 at the
occasion of the graduation of the first class from the Hebrew
Union College, the rabbinic seminary of the Reform movement, which most believed would furnish spiritual leaders for
all American Jewish communities. The banquet went far to
change that belief. "The great banquet hall was brilliantly
lighted," wrote one participant in his memoirs, "the hundreds
of guests were seated at the beautifully arranged tables, the
invocation had been spoken by one of the visiting rabbis, when
the waiters served the first course. Terrific excitement ensued
when two rabbis rose from their seats and rushed from the
room. Shrimp had been placed before them as the opening
course of the elaborate menu . . ." Actually it was not shrimp at
all but little-neck clams which are just as *tref* (unkosher) but far
more exotic. The *"tref* banquet" became a *causus belli*, since it
almost directly triggered a vitriolic war of words in the Jewish
press. The Reformers were accused of everything from having
gone too far to deliberately humiliating those who held to dietary laws. In response, Reform societies in certain Midwestern
cities, perhaps hoping to rub salt into the wounds, deliberately
organized more such *"tref* banquets." Isaac Wise, a moderate
who is believed to have adhered to the laws of *kashrut* (dietary
laws), counselled against fanaticism. The *American Hebrew*, the
most widely circulated Anglo-Jewish journal, argued that authentic spiritual feeling "centers not in the kitchen and
stomach" but ostensibly in the heart. The gap between tradi-

tionalists and Reformers had grown so wide that they no longer accepted the same premises, and a primary basis for communication had been destroyed. Reformers would watch in amazement as the new Eastern Jewish immigrants established separate hospitals where *kashrut* was observed. (They did so even while plagued with kosher meat wars and with numerous cases of bogus *kashrut*.) For them Judaism was a matter of the stomach as well as the spirit. Dietary laws were that encompassing. The perception that an unbridgeable gap had developed led Sabato Morais to establish a separate seminary to counteract "the baneful influences which have perverted the Cincinnati Institution."

The Conservative consciousness has its inception as a reaction to the Reform movement. Its physical existence, however, would depend on the traditionalists. The arrival of massive numbers of Jews from Eastern Europe who, even when they no longer adhered strictly to the tenets of Orthodox Judaism, nevertheless remained fiercely loyal to Jewishness, its cultural, ethnic, and national components. For these Jews, who as yet saw no need to refashion their identity as Jews, Reformism smacked of betrayal. Even if the correctness of much of the Reformist critique was admitted, they could not relate to it since it lacked all the additional components they associated with being Jewish. It saw Judaism as merely a religion, not as the religious civilization of the Jewish people. It had no distinct language such as Yiddish. It understood little of the special Jewish cuisine, or the special ironic humor which was part of Jewish life in Eastern Europe. It was deracinated and offered few cues on how to live one's life. Whereas Reform was for many reasons unacceptable and out of reach for these immigrants, Conservatism seemed eminently suitable. The more moderate reasonable adherence to Jewish law correspnded to their needs. There was a practical reason as well—the traditionalist Orthodox community would produce a surplus of candidates for the rabbinate which could be placed in the growing number of Conservative congregations, especially in the second and third circles of suburban settlement. These pulpits began to materialize in numbers in the twenties and thirties, the period of "Conservative triumphalism." But that triumph, which in some respects sustained itself to 1982, could occur only after the Conservative movement established its institutional structure.

We have noted that a seminary for the training of rabbis established by Morais in 1886 did not fare well. Six of the congregations affiliated with the seminary were won over by the Reform branch by 1900, and only seventeen rabbis were ordained. When Morais died in 1897 the seminary, housed in New York's Congregation Shearith Israel, had few students and verged on bankruptcy. It was a half-way house few would enter.

It was this sad condition that Cyrus Adler, an Arkansas-born pupil of Morais who went on to earn a doctorate in Semitics at Johns Hopkins, observed and resolved to remedy. Together with Adolphus S. Solomon, the acting president of the seminary, he brought the matter to the attention of Jacob Schiff, known for his devotion to Jewish causes. The philanthropist was himself committed to the Reform movement. Would he see the wisdom in supporting the seminary of what might develop into the flagship institution of a rival branch of American Judaism? Schiff not only did, but convinced his monied friends, Leonard Lewisohn and others, to follow suit. The seminary institution was refinanced, reorganized, revitalized, and given a new building. Solomon Schechter, whose reputation as a brilliant reader of rabbinics at Cambridge had preceded him, was recruited to head the seminary. He brought with him a coterie of brilliant scholars, Louis Ginzberg, Alexander Marx, Israel Friedlaender, and others. Soon a new sense of elan radiated from the headquarters on Broadway and 121st Street in New York. But the peculiar sequence of events, establishing a rabbinic seminary first and then recruiting and organizing congregations, has affected the Conservative movement ever since. For while it pays some lip-service to democracy and congregationalism, in fact the faculty of the seminary exercises an extraordinary influence on the movement. That predominance may be one of the sources of the movement's problems.

The role played by Schiff and other wealthy Reform Jews in financing what would become a competing institution to the Hebrew Union College is undoubtedly the most outstanding illustration of intelligence by a patrician leadership in American Jewish history. The patricians saw such an academy not as a competitive institution but one enriching all of American Jewry, and they understood that the masses of new Eastern European immigrants would perceive the Reform branch as alien. Yet contact with them was imperative, and it could be established only through the mediation of the Conservative movement. By buttressing the Jewish Theological Seminary they were also creating a needed link to "downtown" Jewry. In 1913 sixteen congregations affiliated with JTS established the United Synagogue of American Hebrew Congregations. Sometime earlier the Rabbinic Assembly of America had been organized. The basic institutional structure of the Conservative movement was complete.

But what precisely the new movement represented, its theology—which in Judaism really means its approach to the Jewish people as an entity—remained an enigma. Its distinctive practices, rituals, and hymns were readily discernible. They reflected a peculiar middle position. Aesthetic practices were borrowed from the Reform movement. With some exceptions the separate women's gallery was abolished in favor of family pews. There was usually a program of Hebrew education. The prayerbook remained much the same as the traditional one except that the petition for the renewal of the sacrificial system was eliminated, and the tense of the Mussaph service was changed so that it becomes merely a recitation of what the forefathers did. The idea of the resuscitation of the dead (m'hayeh hamaisim) was vacated, of its miraculous aspect. Some prayers in English were now included in the service, and synagogues employed an organ and a choir as in Reform temples. But in matters of law many practices associated with the Orthodox branch were retained. Worshipers wear the prayer shawl (tallith) at the morning prayer and phylacteries (t'fillin). Heads are covered and Rosh Hashanah (New Year) is celebrated in two days rather than the one day customary in Reform congregations. All boys are prepared for Bar Mitzvah, and Bas Mitzvah (confirmation ceremonies) for girls are almost equally popular. Adherence to dietary laws is customary at synagogue functions. Most Conservative rabbis will not perform marriages for divorced persons without a previous Jewish bill of divorcement (the *get*). There is also as formal prescribed course of training before conversion. "Occupying the middle position between Orthodoxy and Reform," noted one authority, "may be understood either as a critique of the former or a protest against the latter trend." The truth was reflected in Conservatism's eclectic practice. Conservatism had no consistent theology or dogma. In one sense that was an asset, for it gave the movement the flexibility to negotiate the middle position and retain the adherence of the largest number of the faithful, who cared little for fine distinctions of doctrine. But it was also a liability, because religion, especially during periods of social crisis and rapid change, needs to project certainty and confidence that it is on the right path. Pragmatism and flexibility are sound principles in all enterprises except a church.

There is a wry story frequently heard before 1950 when the Law Committee of the Rabbinical Assembly voted to permit travel to attend services on the Sabbath. It made short shrift of the doctrinal differences between the three branches. These were all rhetoric, since none of the branches are in fact what they purport to be. The real difference between the three branches was in the distance their respective congregants parked their cars from the synagogue on the Sabbath. The Reform movement provided a parking lot, the Conservatives parked a few blocks away and the Orthodox a few blocks further away. That story gives us a keen insight into the fact that it is objective circumstances, like living a great distance from a synagogue, rather than doctrine, which determines what most worshipers do. We find members of Orthodox synagogues who in fact adhere more closely to the standards of the Conservative movement, and in the left wing of the Conservative movement we find members who would not be uncomfortable with Reform practices. In that respect the branches have grown closer together. We have noted that much of its former ultrarationalism and antinationalism has been abandoned by the

Reform movement. A recent study of the adherents to the Orthodox branch shows that a surprisingly high percentage, perhaps as high as 60 percent, do not strictly adhere to *halakah*, especially its dietary laws. While there are perhaps as many as a million Orthodox Jews in America, there are only two hundred thousand strict Sabbath observers. In the normative sense, Orthodoxy seems closer to the practices of Conservatism. Paradoxically, the steep decline in observance and adherence to Jewish law is even more characteristic of the Conservative movement.

Nevertheless, it would be wrong to conclude that the difference between the three branches of American Jewry is chimerical, or that American Jewry is on the road to religious unity. Institutional interests have understandably developed, and each branch serves a different constituency based on class, region, and degree of observance. In the case of the last mentioned, Orthodox Jews are most observant, Conservative somewhat less so, and Reform least of all. But that hardly tells the entire story. For that we must look back for a moment to the preemancipation period, when Judaism was of a single cloth. It was traditional, and there existed no way of leaving the fold except through conversion. The triangulation of the Jewish religious enterprise occurred with the historic encounter with the emancipation, which progressed furthest in America. In the free secular atmosphere of America, all religions seemed to undergo a kind of fragmentation or denominationalism. The separation of government authority from the church meant that the church could not rely on legal sanction to compel uniformity and adherence. Modern secular citizens were free not to belong if they so chose, or to select from religious dogma what suited them and ignore the rest. In such a society the rule was congregationalism; that is, final authority resting with a congregation voluntarily associated with the movement, rather than obedience to a central authority. And, of course, individual congregants had a parallel freedom to take from the faith what they desired. Their association with the congregation was voluntary.

The Jewish communities responded in three different ways to the challenge of emancipation and the new secular order.

The Orthodox were least accepting of its premises and continued to emphasize the primacy of Rabbinic law, even when that law no longer possessed sanction and depended on voluntary compliance. The Reformists, on the other hand, reshaped their Judaism to stress the high moral and ethical imperatives found in the Hebrew prophets. Not surprisingly, these principles neatly matched those emanating from the enlightenment, so that for some, Judaism, an ancient faith, seemed the most "modern" religion of all.

Considering themselves merely a variant of Orthodoxy rather than a separate movement, the early Conservatives never fully articulated a position. To be sure they emphasized some points that were familiar to the faithful, *Emunat Yisrael*, loyalty to the Jewish faith, and *k'lal* or *knesset Yisrael*, (the universal community or collectivity of Jewry) belonging to the Jewish people. Later Solomon Schechter would speak of "Catholic Israel," by which he meant a holistic approach not represented by any segment of the Jewish nation "or any corporate priesthood or rabbihood, but by the collective conscience of Catholic Israel as embodied in the Universal Synagogue." The practice of Judaism would be normative rather than prescriptive and mandated from above. The problem for the Conservative movement has been that by using as a norm the practices of committed Jews, the norm has tended toward less and less observance. The personal autonomy accompanying modern secular life tends to erode adherence to religious law, especially when there is no longer a means of enforcing it. The question of adherence to Jewish law marks the sharpest difference between Conservative and Orthodox. The latter believe that rabbinic law, as well as the standard procedure for deriving and evolving it, has priority, and they enjoin the faithful to obey it. Their life is shaped by the law they choose to serve. Conservatives also recognize the binding nature of Jewish law, but Jews come first. They make the law, which is continually changing to confront new conditions. *Halakah* is a living, social thing. The law is made for Jews, not Jews for the law. The difference in approach to law among the three branches is succinctly described this way by a Conservative rabbi: "We have felt that Reform

Judaism abandoned Halahah [sic] while Orthodoxy permitted Halahah to abandon us."

An outstanding difference between the Conservative movement and the other two wings developed originally over the question of Zionism. We have noted that the original classic Reform position was anti-Zionist. (That has not been true for a long time. Today the Reform branch maintains a full program for its students and adherents in Israel.) Anti-Zionism also prevailed in the Orthodox wing. Adherents of ultra-Orthodoxy associated with *Agudath Israel* continue to believe that Zionism and the state of Israel are abominations. However, that view has become a minority view in the observant community. In fact, a disproportionately high number of the small trickle of *olim* (immigrants to Israel) from America are Orthodox Jews. But the most comfortable home for Zionism in America, especially its cultural manifestations, has been the Conservative movement. If one considers the commonality of Jewish peoplehood, Zionism is in a sense a kind of secular equivalent of Conservatism. "Catholic Israel" and Jewish peoplehood, which is contained in Zionist ideology, are opposite sides of the same coin. It is thus no accident that American Zionism did not receive initial legitimation until Solomon Schechter gave strong support to the kind of redemption it held out for secular Jews.

The absence of known limits to the accommodation process poses endless problems for the Conservative movement. That can be seen most clearly when the movement is compelled to confront a central tenet of modernity like the equality of women. Practically, the question arises when female congregants ask to be called to read from the Torah during the traditional Sabbath reading or seek to be ordained as rabbis. Predictably, the Reform branch, which is most enthusiastic about the principles of modernity and enlightenment, made the required changes without much turmoil. The *mechitzah* (the object separating men and women worshipers in traditional observance) was quickly and early replaced by family pews. The Reform branch was the first to ordain female rabbis. The branch least in tune with its precepts of modernity has officially done none of these things (although one can note many congregations affiliated with the Orthodox branch where the use of the *mechitzah* is honored more in the breach than in the observance). For the Conservatives, who want to be both modern and traditional, the question of the role of women has caused endless problems. The *mechitzah* has been eliminated without much difficulty, and the question of *aliyot* for women (being called for a reading of the weekly Torah portion) is in practice decided on the congregational level, where it has often proved to be a divisive issue. The question of ordination of women rabbis, however, has proven to be an agonizing one. A resolution by the JTS faculty senate (December 1979) calling for tabling the question in the hope that interim developments will help crystalize a consensus, expressed concern that the question of women's ordination "has provoked unprecedented division at every level of the Movement." The "divergence of opinion" was so bitter that it was felt that it might result in "irreparable damage" to the seminary and "pluralistic unity" of the Rabbinical Assembly. The issue has yet to be resolved. The conflict gives us another perspective on the paradox of the organization of the Conservative movement. It develops that it is more "Catholic" in its hierarchical organization than it is in its practice of peoplehood—Judaism. The compromise between the imperatives of modernity and classical Judaism, as presented by the ordination question, would probably best be solved on the grass-roots level by the membership of the congregations. But that is not where the decisions are made in the Conservative movement.

In practice, the ideals of the Conservative movement—what Alexander Kohut called a "Judaism of the healthy golden mean"—has proven difficult to achieve. But what is the answer? "A reform which seeks to progress without the Mosaic rabbinic tradition is a deformity—a skeleton without flesh and sinew, without spirit and heart," insisted Kohut. What Conservatism desired was a Judaism "full of life—Jewish, yet breathing the modern spirit. Only a Judaism true to itself and its past, yet receptive of the idea of the present, accepting the good and the beautiful from whatever source it may come can command respect and recognition." But Kohut and the leaders of the

Conservative movement could conceive of no formula that would at once "be true to itself, yet receptive to the present." At the juncture in time when the Conservative movement is triumphant in attracting the faithful in the suburbs, where it now predominates over the Reform branch and produces its own leadership partly through the Ramah summer-camp movement, it is beset with ideological and morale problems. The amorphousness of the middle ground position repels those who insist that a religious dogma requires certainty and confidence to inspire a laity. Others are appalled at the waning of observance and general piety. Because the Orthodox branch has somehow retained its sense of elan and its claims to authenticity, it serves as a kind of subtle threat. Much of Conservative leadership seems to be looking over its right shoulder at what the Orthodox are up to. Finally, the movement to which it has given much and from which it has gained as well, American Zionism, is today no longer the lode star for American Jewry it once was. (It may be that we live in a post-Zionist era, or that an ideology that has, after all, achieved its primary goals and is nearly a century old, has reached middle age and thus loses its popular drawing power.) Zionism—or "Israelism", if one prefers that term—nonetheless continues to bind American Jewry together. Zionism is bound together with the Conservative movement in a historical tandem. Both locate themselves astride the broad middle ground of American Jewry, who are moderately faithful and concerned about the welfare of Israel. Conservatism is the religious branch closest to the consensus of American Jewry. The problem with such closeness is that it is bound to reflect the dilemma of American Jewry: how can Jews define their Jewishness in a modern secular society? Conservatism offers no answers to that dilemma, and indeed there may be no ready answers. In the meantime, the Conservative movement lives with a paradox. In the very source of its success, its synthesis between tradition and modernity, may also lie the seeds of failure.

Bibliography

Appel, J. J. "The Trefa Banquet," *Commentary* vol. 41 (February 1966).

Blau, J. L. *Modern Varieties of Judaism.* New York: 1966.

Davis, M. *The Emergence of Conservative Judaism.* Glencoe: 1963.

Karp, A. *A History of the United Synagogue of America, 1913–1963.* New York: 1964.

Neusner, J., ed. *Understanding American Judaism,* vol. 2, especially essays by Waxman, Neusner, and Sklare. New York: 1975.

Siegel, S. *Conservative Judaism and Jewish Law.* New York: 1977.

Sklare, M. *Conservative Judaism.* New York: 1976.

CHAPTER IX /

Israelism/Zionism:
A New Civil Religion

A visiting Israeli friend made an interesting observation about the character of American Jews. He was impressed by the strength of their commitment to Israel. In some cases their defense of Israeli actions is so unreserved that it exceeds that of the citizens of Israel. Yet, he noted that the number of American Jews who choose to migrate to Israel is relatively small, despite this strong commitment. He accounted for the disparity by noting that the basic principle governing the behavior of American Jews—a principle which they share with other Americans—is an unrelenting search for comfort and convenience. "When it is too hot, Americans air condition. When it is too cold, you use central heating. You refuse to leave God's order of things alone." He went on to explain that American Jewish behavior is an exaggeration of this tendency. "If your name is too long or too Jewish, you change it; you do the same for your noses." The same is done, according to my guest, with basic principles of Judaism. Just as American Jewry has conceived of a Judaism without the "yoke of Torah," so you have a Zionism without the "yoke of Aliyah." Nothing in American Jewry takes hold if it is not convenient and comfortable.

Needless to say, although my guest did not make these observations to show disapproval, I was a little taken aback. Sometimes an outsider can make more realistic observations than an insider. Was the observation accurate? Was the basic principle governing American Jewish behavior convenience or comfort? I thought about it for some time and finally decided that, although it has an element of truth, it is a little too facile. It does not tell the whole story regarding American Zionism. In history, a half-truth is often worse than no truth at all.

In a recent study, a select sample of American Jews was asked what being Jewish meant to them. The object of the study was to discover what is commonly known as the "state of the faith." Researchers are interested in measuring the gap between normative Judaism—what Jews actually think and do concerning their Jewishness—and what "professional" Jews— rabbis, officials of Jewish organizations, and sundry researchers—think Judaism should be. The results of the study would not surprise the average American Jew. Close to the top of the list of what being Jewish entailed were two items: helping and supporting Israel and behaving ethically in daily transactions. Following the laws of the faith *(halakah)* was close to the bottom of the list. The high place given to Israel is especially noteworthy because it confirms what many students of American Jewry have determined independently of such studies. Zionism, at least a peculiar American version of it, which we might call "Israelism," has become the centerpiece of a new civil religion that holds sway among American Jews. It is the way most American Jews today come to terms with the fact of their Jewishness. The new civil religion contains many disparate elements. There are religious facets including going to synagogue on holy days, having their male children circumcised, a Jewish wedding and burial. There are new secular elements as well, of which philanthropic giving to the United Jewish Appeal (UJA), a portion of which goes to Israel, and in some cases a periodic hegira to Israel are constants. What we are witnessing is the decline of a purely denominational model based on adherence to Jewish law in favor of a secular–cultural model rooted in a common concern for Jewish people wherever they may reside. Zionism, even the deracinated version of it adhered to by American Jews, contains the Jewish peoplehood idea in its purest form. That is one reason why it continues to win such loyalty from committed Jews everywhere. In fact, other studies also show that the more committed the Jew the stronger the

Zionism: thus the contention that being anti-Zionist is close to being anti-Semitic, especially when the polemics emanate from the Kremlin or Arab sources, is true in a technical sense, since in large measure Zionism is the way Judaism is carried forward in the second half of the twentieth century.

For historians the centrality of Zionism represents a strange twist in American Jewish development. If an American Jew, living in 1900, had been told that five decades later Zionism would become the paste that held American Jewry together, he would have shaken his head in disbelief. Zionism was not popular among American Jews at the turn of the century. Similarly, the handful of Jews who were committed to Zionism would undoubtedly have considered the kind of Zionism finally developed in America as peculiar, or at least different from the Zionism developed in societies—like those of Eastern Europe, from whence many had emigrated—where a virulent form of anti-Semitism prevailed. As my Israeli friend observed, it is a Zionism of convenience. The commitment to the ideology is fulfilled by philanthropic giving rather than by an obligation to resettle in Israel. It is that which our Israeli found most difficult to understand. He was astounded by our disregard for facts which to him were perfectly obvious. Did American Jews not know what Israel is the only place where one could live a full Jewish life? And, after the Holocaust, how could they fail to see the dangers of living in the diaspora? Let us try to discover the historical reasons for American Jewry's fashioning of a Zionism in which neither of these two assumptions finds a place.

That the Zionist movement in America was a slow-starting affair, which really did not achieve a consensus until the late thirties, can only be understood from the perspective of history. The Eastern Jewish immigrants, who sought a haven in America rather than Palestine, were really "voting with their feet" for life in the diaspora. The Zionist ideology, which desired to rebuild a Jewish homeland in Palestine, served as a disturbing counterthrust to the choice they had made. If taken seriously, it could interfere with the delicate Americanization process, already beset with problems. Despite these difficulties, there was always a discernible Zionist presence not only in the

Jewish community but among Christian groups as well. The latter phenomenon, crypto-Zionism, will not be discussed here. Nevertheless, we ought to be aware that it plays an important role in determining the sustained affinity for a Jewish homeland in the American public mind. In the American Jewish community there were Zionist-oriented cultural and fraternal orders, such as the Knights of Zion clubs in Chicago and the *Hibbat Zion* clubs wherever there were sufficient aggregates of East European Jews. Among German Jews there was the *Zentral Verein der Amerikanischer Zionisten*, the German Jews who furnished the first leadership cadre for the American movement. But usually these Zionist clubs were transitory affairs, composed primarily of lovers of Jewish culture and Hebraists.

Most of the organizational expressions of American Jewry were outspokenly anti-Zionist. When the first World Zionist Conference convened in Basle, Switzerland, in 1897, the Central Conference of American Rabbis passed a strong anti-Zionist resolution. It reinforced the opposition of the Reform movement expressed in the Pittsburgh Platform of 1885. On the other side of the religious spectrum, the ultra-Orthodox groups, under the banner of Agudath Israel would be equally adamant in their opposition to Zionism, which they viewed as sinful. They believed there could be no return of Jews to Zion without the prior appearance of the Messiah. The uptown stewards, descendants of the German Jewish migration who established the American Jewish Committee in 1906, were opposed to Zionism for other reasons. Most important was the opposition of the socialist labor wing of the immigrant community. They viewed the problem of anti-Semitism, the major burden borne by Jews of the diaspora, as symptomatic of distorted exploitative relations between the classes. That distortion was inherent in the capitalist system—once the system was transformed to a more rational socialist one, the "Jewish problem," together with many other social problems, would vanish. Zionism, especially the political variety advocated by Theodor Herzl, was viewed by socialists as a reactionary "bourgeois nationalist" throwback, which militated against the principle of universal brotherhood central to the socialist belief system. We

take note of two factors, then, concerning the attitude of organized American Jewry toward the ideology overwhelmingly
accepted today. At the outset, it faced the opposition of all
major movements claiming the mind and heart of American
Jewry. Paradoxically, anti-Zionism was, in fact, the only commonality between the various secular and religious factions in
American Israel. It was the one thing they agreed upon.

Yet the organizational base of the American Zionist movement was laid precisely during this period between 1890 and
1920, when opposition was strongest. Led by a handful of dissident uptowners, such as Richard Gotheil, Judah Magnes, and
finally Julian Mack and Louis Brandeis, the movement attracted new support. There were always those students of the
Hebrew language who understood that a longing for the return
to Zion was deeply embedded in the Judaic religio-culture.
They would now be joined by the refurbished Conservative
movement, which, under its new leader Solomon Schechter,
had broken ranks with other religious branches to support at
least the idea of cultural Zionism and the need for a vital center
controlled by Jews. At the same time, there was a growing
number of Eastern immigrants who took their cues from
Nahum Syrkin and Ber Borochov and preferred to express their
socialist universalism within a Jewish context—the Jewish national home would become a modern classless society in which
there would be no exploitation of one person by another. The
Poale Zion (Zionist labor) was established in March 1903, and its
fraternal order, the *Farband*, in 1910. Meanwhile, the growing
number of middle-class Jews projected a Jewish national state,
or at least community, which would be a model of secular
parliamentary democracy, with a firm guarantee of civil and
religious rights. Joining these advocates of some form of Zionism was a group of religious Jews whose Zionism focused
primarily on what they felt was an urgent need to have a central
locus from which the learning of Torah could go forth. Called
Mizrachi, this religious branch of Zionism was established by
Meier Berlin in 1911.

Sometimes a closer scrutiny of the anti-Zionist camp yields
surprising results. The wealthy uptown Jews who furnished

much of the leadership for the Jewish community were not always opposed to Zionism. Unyielding opposition held true primarily for those like Rabbi David Philipson, whose association with the Reform movement—which sought to convert the dispersion from a curse to a blessing—could not on principle accept an ideology that desired the return of the Jews to a distant Zion. Men like Jacob Schiff and Louis Marshall might be better classified as non-Zionists. They were apprehensive about a separatist nationalist movement among Jews, which would inevitably raise the question of "dual loyalties." The last thing these fiercely patriotic Jews wanted was to have such a question on the American political agenda. At the same time, however, they could and often did find it possible to support the nonpolitical elements of Zionist ideology. They welcomed the idea of Palestine as a Jewish cultural center, and they generously supported the Jews already settled there. It was the question of a sovereign Jewish commonwealth that nettled. Thus, we find Louis Marshall lending his support to the Balfour Declaration and condemning those around Sulzberger who memorialized against it in the *New York Times*. Later, Marshall was one of the non-Zionists who joined the Jewish Agency. Judah Magnes was a staunch Zionist, who eventually became the head of the new Hebrew University but always held some reservations regarding political Zionism. Jacob Schiff, too, had little difficulty in supporting cultural projects in Palestine.

By 1919 there existed a small Zionist movement in America composed of about 180,000 members. The various organizations, reflecting the full political spectrum, were loosely joined together under the Federation of American Zionists (an umbrella organization founded in 1899 by Richard Gottheil and Stephen Wise). From its beginnings the FAZ was beset by problems of unity within its ranks as well as by relations with the world Zionist movement. In the words of one noted historian, it was "dysfunctional". Major components like the *Poale Zion* (labor Zionists) and *Mizrachi* (religious Zionists) withdrew from the FAZ in 1916. The major Zionist women's organization *(Hadassah)* ultimately followed suit. Even the replacement of the uptown leadership with more acceptable representatives like Judah Magnes and Harry Friedenwald could not heal the growing breach between the uptowners, who led the movement, and the downtowners, who increasingly comprised its rank and file.

Paradoxically, it was the two cataclysmic wars in the twentieth century that helped Zionism establish itself. World War I presented an opportunity to realize Zionist objectives, since Turkey, the "sick man of Europe"—which controlled Palestine, then part of Greater Syria—faced dismemberment should the cause of the central powers fail. The war also caused the Provisional Executive Committee of the world-wide Zionist movement to be temporarily transferred to America. Most important was the fact that Louis D. Brandeis, who had been recruited for the movement, became seriously active and finally assumed the leadership of the American movement. With a man of Brandeis's caliber at the helm, there was certain to be an improvement.

There has been endless speculation concerning the reasons why Brandeis, who in his early life had had almost no contact with Jews and things Jewish, should at the age of 50 assume leadership responsibilities in a group and community he barely understood. Was it the positive impression he gained of Jews on both sides of the table when he acted as a mediator during the "great" strike that wracked the garment industry in 1911? Was it a ploy to gain a Jewish constituency and thus advance his political career? Perhaps Brandeis was really seeking a social experiment of suitable human scale to test out his progressive reform notions. The Zionist resettlement experiment in Palestine offered a good laboratory. Was it the Frankist tradition of the Brandeis clan coming to the fore, or perhaps something more mundane, like the influence of his uncle Louis Dembitz? At one point in his career, he had taken Dembitz as his middle name. All these theories and more have been presented to account for Brandeis's precipitous assumption of leadership responsibilities in the Jewish community. Historians will probably never learn the exact reason, since his private letters are not available. We know only that some time during 1911 Brandeis evinced a sustained interest in the cause of Zionism. He became a kind of *baale tshuve* (returnee or repentant) who chose Zionism—at least his own version of it—as his form of Judaism. He was sensitive to his lack of Jewish background and frequently mentioned it. But by 1914, when he took over the Provisional Executive Committee, he had already taught himself a great deal about the Jewish tradition and culture by systematic disciplined study.

The assumption of a leadership role by a person of Brandeis's standing elevated the esteem of American Jewry. His reputation as the "people's attorney" was nationwide, and when he was appointed to the Supreme Court in 1916 it was enhanced further. That was especially true within the Jewish community, where judges were held in extraordinarily high regard. The acceptance of the leadership of the Zionist movement by a man of first rank also did much to make that ideology known and acceptable among Jews. It convinced them of the legitimacy of Zionism, which Brandeis soon strove to underline not only by his presence but by reasoning any sense of disloyalty away. Moreover, Brandeis brought with him a coterie of brilliant, well-connected, highly Americanized people, such as Judge Julian Mack, Felix Frankfurter, Rabbi Stephen Wise and Mrs. Joseph Fels (wife of the soap manufacturer). He placed at the head of the Zionist movement a group of leaders who could easily act as intermediaries between the movement and American leadership elites. The Zionist movement would become as American as B'nai B'rith. Brandeis lost no time in confronting the basic obstacle to the development of American Zionism— the problem of dual loyalty. In an early exposition of social pluralism, he argued that American Society does not demand of its subgroups that they surrender allegiances that are not in conflict with Americanism, and that there was no conflict between Americanism and Judaism: rather, there was a remarkable confluence of principles and values. "To be a good American," he insisted, "one must be a good Jew, and to be a good Jew, one must be a good Zionist." He elaborated on the idea at the American Zionist Convention in 1915: "The highest Jewish ideals are essentially American in a very important particular. It is democracy that Zionism represents and every bit of that is the American ideal of the 20th century." Such statements and the fact of his high-born position in American society helped Brandeis legitimize the Zionist movement. Few understood that there were those in society's mainstream who found Brandeis unacceptable precisely because of his Jewishness. For the Jewish community, the fact that Brandeis could accept Zionism was sufficient to mute the vexing question of dual loyalties, which for many had posed a genuine dilemma. Later, the philosopher Horace Kallen would proffer a more substantial rationale, arguing that democratic societies are healthiest when they are pluralistic. He used the analogy of the orchestra, which has many different instruments but produces wonderful harmonious music when properly directed. The idea that every subgroup possessed something precious, which it should retain, undermined the melting pot theory that there was only one way to be an American. Brandeis began the process of creating social space in which the distinctive Jewish culture, with its Zionist component, could germinate and thrive.

But creating such space entailed a price, for there existed limits beyond which a subgroup could not go. For many Jews, that limit was the question of emigration to Palestine. How could a Jew be loyal to America while preparing to make a new home in another country? Brandeis insisted that an American Jew need not migrate to Palestine in order to be a Zionist. "The place is made ready," he explained, "legal right of habitation is secured; and any who wish are free to go. But it is of the essence of Zionism that there shall be no compulsion." He failed to note that in post-emancipation Jewish communities, there no longer existed a central authority that possessed such coercive power. Zionism would have to rely on persuasion and historical circumstances to attract settlers. In the societies of the West, where until just before the Holocaust many believed anti-Semitism to be a thing of the past, Zionist spokesmen were rarely persuasive enough to convince large numbers of Jews to resettle in Palestine. In America, which did not experience the Holocaust and where a Jewish question has never been part of the political agenda, few conceived of the necessity of resettling in Israel. American Jewry developed a vicarious Zionism; a

Zionism *far yenem* (for others), the *yenem* being persecuted Jewries, wherever they might be—Russia, Poland, or the *Maghreb*—who required a haven.

Perhaps more significant than what Brandeis did to establish an ideological rationale for American Zionism was what he did for the organizational well-being of the Zionist movement. He found a fragmented, chaotically organized, bankrupt movement with no sense of order, no strategy, and no policy. By projecting his own sense of discipline, he welded together a strong viable organization with a sense of purpose. Using the slogan, "Men, Money, Discipline!" he virtually rebuilt the organization from bottom up. Despite his heavy work load on the Supreme Court (to which he was appointed in 1916), and the need to work only from behind the scenes lest he compromise his court position* Brandeis was totally familiar with the minutest detail of organization. He demanded and received daily reports of fund-raising and membership figures. His memory for details was prodigious. His progressive stamp was reflected in the new American-style managerial efficiency in the FAZ, whose name was changed to the Zionist Organization of America (ZOA) in 1918, as if to herald the revitalization of the American Zionist movement. Together with the new operational efficiency there was a rise in membership. The mettle of the new organization and leadership was tested when, during the war, the hard-pressed *yishuv* (settlement in Palestine) required food if famine were to be avoided. The Wilson administration sent ships loaded with potatoes and thereby established the precedent for aid to Palestine. More important was the support the American movement was able to give in the diplomatic arena. The British required a confirmation from the Wilson administration regarding the Balfour Declaration, a quasilegal promise of a national Jewish homeland in Palestine and the protection of the rights of the indigenous population. The Zionist leaders considered that the Balfour Declaration,

*The model of proxy political activism through Felix Frankfurter in the political arena between 1919 and 1937, which came to light in February 1982, was preceded by a similar behind the scenes activism in relation to the American Zionist movement after his appointment to the court.

awarded largely as a result of the influence of Chaim Weizmann, set the legal foundation for a future Jewish commonwealth. British decision makers, it would develop later, were less concerned with the promise inherent in the document than they were with having the Jews, whose power they considerably overestimated, on their side during the Great War. The new American Zionist leadership, led by Brandeis, was able to obtain Wilson's confirmation. Later, when support of the mandate idea embodied in the Treaty of Versailles was required, the Brandeis group again proved able to override anti-Zionist opposition within the Jewish community as well as considerable opposition from Palestinian Arabs, American missionary and naval interests, and the U.S. State Department. This period marks the emergence of a Zionist-oriented leadership within the American Jewish community. The old German Jewish stewards were still on the scene, but many now recognized that the force of Zionism was irresistible.

Yet the path was not altogether clear for the Zionist movement. Almost as soon as it had come into its own, it crashed against the shoals of disunity and popular indifference. Brandeisian Zionism stressed efficiency, scientific management, and the completion of specific, attainable objectives. Building a potash plant along the Dead Sea was more important than the cultural–ideological programs with their emphasis on the *ruach* (spirit) of Jewish peoplehood, the *gegenwartsarbeit* (the ideological propaganda work) so dear to the Eastern Jews, who cared more for ideas, especially the idea of socialism, than for the beauty of a perfectly balanced ledger. For them the American version of Zionism seemed deracinated. It lacked *Yiddishkeit* (Jewish-peoplehood content), and after it became apparent that Brandeis sought reconciliation with the wealthy Jewish stewards who were already cultural Zionists, they suspected that Brandeis was moving back towards *shtadlanut* (court Jewry) of the rich and well-born. When the inevitable split did materialize, it was over a seemingly irrelevant issue, the status of *keren hayesod*, the development fund for Palestine. The conflict came to a head at the Cleveland convention in 1921, where it was compounded by personality conflicts. So acrimonious was the debate that many could agree with Chaim Weizmann's observation that between Pinsk and Washington there could be little in common. The Brandeis group, partly because it had little stomach for the politicking required to impose its rule on the rambunctious movement, lost the battle. The leadership was assumed by Louis Lipsky, who represented the Weizmann faction in the American movement. It was an interesting turn of events. Lipsky, a journalist and well-known theater critic, had been an insider in the American Zionism movement since the turn of the century. The advent of Brandeis and the Americanized leadership had pushed him into the background. Now he emerged, far closer to the immigrant rank and file in disposition and character, yet in mastery of language and knowledge of organization, an easy match for the Brandeis group. He embodied a more precise amalgamation of the two wings of the Zionist movement and American Jewry itself.

It is difficult to say whether the subsequent decline in membership and funding during the twenties should be attributed to the ascendancy of the Lipsky–Weizmann faction. The twenties were a period of the resurgence of a privatism that had an impact on all organizations. Organized labor also declined in membership, after having reached a high point after the passage of the Clayton Anti-Trust Law in 1914. In the case of the Zionist movement, moreover, the decline in membership preceded Lipsky's tenure of office. In 1920, membership declined to 25,000, and by 1921 it went down further, to 18,481. There was a parallel decline in fund raising. Future historians may want to probe the possibility that the xenophobia and nativism of the period embodied in such things as the Red Scare, the Palmer raids, the passage of restrictive immigration laws, the reorganization of the KKK, and finally the Sacco and Vanzetti case did not have a bearing on the decline. That becomes especially noteworthy when it is realized that the nativism of the twenties had, not far beneath the surface, a specific anti-Jewish animus. It could be heard during the congressional hearings over the immigration laws, its tone amplified by Henry Ford's anti-Semitic diatribes in the *Dearborn Independent* and by the imposition of an unofficial *numerus clausus* for admission to Harvard and other desirable universities. Sensitized to the limits of ethnic separatism and the limits of the pluralistic society and wanting more than ever to become American, the Jewish public during the twenties seemed less prepared than ever to welcome the disturbing countertendency represented by Zionism. It welcomed it only from a distance, and then only if it did not interfere with the headlong drive for prosperity and Americanization. In a voluntaristic American society, those willing to expend money had a special place. Many of these wealthy Jews had never accepted the Zionist alternative or Brandeis's rationale. Whereas the movement found it increasingly difficult to raise funds, one wealthy steward, Lessing Rosenwald, then directing Agro-Joint, (the Agricultural resettlement arm of the Joint Distribution Committee), was able to raise millions of dollars to resettle Russian Jews in the Crimea and the Ukraine. As managed by Dr. Joseph Rosen, the enterprise soon dwarfed the kibbutz movement in Palestine upon which so much hope had been placed. Between 1924 and 1928, Rosen resettled 5,646 Jewish families on the land, so that by 1928 there were 112 Jewish Agro-Joint colonies in the Ukraine and 105 in the Crimea.

If the Zionist movement was to progress, money was necessary. That much the successful Agro-Joint and ICA experiments in the Soviet Union and Argentina illustrated. But the enthusiasm of the monied class waned during the twenties. Some willingly participated in the enlargement of the Jewish Agency in 1929, but despite the fact that the Lipsky–Weizmann leadership adopted most of the program originally suggested by the Brandeis group, financial support for the Zionist enterprise remained lukewarm. That was the situation when, in 1930, in the midst of the great Depression, the Brandeis group headed by Judge Julian Mack and Robert Szold again assumed the leadership of the movement. The change was insufficient to halt the unraveling of American Zionism. By 1933, the year Hitler came to power, the membership of the ZOA had declined to 13,000. By 1935 the organization with the largest single membership, Hadassah, had declined from a high of 35,000 to 8,800.

Yet soon after that year, the entire situation was reversed. By 1938 membership in the Zionist organization suddenly began to climb. By 1945, at the war's end, organizations with a Zionist orientation had attained clear predominance among American Jews. The ZOA claimed over 136,000 members, and the total number of members of Zionist organizations stood at 400,000. Five years later the Zionist consensus was so complete that standing in opposition to it could mean the kiss of death. That was, in fact, the fate of the anti-Zionist American Council for Judaism, which as virtually read out of the Jewish community. What had happened to bring the troubled fragmented American Zionist movement to the very center of Jewish consciousness?

The answer, of course, is the Holocaust, which took the lives of one out of every three Jews alive in 1940 and two out of every three European Jews. That catastrophe was more effective than a thousand well-reasoned ideological arguments concerning the need for a national rebirth. The systematic processed murder of millions of their coreligionists convinced American Jews that at least one part of the Zionist rationale—that because anti-Semitism was endemic, some national sovereignty was needed where Jews could find a haven and control their own destiny—was irrefutable. Had such a haven under Jewish auspices been in existence, millions of Jews might have survived. The change of mood became apparent at the Biltmore convention, held in May 1942. At that convention something was done which would have been unthinkable less than a decade before. A Commonwealth resolution, pushed by the militant rabbi Abba Hillel Silver, was passed openly advocating a political solution to the perennial Jewish problem: the reestablishment of a Jewish commonwealth. American Zionism had been radicalized by the Holocaust; All prior reservations and special constructs were pushed aside, for the moment at least, so that Jews could support the idea of a state in Palestine.

The earnestness and generosity of American Jewish support of the *yishuv* and the movement for statehood after the war is well known. It is no exaggeration to claim that without that unstinting support, the Jewish state would never have been founded in 1948; and, further, that without that same support, probably could not have survived. Not only was American Jewry strategically placed within the nation that had emerged from the war as most powerful, it was also developing the financial resources required to set the state on a firm foundation. Perhaps because it keenly felt a sense of guilt regarding its lack of success in moving the Roosevelt administration to play a more active rescue role, American Jewry now tended to be so generous in distributing financial resources to develop the various facets of the Israeli economy that it neglected the development of its own communal institutions. A relationship of mutual dependence developed between Israel and American Jewry. Israel required the influence as well as the financial resources of American Jewry. It would have liked human resources as well. American Jewry saw in Israel not only a haven, if the need for one should become necessary, but also an important instrument in strengthening the weak identity of the diaspora Jews. Israel was viewed as an imperative for Jewish survival.

Yet it is not a relationship without problems, some of which have been concealed by the overriding concern for the survival of a threatened Jewish state. Particularly incomprehensible for the Israelis was the absence of *Aliyah*, American immigrants seeking to resettle in Israel. Greeting American volunteers who rushed to Israel to help during the 1967 war, Golda Meier wondered out loud why young Americans would come to die for Israel but not to live there. Israelis seem unable to fathom the philanthropic, nonideological character of American Zionism, which nevertheless is intensely concerned about Israel's survival. There is an interesting mutuality even here. Committed Zionists who live in Israel are no less concerned about the survival and the danger facing Jews who continue to live in the diaspora. That is why they insist on *Aliyah* . That fear is one of the major themes of an eloquent Zionist polemic, *Letters to an American Jewish Friend*, by Hillel Halkin. (1977.)

On the American side, too, there has been much concern about the relationship with the Jewish community of Israel. There is fear that Israel has become so important in the

American Jewish gestalt that it is in fact a new form of idolatry which cannot be sufficient to assure the survival of American Jewry. Other sources of potential strength, such as Jewish education, have been neglected in the all-encompassing concern for the welfare of Israel, which has been placed at the center of a survival strategy. American Jewry, the argument runs, has become dependent for its cultural and even political cues on the small community of Israel, which itself has inherited a fragmented, problem-ridden Judaism whose political interests, fashioned by reasons of state, are not always identical with those of American Jewry. It is argued that not only do Israel and the Jews of America have to acknowledge such divergence of interest, but both require that their mutual dependence be counterbalanced by respective self-confidence and autonomy. There is also concern that Israel, like European Jewry during the Holocaust, misperceives the nature and character of Jewish power in America and thereby overestimates its ability to influence the American government. The history of American Jewry's efforts to influence that government to intercede for its coreligionists has not been particularly glorious. Meanwhile, the sharpening energy crisis has generated a fear that the "dual loyalties" question, which was so vexing in the early decades of the century, may be disinterred in the 1980s. Energy is at the very heart of America's well-being. No culture has had a longer, more sustained "love affair" with the automobile. If America's culture is anything, it is a turnpike culture. It would not be abandoned for light and transient reasons. What would happen if American policy, like that of France, finds it necessary to tilt ever further toward the oil-rich Arab world, in the process compelling American Jews to choose between what is generally conceived to be the American national interest and the Jewish? The energy crisis together with a resurgent Cold War mentalité which exaggerates the need for Arab bloc support contains the possibility of making the American Jew "odd man out" in the American polity. That is a source of much apprehension.

If that general problem were not difficult enough, American Jewish–Israeli relations have been troubled by the inability to resolve certain internal problems. There is unhappiness that Israel is not a fully secularized state, especially in the area of separation of church and state. Because of the dominance of the Orthodox branch, whose political wing, the National Religious Party, plays a key role in the political coalitions that govern Israel, the Conservative and Reform branches of American Judaism have been ignored, particularly in the area of *gettim* (religious divorces) and conversion.

The conversion issue, especially, is crucial to the future of American Jewry, since it relates to the question of intermarriage, a growing phenomenon in America, and therefore impinges directly on the demographic crisis. Yet another source of concern is the unresolved West Bank settlement policy, which many liberal Americans believe is unnecessarily provocative. The issue is as divisive among concerned American Jews as it is among Israelis. Many American Jews, who perhaps unrealistically expect a Jewish sovereignty to be "holier" than others, are particularly distressed at the many recent revelations of corruption in Israeli society. It disturbs their image of themselves as Jews and the total commitment to Israel which that entails. Finally, many American Jews have gotten a disturbing alternate view of Israel from the hundreds of thousands of *yordim* (Israeli immigrants who now reside in America). It has not proven easy to integrate these new immigrants into Jewish communal affairs, and there is the nagging question of why so many Israelis have chosen to leave the "Promised Land." It makes the quest for American *olim* (immigrants, literally "those who ascend to Israel") merely an exercise in exchange of population. The very basis of the dialogue between the two communities is made problematic by the Israeli insistence that on certain internal issues, especially those relating to security, the intrusion of American Jews is unseemly, as those decisions belong to those who risk their lives for the country. Yet surely the kind of sacrifices American Jewry has made, and its centrality in Jewish culture, warrant something more than playing the role of financial supporters. For some American Jews, Israel is simply too crucial to leave to the Israelis alone. Moreover, Israeli leaders—using the position of Israel as an independent sovereign

nation with an especially supportive constituency in America—
have not hesitated to intrude into American politics when they
thought the national interest of Israel required it. The problem
of mutuality between a sovereign nation and an amorphous
voluntary community is not easily resolved.

Naturally, in the post-Zionist period, the promises and aspirations of the founding ideology look somewhat different, and
that sometimes disappoints those American Jews who traditionally have viewed Israel as a sacred place. Clearly there is
something transcending a normal relationship between Jews
who live in other countries and the State of Israel. For their
own reasons, American Jewry and Israel retain a compelling,
even unreasonable, need for each other. They are, after all, all
that remains of a once-vibrant civilization, and both have ample
evidence in the post-Holocaust period that the world has not
grown less hostile to Jews. From their perspective of catastrophe, many American Jews want Israel to be there, just in
case. Similarly, many Israelis are aware of how crucial an active
and committed American Jewry is to their own survival. Israel
may well one day be in a position where the only element it
may rely on is the loyalty and commitment of Jewish communities in the diaspora, the most viable of which is American
Jewry.

It is altogether likely that for the foreseeable future, American Jewry will continue to cling to Israel as to a sole surviving
relative, and Israel will undoubtedly continue to make inordinate demands on American Jewish resources and influence.
What has developed is a kind of mutual dependency in which
each is compelled to lean on the other. When one thinks about
it, there is nothing new in such a relationship between two
Jewish communities in a threatening world. It has, in fact, been
one of the secrets of Jewish survival.

Bibliography

Feinstein, M. *American Zionism, 1884–1904*. New York: 1965.

Halperin, S. *The Political World of American Zionism*. Detroit: 1961.

Kaganoff, N., ed. *Solidarity and Kinship: Essays on American Zionism*. Waltham: 1980.

Lipsky, L. *Thirty Years of American Zionism*. New York: 1972.

Shapiro, Y. *Leadership in the American Zionist Organization, 1897–1930*. Detroit: 1971.

Sklare, M. *The Impact of Israel on American Jewry*. New York: 1969.

Urofsky, M. *American Zionism from Herzl to Holocaust*. New York: 1975.

Urofsky, M. *We Are One: American Jewry and Israel*. New York: 1978.

Urofsky, M. *A Voice That Spoke for Justice: The Life and Times of Stephen S. Wise*. Albany: 1982.

Wise, S. *Challenging Years*. New York: 1949.

Woocher, J. "Civil Judaism: The Religion of Jewish Communities," National Jewish Conference (Resource) Center. New York: May 1979.

"Zionism in America." *American Jewish Historical Quarterly*, vol. 60 (September 1970).

"Zionism in America: Magnes, Kallen and Brandeis." *American Jewish Historical Quarterly*, vol. 65 (December 1975).

CHAPTER X

Orthodox Judaism:
A Problem Becomes a Prospect

THERE is a well-known story of a very observant Orthodox Jew who ekes out a bare living selling religious items, phylacteries, prayer shawls, books, and an occasional *mezuzah* (a small piece of parchment containing a passage from Deuteronomy 6:4–9 and 11:13–22 rolled into a container and affixed to the doorframe of a Jewish home). When a friend comes to visit, he notes the merchant's dire poverty; but when he calls again four years later, he is amazed as the transformation. The merchant is wearing a well-tailored suit, his wife is bedecked with jewels. The store is now crowded with customers, but in the showcase there are also displayed crucifixes, incense burners, St. Christopher medals, and copies of the New Testament. Astonished, the friend asks the merchant what he has done, and receives in response a shrug of the shoulders and a plaintive cry: *"Fun ein Got, ken man machen a leben?"* ("Can one make a living from only one God?")

The story, of course, is apocryphal. Perhaps originally it was used to illustrate Jewish awareness of the price entailed in stubbornly retaining faith. Here we use it to remind ourselves of the special problem faced by observant Jews in accommodating to the free environment of America. Orthodox Jews who clung faithfully to the myriad requirements of *halakah* (Jewish law) often did so at the expense of economic mobility. They would not work overtime or keep their businesses open on the Sabbath. Inability to enroll in a secular university meant that a favorite route of mobility, formal education and certification, was closed to them. Strict adherence to *halakah* made it more practical to live in enclaves with other observant Jews. There had to be a ready *minyan* (quorum of ten men required for Jewish prayer service), a *shul* or synagogue within walking distance, a *mikvah* (ritual bath for women), a kosher butcher, and a myriad of other things the observant require to live their lives. Not surrounded by like-minded Jews, they would face the temptations of the outside world alone and would risk succumbing like the merchant of the story. It was more difficult to retain one's piety in the affluent environment of America. For many the problem was simply solved; they took themselves out of the economic race for wealth and achievement. It was almost as if they were compelled to choose a life of poverty. Before World War II, it was apparent to Jews whose ambition and talent had been inhibited for generations of ghetto life in Europe—the same energies that were now being released with the force of a steel coil—that Orthodox Jews were less prosperous than those who adapted. It was hardly a good selling point for Orthodoxy. In fact, under such conditions it was difficult to teach one's faith to one's children as a Jew is commanded to do. Children raised on the streets of the ghetto, who were exposed daily not only to the corruption of congested urban living but to the possibility of amassing wealth (the key to removing themselves from the shoddy environment of their parents), often strayed from the faith of their fathers. It required a sacrifice they were unwilling to make for a faith they no longer understood.

The development of the Orthodox branch's leadership was hampered by these conditions. Its vital center was in the *yeshivot* (religious training academies) of Eastern Europe. "Learning," meaning a specific skill in interpreting Talmud rather than forensic ability in the pulpit or talent for ministering to a flock of the faithful, was central to the Orthodox conception of religious leadership. Aware of the great difficulties of living an observant life in a *tref medinah* (slang, referring to the low level of observance in America), learned Orthodox leaders were reluctant to settle here. Unlike the Conservative and Reform branches, the Orthodox did not develop sufficient *yeshivot* where an indigenous leadership might be trained. The reputation for "learning" in America was in any case too low to compete with the *yeshivot* of Europe. Thus, as late as 1900, some Orthodox circles banded together to import a "chief Rabbi" from Europe, Rabbi Jacob Josef. The attempt was a failure, which exposed to public view an inability of Orthodox leaders to accept the new terms of post-emancipation community organization. Not only would the Jewish community not accept the imposition of a religious leader from above, Orthodox circles themselves found the idea odious, especially when his salary would be paid through a special tax on kosher meat. The Orthodox wing was slower in mastering the new organizational techniques and institutional forms required to sustain a religious enterprise in the free secular environment of America. Its first attempt to establish a single central authority in 1902, the *Agudat Harabonim*, was similarly unsuccessful.

The absence of a central authority to furnish the Orthodox community with the many special requirements for observant living was keenly felt. Orthodox congregations tended to be small and transitory. A proliferation of *shtiblach* (rooms used for worship and learning) characterized Jewish neighborhoods. This system allowed a postponement of the establishment of permanent congregations, with the ability to support a rabbi and a religious school. The absence of a central yeshiva meant, in effect, a haphazard process of granting *semichah* (similar to the ordination given Christian ministers but not quite the same, since technically Judaism does not require a priesthood). Confusion based on absence of legitimate authority was reflected in the chaos of supervising *kashrut* (kosher dietary rules). The scandals in *kashrut* supervision were faithfully reported in the secular Yiddish press and further demeaned the Orthodox community. The large Orthodox community, in the absence of proper leadership, could not meet even its basic requirements. They did not provide themselves with sufficient schools of quality to train the next generation or *mikvahs* for the women's ritual cleanliness.

Given these utterly chaotic conditions, and the special seductiveness of the new environment, an astute observer at the turn of the century would not have given the Orthodox enterprise much hope for sustaining itself. Of the three branches, Orthodoxy clearly had the least possibility of survival. Yet today, although far from free of problems, the Orthodox branch is full of vitality. To state, as one scholar recently did, that Orthodoxy has entered a period of "triumphalism" may be an exaggeration, but clearly there is a new-found confidence and elan in the Orthodox movement. We have noted how its influence sometimes extends even over the right wing of the Conservative movement. It is another indication of how difficult it is to make predictions about anything in Jewish history. If one could, Orthodoxy should have vanished together with the Jewish people. Yet they are both here, more vital than ever. Can we find an explanation?

Given the monolithic character of the Orthodox approach to faith, one would imagine that its organizational structure would be hierarchical. The rabbis would be at the top, interpreting the law, and the rank and file below, dutifully obeying it. But that is hardly the case. The Orthodox wing remains the most amorphous in its structure, with several power centers competing for the allegiance of the faithful. As with the other branches, there are umbrella organizations for congregations and professional organizations for rabbis. The Rabbinical Council of America, the largest rabbinical body in the United States, and the Union of Orthodox Congregations of America and Canada were established in the second and third decades of the century. But, unlike the other branches, no single umbrella organization ever included the movement in its entirety. Many Orthodox congregations were transitory, little more than quorums organized for daily prayer. These were not interested in distant affiliations. During and after the Holocaust American Orthodoxy was replenished by the remnants of the Orthodox community of Eastern and Central Europe. Some of these groups, either because they were members of chassidic courts with primary loyalty to the rabbinic dynasty, because they cherished their independence, or because they thought of themselves as the sole guardians of the true faith, refused to affiliate with the existing Orthodox community. The ultra-Orthodox

Agudath Israel movement, which was organized in America in 1912, rejected the notion of acting in unison with any other organizations claiming to represent observant Jews. Orthodoxy remained a world unto itself. It "had not yet matured to the point of assuming a definite cast of thought or pattern of practice," according to one observer. Its ultratraditionalist wing rejected the idea of working together with the Conservative or Reform branches, which they considered as proposing an unacceptable departure from true "Torah Judaism."

The several shades of Orthodoxy locate themselves on a spectrum reaching from the ultratraditionalist–fundamentalist groups, to the ordinary traditionalist and modern or neo-Orthodox groups in the center, to nonobservant Orthodox. The last-mentioned group is only nominally affiliated, and gives the reader an indication that the Orthodox community is the least churchlike of the three branches. The gap between the traditionalist Orthodox members of Agudath and neo-Orthodox Jews who tread the path originally laid down by Samson Rafael Hirsch is wider than the difference between right-wing Conservative and liberal Orthodox Jews. There is a great deal of truth to the observation made by one knowledgeable observer that American Orthodoxy has yet to settle down "to the task of rendering an intelligent account of itself in the American idiom of thought and culture."

In the absence of a vital center and a clear organizational structure, the actual leadership and administration of the Orthodox enterprise is assumed by a combination of geographic Orthodox population centers, several institutions of learning, and, finally, a handful of charismatic religious leaders. Geographically these population congregation centers cluster around the New York metropolitan area: Boro Park, Bensonhurst, Williamsburg, Crown Heights in Brooklyn; Washington Heights (the locale of the Breuer group) in Manhattan; Far Rockaway, Forest Hills, Kew Gardens in Queens; Spring Valley and Monsey in Rockland County. There are other centers in Boston, Chicago, Baltimore, and Philadelphia, and a growing presence in Los Angeles. These centers are not, of course, the only places where Orthodox Jews live, but they are the vital centers containing the critical mass adherents to generate the special *ruach* (spirit) that identifies Orthodox communities everywhere. The organizational buttressing consists of the aforementioned Union of Orthodox Jewish Congregations and the Rabbinical Council of America, but also the National Conference of Synagogue Youth, YAVNEH (the Orthodox Jewish Student Association), the Association of Orthodox Jewish Scientists, and numerous other organizations. One such is Young Israel, which was founded by Conservative Jews in 1912, but split away in 1920 and is now firmly in the Orthodox camp. Another is the Religious Zionists of America (RZA), founded in 1957 and composed largely of Mizrachi and Hapoel Hamizrachi.

Of the institutes of learning, Yeshiva University, the largest Jewish university in America, is a center in itself. Founded originally when the Isaac Elchanan theological seminary merged with Etz Chaim talmudic academy in 1915, it became the nucleus of the university under the skillful guidance of Bernard Revel, a practical business-minded leader. Additional components, including the Albert Einstein Medical Center, were added by Samuel Belkin, Revel's successor. It receives its Orthodox legitimation not only from its origin as an Orthodox rabbinic academy but from its ongoing association with one of the charismatic rabbis and outstanding talmudists, Rabbi Joseph Solaveichik. Other Orthodox yeshivot such as the Hebrew Theological College (of Skokie) boast no such star in their firmament. The Breuer group, K'lal Adath Jeshurun, which was transplanted to New York City from Frankfurt Germany in 1940, maintains its distinct character but geographically exists in tandem with Yeshiva University. Unlike other ultra-traditionalist groups, the Breuer group did not view secular education with apprehension.

Of a different character but no less influential in the Orthodox community is a group we might simply identify as *rosh yeshivot* (heads of religious training academies). The best known of this group is Rabbi Aaron Kotler, who established America's first *kolel* (a *yeshiva* for advanced learning) in Lakewood, New Jersey. There are also less well-known centers of Orthodoxy.

The Sephardic community in America, supplemented by an infusion of immigrants in the twenties and thirties as well as in the postwar period, boasts about 63 congregations, including two of the most renowned: Shearith Israel in New York and Mikveh Israel in Philadelphia. Although their adherence to *halakah* is often considerably looser than the ultratraditional Ashkenazic Orthodox (German or Eastern-European Jewries), they are nevertheless in the Orthodox fold. There is also the aforementioned Aguduth Israel—a group of ultratraditionalists, which boasts about twenty thousand members and sympathizers. More problematic are the various Chassidic dynasties, which in the nineteenth century deemphasized a prime hallmark of Orthodoxy, the study of Talmud. Since the Holocaust, or, perhaps more precisely, since the end of World War I, the Chassidic courts have become—in their piety and devotion to study—indistinguishable from the *mitnagdim* ("rationalistic" rather than mystical groups). The most interesting and vital of these groups is the Lubavitch, headed by Rabbi Menacham Mendel Schneersohn. Unlike other Chassidic groups, the Lubavitch is not cloistered and maintains a well-organized outreach program. The movement, rumored to have special ties to followers within the Soviet Union, now maintains branches in all parts of the country, and supports *chabad* houses, special meeting places for worship and other Jewish activities on major college campuses, fourteen Lubavitcher day schools, and a growing number of *beth rivka* schools for girls. (So called after the matriarch Rebecca.)

What we see in the organizational structure of the Orthodox branch is a complex of many overlapping and conflicting elements forming a world unto itself. Many of the ultratraditionalist elements simply do not acknowledge the existence or validity of an outside Jewish world, with beliefs, interests, and claims on leading the entire Jewish people. They reject overtures from other sections of the Jewish community, to whom they nevertheless look for funds and to whom they hope to furnish leadership.

It should be fairly simple to describe what Orthodox Jews believe, or, at least, precisely how they differ from adherents to the Reform or Conservative branch. But that is not the case, partly because there are variations in emphasis between the various Orthodox groups, and partly because Judaism does not really produce theology, that is, a body of explicatory texts that seek to mediate between God and the faithful. Even if there were such a body of dogma and rules, the Orthodox community has no sanction to impose them on the faithful, who are, in modern times, only voluntarily associated with the "church." In the absence of such doctrine from on high, a strange phenomenon occurs in the Orthodox community: Devoutness is measured by compliance to the myriad rules of *halakah*, or degree of *fromkeit* (religiosity). There exists a status system, at the top of which are those most involved in obeying the laws. It is illustrated by the story of the two young Orthodox mothers tending their children on a festive Sabbath. A third Orthodox mother approaches, her children in tow. All three women wear long sleeves and *sheitels* (wigs), as is the rule among the Orthodox observant. As if the most wondrous thing has just happened to her, a beatific smile plays on the lips of the last mother to appear. Curious, the other two inquire what has made her so content and happy. She answers: "I just found yet another thing forbidden on the Sabbath. Life is so full, if only you seek for it." Being a good Jew does not depend on finding yet another source of the divine or argument to prove his presence: it has nothing to do with the elaboration of a theology. For the Orthodox it means, more than anything else, compliance with halakah. There is no distinction between piety, devoutness, and spirituality. They are all encompassed in careful attention to the detail of ritual and to the myriad laws that shape the life of the traditional Jew. The status system itself is based on such compliance: the more detailed the compliance—the *frommer* (more religious) one is—the higher the status reward within the community. In that way, devoutness is always reinforced among genuinely Orthodox Jews.

But what is the nature of this law and how is it developed? Space limitations will not permit a full elaboration of the difference between the *halakic* (written) and *aggadic* (oral) traditions, which together serve as the wellspring of Jewish law. Briefly, the former are laws developed by rabbinic interpretation of *Torah* (Pentateuch) through a formal procedure. The laws of *kashrut* and of Sabbath observance are good examples. *Aggadic* law is not directly derived from Scripture and concerns the ethical and moral behavior of the individual and the community. Laws governing the behavior of the *agunah*, the wife whose husband is missing in action, is a good example. According to some, the Orthodox life can be reduced to three basic principles. The first is *halakah*, compliance with Jewish law; the second is *mitzvot*, the actual deeds required for holiness, such as charity; and the third, *ahavat Yisrael*, love and concern for the Jewish people. Orthodoxy differs from the two other branches of Judaism in two important ways. The Orthodox accommodation to modernity is more reluctant and occurs on different terms. Primacy is given to the internal group behavioral cues of Judaism, which are maintained even if such maintenance requires a dual life. The second concerns the sacred law itself. Reform and Conservative Jews frankly recognize the difficulty of following Jewish law in daily life. They see that law as a living body, ever-changing. They would tamper with its substance, and even short-circuit the elaborate procedure for deriving it, in order to live with some ease in the modern world. Families can sit together in synagogue, and one can ride the elevator on the Sabbath. The premise of Orthodoxy is different, because it begins with the recognition that sacredness means apartness. Jews are made for the law, not the law for Jews. Therefore, few concessions to convenience can be made. In the end, one should note that the life of Orthodox Jews is sometimes much more demanding. What distinguishes them from other Jews is that they are willing to sacrifice a great deal for the sake of living a Jewish life. More than the others, the Orthodox life is shaped by its conception of Jewishness. The desire to be Jewish every moment of the day has the highest priority. In the sense that a religious ethos and the rules it brings with it are permitted to structure their lives or at least deeply intrude into them, Orthodox Jews are more committed.

Yet in the actual practice of living a highly observant life, things are not nearly so clear. Knowing the rules and the principles behind them does not mean that it is convenient to live the Orthodox life style in a society like ours, which is relentlessly secularizing. Increasingly, a total Orthodox environment offering a support structure for observance is unavailable. It requires an almost daily decision to be observant: from watching certain television programs to selecting kosher restaurants, to wondering if the dinner you have been invited to is sufficiently kosher. Under such circumstances, it is not surprising that there is a perceptible gap between those in the Orthodox community who actually do so and those who make some accommodation while remaining nominally Orthodox. One researcher has classified this group as "nonobservant Orthodox," by which he means a growing group affiliated with the Orthodox wing out of convenience or background who do not follow its precepts. The size of this group is undeterminable but it may be more than half of the one million American Jews who classify themselves as Orthodox. One indication is that from 25 to 60 percent of Orthodox Jews do not purchase kosher meat on a regular basis. We have seen that only 4 percent of American Jews observe the Sabbath. Even of these approximately 200,000, many are members of the Conservative wing. If we permit an *Agudath* interpretation of what is entailed in Sabbath observance, the figure would undoubtedly be still lower. Getting a picture of the actual situation in the Orthodox community is made complex by its amorphous, fragmented condition, and by the general difficulty of accurate information retrieval. Few of the Orthodox centers preoccupy themselves with membership files or the compilation of statistics. One estimate is that there are approximately 205,640 adult males who are affiliated with 1,603 Orthodox synagogues of varying sizes. But this figure does not take into account the hundreds of informal Orthodox congregations and the existence of the aforementioned "nonobservant Orthodox." Some of this group affiliate with Conservative synagogues and others are in reality fully secularized Jews who experience some nostalgia for the organized religious life in which they were raised. According to the 1970 National Jewish Population Study, 82 percent of the 5.5 million American Jews identify themselves with one of the three branches of religious Judaism, and 18 percent simply state that they are "just Jewish." But such figures tell us very little about the Orthodox branch. On the grass-roots level, most Jews are secular, but they find no problem in affiliating with a congregation, since being secular no longer means being antireligious. That definition, however, cannot apply to the Orthodox group, since they reject amalgamation between secular and observant modes. The thrust of Orthodoxy is toward ever purer forms of piety and adherence. It may well be that the large group of nonobservant Orthodox Jews results from the tendency of the Orthodox to become more observant. As the outer periphery of nonobservant Orthodoxy falls away, the intensely pious remain to establish their own stricter norms.

Talk of "falling away" brings us directly to the problem of attrition among the American Orthodox. Clearly, a branch of Judaism that requires a high degree of commitment will have difficulty holding its adherents, who are also members of a society whose major characteristic is multiple allegiances— pluralism. It is the exclusivity demanded by Orthodoxy that makes it at once attractive and repellent to modern American Jews. There may in fact be a revolving-door effect, a constant flow out of the Orthodox fold that is partly replaced by an infusion of young "returnees" anxious for the certainty and sense of community furnished by the Orthodox branch. There has always been attrition in the Orthodox branch. A 1975 survey of Jews in metropolitan Boston revealed that Orthodox Jews composed the largest percentage of first-generation immigrants but that the figure declined thereafter from generation to generation. Among second-generation Jews whose parents were Orthodox, only 6 percent considered themselves so. But so sustained is the early Orthodox influence that most continue some involvement in the Jewish community. The presence of an Orthodox wing, it seems, strengthens all other facets of organized Jewry. Of the second-generation group, 61 percent had joined the Conservative movement and 22 percent had become Reform Jews. The National Jewish Population Study (1970) told a similar story of attrition in the Orthodox branch. It estimated that 26 percent of the first generation defined themselves as Orthodox Jews, but that only 9 percent of the second and 3 percent of the third generation did so. (Nonetheless, as we have noted, the normal projections concerning declining mass, rising age level, and general diminution in influence, cannot be made.)

The internal vitality and the general impact on American Jewry of Orthodoxy is, in fact, on the upswing. The loss of numbers occurs on the outer periphery. It leaves a confident, elitist hard core, more convinced of the correctness of its path and less willing to make concessions to other branches or to work with them. There is some suggestion in the data available that, after the initial loss of the nonobservant Orthodox, the remaining hard core is more successful in solving the transfer problem, passing the faith and life-mode to the next generation, since they project a clearer message without the disturbing background noises made by the nonobservant Orthodox. Add to this the infusion of the remnants of European Orthodoxy, the surviving Chassidic dynasties, now virtually indistinguishable from other Orthodox Jews, the dominance of Orthodoxy in Israel, and a high birth rate, and one possesses the ingredients for the minor Orthodox triumph we have witnessed in the sixties and seventies. The prognosis for American Orthodoxy is good, or, at least, better than it has ever been before. Its influence goes far beyond its limited numbers. Not only do the several factions within the Orthodox community look anxiously over their right shoulders at what the most observant Jews are doing, but increasingly, so do many Conservative Jews.

What a paradox! What has been described here would drive a sociologist mad. A decline in proportionate numbers would normally indicate that a movement is moribund. The reverse appears to be true for the Orthodox community. It has grown more vital and more influential even while flaunting every known principle of demography and organizational dynamics. The continued development of Orthodoxy, moreover, undermines the assumption that the strength and endurance of a movement is related to the use of democratic forms and the allowance for measured change and accommodation. It is a further sign of how inapplicable the laws of social science are when dealing with Jews and their idiosyncratic history. Normal patterns of development do not seem to apply. Historians like Arnold Toynbee found that extremely disturbing. Imagine what he might have thought if he were to examine the strange development of American Orthodoxy.

But why is this happening? How did the Orthodox movement defy the prediction of its decline pronounced at the turn of the century? Several basic reasons deserve attention. First is the fact that the Orthodox movement produces Jews. It is not so much the numbers that are important but the kind of Jews. They are not ordinary Jews, such as are produced by secular families. Every test we possess demonstrates that Orthodoxy produces the most totally committed Jews within American Jewry. In its passion and devotion to Judaism, Orthodoxy acts like a priesthood. We have seen that even when children of the Orthodox join other centers of the community, their residual commitment to Judaism continues. It should not surprise us to discover that the most passionate of Zionists or the most faithful of the Conservatives had at one point in their lives been connected with Orthodoxy. In that sense, Orthodoxy is a boon to Jewish survivalists; its overflow strengthens all sections of the community.

Second, Orthodoxy has at long last solved the mobility dilemma. Today it is possible to achieve status, wealth, and fame while retaining one's Orthodoxy. It may have been that roadblock, more than any other, that caused attrition in the first and second generations. Not too long ago an Orthodox observer noted that it was no longer necessary to live in squalor on the Lower East Side in order to maintain one's Orthodoxy. Today the Orthodox community is as firmly ensconced in the middle class as other segments of American Jewry, and some Orthodox have attained the highest peaks of affluence. This fact is revealed in strange ways: an agitated community when it is proposed that a *mikveh* be built in an affluent Jewish suburb; the sight of bearded Orthodox Jews driving the latest model automobiles. The most certain sign that the Orthodox have "arrived" is in the area of philanthropy. Programs and projects sponsored by Orthodox organizations and congregations are able to attract affluent givers not only from within their own ranks, but from non-Orthodox areas as well.

Its resistance to the blandishments of modern secular culture has exacted a price for the Orthodox branch, since Jews are avid in their acceptance of that culture. But it has become increasingly clear that it may also prove to be a powerful asset for the Orthodox community. The malaise at the very heart of modern secular culture has become abundantly clear: family break-up, loneliness, anxiety, and loss of confidence. These and many more tensions were foreseen as inevitable by Orthodox spiritual leaders. The Orthodox have not, of course, been immune from all the stresses of modern life, but their tightly knit communities with built-in support structure and clear principles of behavior can prove very attractive to those who are confused and crave such structure. For many, life based solely on secular values has proven to be a total failure, and the recruits for Orthodoxy—which is certain, clearly defined, and, above all, authentic—are drawn from this group. Orthodox Jews, it is reasoned, believe in Judaism, and the proof is that they shape their entire lives by its tenets. They have instinctively understood the importance of ritual and celebration in life. They have been least seduced by the arrogance of modernity, which places weak fallible humankind in the center of the universe with catastrophic results. In an age of ultrascientific rationality, the Orthodox did not forget the extrarational and irrational elements which also play an essential role in human development.

One must take note of the fact that certain Orthodox communities have apparently found a solution to the leadership–followership aberrations that have plagued American Jewry for generations: leaders cannot lead because Jewish followers do not follow. The Orthodox branch alone has the ability to generate charismatic leaders. This is one of Orthodoxy's strongest drawing cards, because a strong charismatic rabbi is precisely what a confused laity, which has lost direction, seeks. Many people today, not only Jews, are willing and anxious to surrender their autonomy, to heed someone "holy" who will show them the way. These charismatic leaders are not confined to the wondrous miracle workers who lead the Chassidic sects, they stem from other sections of the Orthodox community as well, and their influence is hardly confined to Orthodox Jews. But whether charisma is in fact an affirmative force, which can be useful for a community's development, is an open question. For some, it smacks of the rainmaker phenomenon prevalent in some Protestant fundamentalist sects; it borders on charlatanism. Yet there have been rebbes who are perceptive and benevolent, and whose intrusion into the lives of their followers has been as helpful as the paid intrusions of the psychotherapist. It is a difficult time to live, and many people need outside help and support. Yet the question remains whether charismatic leaders can be sustained when the laity is educated and self-confident. Some argue that the phenomenon is educated and self-confident. Some argue that the phenomenon is most prevalent among the Orthodox because there the level of education is lowest and modern individuation has progressed least far. That is to say, "flocks" and "shepherds" are only possible where there exist people willing to surrender responsibility for themselves. The thrust of modernity, however, is for human beings not to regard themselves as sheep. The Jewish world, no less than others, longs for a clear-minded leader. From the time of Abraham and Moses to Elijah of Vilna, Jews have recognized the value of such leaders. But they have also been suspicious of the phenomenon we call leadership, and many of their cherished leaders have also been pilloried. That tension exists in evaluating the contemporary charismatic figures arising mainly in the Orthodox world. Granted that their influence may be affirmative, is the prominent role such leaders play a reflection of a lack of sense of self among their youthful followers? Is there in such charismatic types the potential for a catastrophe such as Shabbateanism, which came close to destroying Jewish civilization?

Finally we need to examine what the resurgence of Orthodoxy means for American Jewry. I have several times suggested that the mere overflow of affirmative spirit—even of the "nonobservant" Orthodox—into neighboring areas of Jewish life has proven to be an enormous asset for the Jewish enterprise. It is acting out in an American context a phenomenon that was already well known and commented upon in prewar Europe. A Bundist member of the Warsaw Kehillah, perplexed by the vote of his fellow party members for a very high appropriation for an Orthodox institution of learning, requests an explanation, and receives the simple reply: "That is where our new leaders are coming from." Indeed, of all the leaders of Jewish agencies and organizations at the time, the overwhelming majority boasted *cheder* (room where pre-adolescent Jewish children received their first religious instruction) and even *yeshivah* training. Such training produced Jews devoted to their people and their traditions and yet also open to change.

The resurgence of Orthodoxy is a hopeful sign for American Jewry from yet another point of view. Clearly, survival in America requires not the choice of one strategy over another but a rebuilding of a specific tension, which has for millenia been a key to the historic survival of the Jewish people. In the post-emancipation world it is reflected in the basic tension between those who see change as imperative and welcome it with open arms—even with willingness to drop the burden of their history to embrace it—and those at the other end of the spectrum who want at all cost to hold fast to the tradition and who see even the slightest accommodation as surrender. Most Jews fall somewhere in the middle, but several historical factors, including the Holocaust, have weighted the scales in favor of the change agents. On the one hand, we have secular Jews, Reform Jews, and to some extent Conservative Jews, all welcoming change; on the other, a relatively small group of Orthodox Jews, who are stand-patters. But it is the tension between the two, the fact that there exists a group who puts a brake on the speed of change, which furnishes American Jewry with a practical survival strategy. One can argue that without the Orthodox the Jewish enterprise would lose its moorings and ultimately its meaning. So avid is the desire for change among Jews that they would forget what they are changing from. Yet without pressure for change, there would be a matching danger, since all living things, Hegel informs us, must change in order to thrive. The tension between traditionalist and innovator gives the Jewish community something rarely achieved—measured change. In an uncertain world, that can be of crucial importance. Things have not really changed so much from the days when the tribes of Israel lingered near Mount Sinai. A small group held rigidly to the faith, and the remainder worshipped the golden calf. They returned when summoned. The point is that Jews need to be summoned, and historically that role has fallen to the traditionalist. That is the reason why the separatism and exclusivity of the ultratraditionalist faction is not an innocent preference. There is hope for improvement even here. Recently Dr. Norman Lamm, a highly regarded Orthodox leader and president of Yeshiva University, reminded his brethren in the Orthodox community of the *halakic* principle of *areivus* (mutual responsibility). He recognized the peril involved in abandonment of that principle. "We do not have the moral or halakhic right to renounce our responsibility for even one Jew, let alone all Jews or most of them," he told the convention of the Union of Orthodox Jewish Congregations. Now that the Orthodox are on the road to finding a new confidence and security, they may well be ready to heed the entreaties of Dr. Lamm. A great deal depends on it.

Bibliography

Heilman, S. C. *Synagogue Life.* Chicago: 1976.
Helmreich, W. *Wake Up, Wake Up, To Do the Work of the Creator.* New York: 1976.
Jung, L. *Men of the Spirit.* New York: 1964.
Klaperman, G. *The Story of Yeshiva University.* New York: 1969.
Kranzler, G. *The Face of Faith: An American Hassidic Community.* Baltimore: 1972.
Liebman, C. S. "Orthodoxy in American Jewish Life." *American Jewish Yearbook*, vol. 66. New York: 1965.
Neusner, J., ed. *Understanding American Judaism: Toward the Description of Modern Religion*, 2 vols. New York: 1975.
"Orthodox Judaism in America: A Special Issue." *American Jewish History*, vol. 69 (December 1979).
Poll, S. *The Hassidic Community of Williamsburg.* New York: 1969.
Rothkoff, A. *Bernard Revel, Builder of American Jewish Orthodoxy.* Philadelphia: 1972.

CHAPTER XI /

Anti-Semitism and the Anti-Semitic Imagination in America: Case Study—the Twenties

ANTI-SEMITISM exacts a hidden price from the individuals who suffer its slings and arrows. That fact is illustrated by the well-known story of the Jewish aspirant for a position as a television newscaster who suffers from a severe speech imped-iment. He finally is interviewed for a position, which, predict-ably, he does not get. When friends and family inquire whether he got the job he shakes his head sadly and painfully stammers: "The, the . . . there's a . . a . . . a . . . anti-Semitism everywhere." The young candidate for the position did not have to confront his painful disability, he simply blamed it on anti-Semitism. Yet the story has an interesting twist. Individu-als and groups who are the victims of discrimination have an excuse for not making the attempt to achieve. That did not happen in this case, and in a larger context, anti-Semitism has not prevented American Jewry from aspiring and achieving. By doing so they have enriched themselves and the society of which they are part. American anti-Semitism has most often been a painful personal experience. At times, especially in the nineteenth century, it has had a collective effect on the Jewish sense of security. But its impact on American Jewish history has been minima despite the fact that the Jewish community is very apprehensive about it.

One of the reasons for that is that it has proven difficult to measure its intensity and to agree on a conceptual framework that will warn of impending danger. Jewish defense agencies like the Anti-Defamation League of B'nai B'rith anxiously monitor the pulse of the nation for signs of anti-Semitism. But they are in the business of finding it, so it should not surprise us that they do. That was the conclusion of the MacIver Report, which appeared in 1950; it found, among other things, that the conceptual approach of the defense agencies measuring anti-Semitism was weak. In a nation composed of many ethnic groups contending for a place, how does one differentiate classic anti-Semitism from normal group antagonisms which are bound to appear in such societies? It may well be that hostility directed toward the Jewish community is part of such residual group antagonism, which, because of the long history of anti-Semitism, expresses itself through an anti-Semitic metaphor. There is, after all, no way to being anti-Jewish other than to be anti-Semitic. Yet other subgroups have perhaps a greater claim to being discriminated against, because official government sanctions and politics were involved. The anti-Catholic animus of the nineteenth century actually became part of the American political agenda in the 1850s, and a political party, the American or Know Nothing Party, was organized to carry its anti-Catholic program forward. The Jewish experience in America fortunately furnishes no parallel, nor can anti-Semitism match in intensity the antagonism aimed at American Blacks. Yet those who have felt the sting of anti-Semitism cannot be assuaged by such comparisons; their pain is real. We need to know not only the character of American anti-Semitism, but its effects on American Jewry. Has it prevented Jews from gaining affluence and influence? Most important, does it pose a threat to Jewish group survival in America?

The period of the twenties, which witnessed the crystallization of certain anti-Semitic strands in American culture, permits us to formulate some tentative answers to these questions. The first of these strands is the pervasive yet intangible anti-Semitism embedded in the restrictive immigration laws, the second concerns the private anti-Semitism of a powerful American folk hero, Henry Ford, and the third is the anti-Semitism of a private educational institution, Harvard University. But first a few words on the peculiar character of the twenties, which makes that decade a good prism through which to view the phenomenon of American anti-Semitism.

Historians are fond of designating certain decades as watersheds because they supposedly contain all the problems and motifs which are subsequently played out. The period beginning with the end of World War I and lasting until the great crash of October 1929 is one such. It seems as if this particular time span, sometimes called the "Jazz Age" or the decade of the "Lost Generation," served as a container for all the social and economic problems which had developed since the Civil War. World War I marked the full debut of America on the world stage as a great power, but the domestic unity furnished by the war, sold to the American people as one "to make the world safe for democracy," also came to an end with the bitter conflict over ratifying the peace treaty. The end of the war brought conflict to the fore and punctured the myth of the great harmonious democracy Americans preferred to believe about their society. The decade after the war is known in history for its extreme xenophobia and nativism and the resumption of conflicts generated by the industrialization process. The great steel strike of 1919 again saw pitched battles between the forces of organized labor and of management. That same year a hysterical fear of communism triggered by the successful revolution in Russia enabled Attorney General Palmer to mount the so-called Red Scare. It led to the deportation of thousands of alien subversives, a goodly number of Jews among them, and the purging of "alien" ideologues such as socialists from the political process. More important, the relative ease with which the scare was implemented by government authorities on the federal and state levels taught some that public hysteria could be used to build a political career. Where Palmer failed in the twenties, politicians like McCarthy and Nixon were more successful in the fifties. Hatred and fear of foreigners were also reflected in the renewed growth of a refurbished Ku Klux Klan, which had added Catholics and Jews to the list of undesirables. The trial and execution of Sacco and Venzetti served to exemplify the notion that foreigners were unassimilable radicals prone to criminality. Whether in the form of a crusade against alcohol or evolution or some other manifestation of Protestant fundamentalism, the basic thrust of these activities was antiurban and antialien. We can view them as a kind of last stand of rural America before another America emerged, symbolized by the Model A Ford, more permissive courting patterns, and liberated women—an America whose hero was the city slicker rather than the rural "rube." That old America would strike out at the forces it was convinced were taking the country away from it, and one of these forces was unlimited immigration, a policy that permitted America to act as a haven for the oppressed. The immigration laws of 1921 and 1924 not only called for restriction, they embodied the very prejudices that distinguished rural America, by making invidious distinctions between the "old" immigration from Northern and Western Europe, from which rural America largely stemmed, and the "new" immigration from Southern and Eastern Europe, which flowed to the cities and was neither Protestant nor Nordic. The Jews were included in the latter group. The idea of "Nordic supremacy," written into the law, was not innocent. It was a theme soon to be echoed in Berlin, where it would be called "Aryanism."

Technically, the move to restrict immigration was not new. The Chinese were excluded as early as 1882, and there was a Gentlemen's Agreement in 1907 to limit immigration of the Japanese. The movement to restrict the genetically defective and illiterate had also gained momentum. But the restrictionist movement of the 1920s contained a new overt racist ingredient embedded in the national-origins quota system, which distinguished between members of the Caucasian group. Jews, as part of a "lesser breed" from Eastern Europe, could now be distinguished under the law. Restrictionists argued not only that a mature economy could no longer absorb all who wanted to come, but that it was necessary to preserve the ethnic composition of America lest it become "mongrelized" by the influx of inferior racial stocks.

It is important to note that the Jews were not attacked directly by the new immigration laws. They were merely part of a larger category of undesirable Mediterranean and Slavic types. But many of the restrictionists did, in fact, harbor a specific fear of being inundated especially by Jews—who, according to American understanding, were poised, after the travail of war, to come to the United States in mass. This fear came out in the hearings held on the Reed Johnson Act of 1923 and 1924. The proponents of the act repeatedly cited Jewish criminality, avarice, and unwillingness to do productive work, as reasons why the law was needed. The arguments of restrictionist congressmen came from men like Professor Henry Pratt Fairchild, who furnished pseudodata drawn from the records of the United Hebrew Charities, purporting to show that Jewish immigrants became dependent on public welfare. Burton J. Hendrick, a journalist who had called for bars against further Jewish immigration in 1913, admitted that the new law was "chiefly intended to restrict the entrance of Jews from Eastern Europe." Yet the law itself nowhere featured the word "Jew." It was simply one group among many to be shunned. It was difficult to argue that it was motivated by a specific animus against Jews, even though future developments in Europe would prove particularly dangerous to Jews and make the finding of a new haven particularly urgent. The Reed Johnson Law made no distinction between ordinary immigrants and refugees in dire need of a haven. When the Nazis began their anti-Jewish depredations in 1933, it soon became apparent that the law would be a part of the millstone that literaly ground European Jewry to death. The Jews of Europe found themselves caught between Nazi extrusion policy, which pushed them penniless out of homes they had inhabited for many centuries, and the restrictive immigration laws, which meant that they could not find the traditional haven in America. Chaim Weizmann, the Zionist leader, testified before a congressional committee that the world appeared to be divided into two groups, those who wanted to get rid of their Jews and those who did not want to receive them. Only in 1939 were the relevant American quotas filled. Another bitter resonance of restrictionism has already been noted. Nazi extrusion of Jews, and ultimately mass murder of Jews, was based on the racial concept of Aryan supremacy. It was the same concept, Nordic supremacy, that kept Jewish immigrants out of America. The promulgators of the restrictive immigration laws had no way of knowing how murderous the law would become during the thirties, but certainly the racist principle behind restriction, the same as the one behind the "final solution," gives America a peculiar relation to one of the ugliest pages in human history.

The details of Henry Ford's conversion to anti-Semitism and the subsequent use to which he put his influence and power to proselytize need not detain us here. They are well known. Here we have a case of private anti-Semitism, which, because of the power of its holder, was amplified far beyond that of a normal citizen. Not only did Ford have money and power to own a newspaper, the *Dearborn Independent*, which could devote itself to spreading an anti-Semitic message, including the publication of the notorious forgery *The Protocols of the Elders of Zion*, but Ford's personal influence was widespread. He was a model, a rustic folk hero, for millions of Americans. Like so many of them, he loved to tinker with machines, he had a humble, rural upbringing, and he boasted little formal education. He exemplified the "rags-to-riches" dream that propelled many Americans. His reward was fame and even the right to eccentricity. A poor humble farm boy changed the way America lived, indeed, the way it conceived reality. If the man who placed the automobile within easy reach of the average American had no use for Jews, then perhaps there was something to what he said.

There is an interesting link between Ford's anti-Semitism and the sources of general American anti-Semitism. Some historians are convinced that American anti-Semitism is rooted in the populist imagination. That turn-of-the-century reform group, which developed out of the discontent of the farmer, typically externalized the source of farmers' problems. The populists imagined that their problems were caused by unproductive middlemen, that currency manipulation by far-away bankers worked against their interest, and that the conspiracy was somehow rooted in the city. Their imagination of the Jew fit all three categories, and Populist publicists—Ignatius Donnelly, among others—made a direct connection. Henry Ford was a kind of latter-day Populist. He possessed a typically simplistic view of how a complex industrial economy operated. His conversion to anti-Semitism correlates closely with the financial trouble faced by his far-flung industrial empire. During the war, Jewish pacifists were involved in his visionary peace-ship venture. But in the early twenties the Ford Motor Company fell upon hard times, and could no longer capitalize itself internally. It faced competition from new cars like Chevrolet. The company was compelled to turn to "Wall Street" to get the necessary capital for retooling. Ford, sensing that he was losing control of his empire, reverted to his rural Populist upbringing: Jews controlled Wall Street in far-away New York City. "The Jewish problem in the United States," wrote the *Dearborn Independent,*

> is essentially a city problem . . . As a population, the Jews exert more power in New York than they have ever exerted during the Christian era in any place, with the exception of present Russia. The Jewish revolution in Russia was manned from New York . . . Politically, while the rest of the country is entertained with the fiction that Tammany Hall rules the politics of New York, the fact is rarely published that the Jews rule Tammany.

It was all there: a deep distrust of the city, which is identified with Jews; a suggestion of a conspiratorial Jewish power operating behind the scenes; Jewish radicalism—they sponsored the Russian revolution; and, finally, assignment to Jews of responsibility for municipal corruption, since they really control Tammany. That was the classic anti-Semitic fantasy: the consignment of enormous power to Jews who exercise it for evil purposes.

The Ford case illustrates something more encouraging, too. It taught Jewish leaders that anti-Semitism could be fought openly and forced to retreat. When Ford began his propaganda, the American Jewish Committee requested a congressional investigation of his anti-Semitic campaign. B'nai B'rith fought for stronger libel laws so that Ford could be brought to court; individual Jews actually brought lawsuits against the company; and, finally, an effective boycott against Ford products was organized. Ford learned that his anti-Semitism would entail a price. By 1927 sale of Ford automobiles was severely affected. Two years later a half-hearted apology, demanded by Louis Marshall, was forthcoming, and the vicious diatribes of the *Dearborn Independent* finally came to a halt. By the late 1930s the cranky industrialist had done a complete about-face. On 1 December 1939 the *New York Times* carried a story in which Ford praised his Jewish workers extravagantly, and wished that he had more and that they would stay longer. In 1941 he offered three rubber plantations in Brazil, including the famous Fordlandia, for the resettlement of Jews who were in desperate need of refuge. Ford, like Lindbergh, had accepted a medal from the Nazi government in Berlin, and the antipathy he felt for Jews probably never left him; but he had learned that in America such sentiments would be unacceptable and entailed a price. He had learned to keep his feelings private.

The third anti-Semitic episode of the twenties is perhaps more remarkable for what it tells us about American Jewry's posture at the time than for the fact that there was anti-Semitism in the admissions policy of a preeminent educational institution, Harvard University.

Observers have had little difficulty in pinpointing the reason why some leading educational institutions suddenly reversed their liberal admissions policy in the twenties and tried to restrict Jewish admission. The noted historian Samuel Eliot Morison, in his *Three Centuries of Harvard*, (1936) believed that it had something to do with the appearance of a new type of Jewish student at Harvard: "The first German Jews who came were easily absorbed into the social pattern; but at the turn of the century the bright Russian Jewish lads from the Boston public schools began to arrive. There were enough of them in 1906 to form the Menorah Society and in another fifteen years Harvard had her Jewish problem." A similar problem appeared at other prestigious universities, which began, unofficially, to impose a numerical quota on Jewish applicants. What was it about "the bright Jewish lads" that created such a problem? For the first time they were visible as a distinct group. It was not only that there were more of them, but that they were different. Unlike their German-Jewish predecessors, they did not

seek to adapt themselves to the "genteel tradition," the antiin-
tellectual value system that dominated student behavior in
America's leading universities. At the turn of the century the
college campus was considered a place where one sowed one's
"wild oats." Serious intellectual endeavor earned no great status
and received little financial reward. The most reputable grade
was the "gentleman's C." College was a place for leadership
training, which was thought to be achievable through socializing with one's peers and through athletics. As one Morison put
it:

> What mattered for so many young men was not the course of
> study but the environment of friendships, social development,
> fraternity houses, good sportsmanship, athletic teams. The
> world of business was a world of dealing with people. What
> better preparation would there be than the collegiate life outside
> the classroom—the club room, the playing field, where the qual-
> ities that showed what stuff a fellow was made of were bound to
> be encouraged.

The prevailing ethos was what Thorstein Veblen called "the
cultivation of gentility"; and ambitious Jewish students, who
viewed education not only as an instrument of mobility but as
something inherently worthy, disturbed that ethos. "Jews
worked far into each night," recalled one Harvard alumnus in
his memoirs.

> Their lessons the next morning were letter perfect, they took
> obvious pride in their academic success and talked about it. At
> the end of each year there were room prizes given for excellence
> in each subject, and they were openly after them. There was
> none of the Roxbury solidarity of pupils versus master. If any-
> one reciting made a mistake that the master overlooked, twenty
> hands shot into the air to bring it to his attention.

They were hands of Jewish students, who not only studied
hard but were probably working at menial jobs to put themselves through school. There was little time for the gay socializing of the fraternity house. Small wonder anti-Semitic feelings

began to surface. These "bright Russian lads" not only did not play by the rules, they brought their own and thought them superior. Jokes, slurs, and social ostracism became commonplace. Harvard housed its Jewish students in a segregated dormitory, which was soon dubbed "little Jerusalem," and an unflattering ditty made the rounds of the fraternities in 1910:

> Oh, Harvard's run by millionaires,
> And Yale is run by booze.
> Cornell is run by farmer's sons
> Columbia's run by Jews.
> So give a cheer for Baxter Street,
> Another one for Pell
> And when the little sheenies die,
> Their souls will go to hell.

The response of the university administrations was to limit the admission of Jews, through complex formulas stressing regional distribution, or by rationalizations, such as limited dormitory space, or, as at Harvard, that rising enrollment of Jewish students would result in inciting anti-Semitism in the university community. Abbot Lawrence Lowell spoke candidly of a developing "Jewish problem" posing a threat to the traditional character of Harvard.

The idea of a *numerical quota* began at Columbia University, whose location in New York City, within easy proximity of the largest concentration of Jews in the world, had caused its Jewish enrollment to climb to 40 percent by 1920. New York University, subject to the same conditions, followed suit, as did other leading universities, fearing a Jewish inundation. But it was not until Harvard imposed quotas that a cry of outrage arose from the Jewish community. Jews were aware that Harvard was the premier educational institution. If Jewish students were to have their access limited there, the precedent would take hold in every elite institution. The practice of imposing Jewish quotas had to be challenged lest it spread to other sections of the economy. Louis Marshall, whose reputation as an intrepid fighter for Jewish rights went before him, challenged Lowell directly. He found allies among the Irish of Boston, who had little love for the Protestant Brahmins who ran Harvard like a private club. A considerable number of the Jewish alumni joined in the campaign against quotas. Finally, in 1923, a special faculty committee report repudiated the quota concept. It was inconsistent with the traditions of Harvard, which was one of "equal opportunity for all regardless of race and religion." The problem of limiting Jews lingered on for some time, however, since various subterfuges could be used to keep the number of Jews within "reasonable" proportions. Educational theory mandated a "balanced" class, composed of different types from different backgrounds, lest Harvard become provincial. Not until the cold-war period, and specifically the orbiting of the Russian sputnik, was there a full realization that talent was a national resource that could not be wasted. That realization noticeably improved the chances for Jewish students' acceptance at Harvard and other prestigious institutions, although to this day the concept of merit is interpreted very broadly and can be applied to a moderately gifted swimmer as well as to a brilliant physics student. Nevertheless, in terms of students and even more of faculty, Jews have won a place in America's most prestigious educational institutions far beyond their proportion of the population.

These then are three classic examples of American anti-Semitism, drawn from one decade, the twenties. We might have broadened our scope and cited dozens more, for there are no shortages of examples of private anti-Semitism: the rejection of Joseph Seligmann from a hotel in Saratoga in 1877, which received much attention from the Jewish community; the lynching of an innocent Leo Frank in 1913; the activities of Fritz Kuhn, Father Coughlin, and others who were part of the virulent anti-Semitism of the thirties; and, of course, the vicious subterranean anti-Semitic literature, which is perennial.

Yet a prudent observer ought to question whether anti-Semitism poses a threat to Jewish survival in America. We can note that even in the twenties the picture was a mixed one: the anti-Semitism of the decade never was strong enough to deny Jews access to the good things, material and spiritual, offered by American society. That decade also witnessed the rapid

professionalization of many second-generation Eastern immigrants, a growing affluence that enabled many to leave the
ghetto for greener pastures, and an astounding rise in the number of synagogues, especially of the Conservative branch. Today American Jewry composes 2.7 percent of the population
but 20 percent of the nation's attorneys, 11–12 percent of its
physicians, 13 percent of its professors (in the nation's most
prestigious institutions the figure reaches 33 percent), and generally has gone considerably beyond the founding Protestant
groups in income and occupational status. Such a record makes
the claim of discrimination appear hollow.

The most critical moments in the nation's recent history have
not seen a direct attack on the Jewish community from elements
from which historically such attacks might have been expected.
The McCarthy period of the fifties did not produce an anti-
Semitic fallout. The senator preferred to confront the citadels
of Americanism, Harvard University, the State Department,
and the United States Army. Any American Jew with a good
memory might have silently chuckled to himself at the trouble
faced by the first two mentioned institutions when they came
under McCarthy's attack. George Wallace, the right-wing
populist-minded governor of Alabama, never attacked Jews directly, and, in fact, received 22 percent of the Jewish vote in
cities like Mobile. Other demagogues have found it convenient
to conceal their distaste by euphemisms such as "effete intellectual snobs," or a hostility towards cities or liberals, rarely Jews
per se. Even the energy crisis caused by OPEC, to which Israel
is at least indirectly linked, has triggered no perceptible increase in anti-Semitism.

One might even argue that the prognosis for the future of
anti-Semitism, its ability to win a mass base in popular sentiment, is not good. The old sources for such an animus, notably
the teachings of the churches, are eroding. The Ecumenical
Council has eliminated some of the most blatant charges of
deicide in the Catholic liturgy. More important, the inroads of
secularism are also well advanced among Christians, and the
churches have experienced a decline in influence. Like the Jews
of modernity, Christians are no longer taking their behavioral

and moral cues from their churches. The populist mentality believed by some to be a key feeder of the anti-Semitic imagination has lost much of its glitter. It was, we have noted, primarily a rural phenomenon. Many of its original adherents had never seen a Jew and merely displaced much of their hostility to cities and the Jews who were imagined to dominate them. But today most Americans have become what Populists imagined Jews to be: involved in nonproductive jobs, using credit cards, and living in cities or adopting the urban style of life wherever they live. It would be difficult for American public opinion to target-center Jews for such real and imagined trespasses without condemning itself in the process. Yet such an approach assumes that in order to sustain itself, anti-Semitism requires a base in rationality. The reverse may actually be the case. One suspects that the anti-Semitism of a Tom Watson, Henry Ford, or Spiro Agnew, and a vociferous number of Black radicals, continues to be linked to a Populist conception without roots in contemporary reality. Thus, there is probably a great deal of realism in the apprehension expressed by many Jews, that their conspicuous affluence offers a ready target for anti-Semitism. That can be so because it makes little difference that today Jews are not the only American subgroup that has been conspicuously successful, and that in achieving that success they have merely acted out America's success ethos, which is the force behind the nation's driving energy. In the twenties, the sociologist Robert E. Park suggested that Jewish history be taught in the schools so that Americans can learn what America is. Park argued that in their energy and drive for achievement Jews were quintessentially American. Yet today one can no longer assume that because such attack would challenge the defining principle of the national community, a group cannot be attacked for succeeding. The success ethos itself is increasingly questioned by many groups in the nation. It is challenged as insufficient to achieve national goals.

Yet an observer of the American scene cannot help noting that in large measure American anti-Semitism has not received official sanction by government and that a Jewish question has simply not become part of the nation's political agenda. It was this factor in Europe—the amplification of anti-Semitism through the state and the polity—that made it such a dangerous phenomenon. Except for Federal Order Number 11,* we can find nothing like the Dreyfus affair in France, the May Laws of tsarist Russia, Rumania's Artisan Law, or Nazi Germany with its Nuremberg Laws, its *Kristallnacht*, and its "final solution." In fact, if one examines certain diplomatic dispatches one can find remarkable evidence of philo-Semitism in the dispatches of James Blaine or John Hay, protesting discrimination against Jews abroad or private documents such as that of the Rev. William Blackstone, whose memorial in 1881 passionately advocated that Jews be encouraged to reestablish a Jewish state in Palestine.

That brings us to an important observation regarding American anti-Semitism, borne out by the examples cited: it has been largely confined to the private sector, and its assault is by indirection. It was never spearheaded by a political party, and it was never officialized and amplified by government policy. One should approach with great care here. To say that American anti-Semitism is primarily a private phenomenon is not to say that it is unimportant. The most important things that happen in America still happen privately, and private anti-Semitism can be devastating in its impact. Witness the Skokie case.* Neither does it mean that it cannot become "official" at some future time. The energy crisis, with its unmistakable links to conflict in the Middle East, or the fact that the recently concluded Israeli–Egyptian peace treaty calls for American taxpayers to contribute six hundred dollars for each Israeli man, woman, and child, can easily bring a "Jewish question" to the fore in the American political dialogue. What seems fairly certain is that thus far anti-Semitism in America has, because of its private character, posed far less of a threat to Jewish well-being than in other areas of the world and other periods of Jewish history.

*An order issued by the headquarters of General Grant in December 1862 for the evacuation of all Jews resident in the Tennessee Department. It is the only instance of government-sponsored collective punishment of Jews in American history.

*This case concerned the right of a virulently anti-Semitic group to parade in full neo-Nazi regalia in the town of Skokie, Illinois, in 1978.

We come finally to the question of whether anti-Semitism in America poses a threat to Jewish survival. It is abundantly clear that, viewed from a historical perspective, the greatest danger for Jewish survival stems not from anti-Semitism but its reverse, and perhaps, if one can be allowed some cynicism, its absence. It is the benevolent absorbency of American society— evidenced by such things as the accelerating intermarriage rate—that poses the real threat to American Jewish continuance. It is that, rather than the imminence of a parade in Skokie, or a Christmas creche in the public school. It is the fact that Jews are accepted and even envied rather than despised, which ought to create apprehension. Where once they used to be indicted for clannishness or eccentricity, for not fitting in, today they are often undifferentiated and indistinguishable.

Yet, given the idiosyncratic character of Jewish history and the compelling analogy between contemporary American Jewry and the Jews of Germany in the twenties and thirties, and observing the American Jewish condition through the prism of the Holocaust, no prudent observer could argue for complacency. That would be denying an early warning system which Jews have developed at a terribly high price. That warning system tells Jews that there are always factors, known and unknown, which could change their situation overnight. It could happen anywhere; it could happen in America. Somehow, anti-Semitism is linked to Jewish history, which means that it is as unpredictable as that history itself.

Bibliography

"Anti-Semitism in the United States," *American Jewish History* (Special Issue) vol. 71, (September 1981).

Belth, N. C. *A Promise to Keep: A Narrative of the American Encounter with Anti-Semitism*. New York: 1979.

Dinnerstein, L., ed. *Anti-Semitism in the United States*. New York: 1971.

Dobkovsky, M. N. *The Tarnished Dream: The Basis of American Anti-Semitism*. Westport: 1979.

Glock, C. Y., and R. Stark *Christian Beliefs and Anti-Semitism*. New York: 1965.

Higham, J. *Strangers in the Land.* New York: 1968.
Moore, D. D. *At Home in America: Second Generation New York Jews.*
New York: 1981.
Morison, S. E. *Three Centuries of Harvard, 1636–1936.* Cambridge:
1936.
Rosenstock, M. *Louis Marshall, Defender of Jewish Rights.* Detroit: 1965.
Steinberg, S. *The Academic Melting Pot.* New York: 1974.
Weisbord, R. G., and A. Stein *Bittersweet Encounter.* Westport: 1970.

CHAPTER XII

American Power and Jewish
Interest in Foreign Affairs

S OME are familiar with the story of two Israelis commiserating on the insecurity and poor economic conditions of their country. Suddenly one announces to the other that he has hit upon a brilliant idea for a solution. Let the Israeli Knesset declare war on the United States. Israel would, of course lose, but then the United States could be depended upon to follow its customary pattern of generosity to the vanquished. The States would become committed to protect and support a defeated Israel. There is a moment of silence, and then the other Israeli shakes his head and mutters: "But with our luck we would win."

That story illustrates the link Jews feel between their well-being and security and American power. The brilliant idea was to somehow inveigle America to commit itself to the security of Israel, which is a central Jewish concern. One major objective of American Jewry in the foreign-policy arena is to assure that American wealth and power are used to buttress the survival of Israel, at least in the diplomatic realm. (Israel has never requested direct military intervention.) The strength of the American commitment to Israel depends in some measure on the political leverage of American Jewry, which historically has been called upon to use its influence on behalf of its beleaguered coreligionists everywhere. How effective has American Jewry been in playing this role? An examination of that problem and the complex conditions of making foreign policy in a democracy is the subject of this chapter. The reader may be surprised to learn that the influence of American Jewry, like that of other special-interest pleaders, is actually quite limited. In the case of American Jewry, it reached a high point with the speedy recognition of Israel in May 1948, an episode we will discuss later. Even here, however, special circumstances made it more the exception than the rule.

There is another reason for studying the influence of American Jewry on foreign policy. How a group behaves in the foreign policy arena is based in some measure on the externalization of its inner value structure. By carefully examining how a given group views itself in relation to the world it can inform the historian about its assumptions concerning the world order. Those assumptions, together with a group style and habits stemming from its historical experience, make up its political culture. Some interesting observations can be made regarding the political culture of American Jewry from its long experience in this area. It is especially informative because American Jewry conceives its identity in terms of its concern for Jewish communities abroad. There are some observers who are convinced that it is the most Jewish aspect of American Jewry.

Compared to other subgroups in America, the Jews have been hyperactive in the foreign policy area. Studies show that Jews are generally better informed about the foreign scene, their organizations are more likely to express opinions and transmit them to decision makers, their leaders are more likely to speak out on foreign-policy questions, and they are more prone to devote time and study to them than other groups in America. An examination of Jewish organizations and the flow of philanthropy would show that a disproportionate share of their organizational energy and financial resources is earmarked for the welfare of Jewish communities abroad. The major Jewish organizations established in the first two decades of this century—the American Jewish Committee, the American Jewish Congress, the Joint Distribution Committee, and the full panoply of Zionist organizations—were founded, and to some extent continue, to focus on supporting and protecting endangered Jewish communities abroad.

If we had to pinpoint a single reason for the Jewish interest in foreign policy it would relate to the continued strength of the tie to *k'lal Yisrael*. (These are the religious, cultural, and family bonds that loosely bind Jews together in a world community.) There seems always to be a beleaguered Jewish community somewhere in dire need of aid from American Jewry. American Jewry often acts as an interested agent for such communities to the American government. But it would be an oversimplification to view this tie as the sole reason for the Jewish preoccupation with foreign relations. One ought to take note of the fact that American-Jewish interest in foreign affairs is amazingly broad and hardly confined to the welfare of Jews in Israel, the Soviet Union, or Iran. Jews were very poor material for the hysteria that accompanied the Cold War in its heyday. They sensed early that the involvement in Viet Nam was a debacle of the first magnitude. All foreign-policy questions draw their interest. That becomes understandable when one becomes aware that a general universalist thrust is characteristic of much post-emancipation Jewish thinking. By the last quarter of the nineteenth century Jews were enthusiastic participants in the socialist movement, which contained the ideal of universalism in its most pristine form but also in more mundane forms, such as the creation of an international language like Esperanto. They were also disproportionately represented in the development of modern science, whose truths were universal. There could be no German or French physics or chemistry. Their social configuration in Western Europe, and increasingly in the East as well, was cosmopolitan and urbane. They boasted the highest level of formal education, and it is precisely such groups that break through purely parochial interests to view the world in global terms. Jewish universalism was a physical as well as an ideological datum. No less important was the growth of the Zionist consensus, which focused attention on a foreign sovereignty, "Israel," whose welfare depends on the play of international power. The historical development of Jewry itself seems to have conspired to give it a special interest in international affairs.

Let us see how this interest was reflected in the early decades of the twentieth century. We focus our illustrations on three foreign-policy problems of deep concern to Jews. The first was the so-called passport question, which includes the Jewish reaction to the Kishinev pogrom and the orchestrated attempt by Jewish leaders to force the intercession of the Taft administration by abrogating the Commercial Treaty of 1832, which gave tsarist Russia a most-favored-nation status. It is a classic and discrete case. The second example was the attempt by the nascent American Zionist movement between 1917 and 1922, first, to get the Wilson administration to protect the *yishuv* (the Jewish community in Palestine); then, to confirm the Balfour Declaration; and, finally, to dispose favorably of the mandate in Palestine. The third was the effort by Louis Marshall to insert a national minority-rights clause into American treaties with Poland and other nations to guarantee the civil rights and ethnic autonomy of the Jewish communities in these countries. (The classic attempt of American Jewry to influence Franklin D. Roosevelt's administration toward a more active rescue policy during the years of the Holocaust is the subject of a later chapter.)

The first observation to be made in analyzing these three examples is that the notion that there is a secret Jewish power operating behind the scenes—a mainstay of the anti-Semitic imagination—is not borne out by the facts. In the arena of American decision making on foreign affairs, Jews have been neither more nor less successful than other special-interest groups in putting their stamp on foreign policy. We shall learn that all ethnic and special-interest pressure on American foreign policy has been circumscribed. During World War I, the German-Americans were a larger and more coherent group than the Jews would come to be. They had only one firm desire, to keep America out of the war with the "Fatherland." When, during the presidential campaign of 1916, Woodrow Wilson ran on a slogan "He Kept Us out of War," enough Midwestern German-American Republicans switched their party allegiance to grant Wilson a narrow victory. But in February 1917, when the German High Command in Berlin redeclared unrestricted submarine warfare, the resultant loss of American ships and lives was so appalling that, according to the historian Arthur

Link, Wilson was compelled to declare war in April, only a month after his inauguration. It suddenly became very uncomfortable to be a German-American. Sauerkraut was renamed "liberty cabbage," frankfurters became "hot dogs," and hamburgers, "salisbury steaks." German was dropped from the curriculum in many schools. German-Americans, having learned the price of being out of step with the political consensus, never dared such a step again. They did not attain their foreign-policy objective. Neither did the most politically astute ethnic group on the American political landscape, the American Irish. Their principal goal in the post-Civil-War period was somehow to damage Britain, and in 1867 they went as far as staging a minor invasion of Canada to make their point. It was part of a tactic employed by the Irish that came to be known as "twisting the lion's tail." Yet, despite their formidable political power, manifested primarily on the local municipal level, and the coherence given the group by the commanding presence of the Catholic Church, the Irish-Americans could not forestall the Anglo-American rapprochement, which began in 1895 after the Venezuela–British Guiana boundary dispute. It was that unofficial alliance which profoundly influenced international relations during the first half of the twentieth century. Some historians are convinced that America actually rose to world power through a British conduit, and did so at the expense of other contenders, such as Germany and Japan. Polish-Americans were not able to prevent what they called the "crime of Crimea," the surrender of part of Poland to the Soviet Union at the Yalta Conference. One observer actually formulated a rule for the limited influence of special-interest groups, which he called the "rule of marginal effect." "The sentiment of the American Jewish community," he observed, "no matter how strongly pressed will influence American foreign policy only to the extent that it doesn't make any substantial difference to what are otherwise considered the best foreign policy interests of the United States."

The reason why that influence is limited stems from the fact that the Jewish interest on a specific question rarely stands alone. Decision makers simply do not recognize a "Jewish question" per se. The Jewish aspect of a foreign-policy issue is customarily part of a larger nexus of issues whose disposition determines the Jewish interest. At the same time, the moment Jewish leaders bring their own interest to the fore, countervailing interests make their weight felt.

That process is illustrated by what happened when, between 1911 and 1914, Jews pressed for the abrogation of the commercial treaty with Russia—a strategy initiated by Jewish leaders to wring better treatment for their coreligionists. The basic question facing policy makers only incidentally concerned the Jews of Russia. They wanted to maintain a balance of power in the Far East to act as buttress for the Open Door Policy. After the remarkable Japanese victory in 1905, that required a strong Russia to balance Japan. The attempt by Jewish leaders to weaken Russia, first by extending financial support to Japan during the war, and then by threatening the market for Russian goods in America, was not in consonance with larger American policy objectives. It aroused the opposition of the State Department as well as companies like Singer Sewing Machine and the International Harvester Company, which had built profitable markets in Russia. Jewish leaders did succeed in organizing a powerful coalition of forces, and finally the treaty was abrogated; but by that time Russia had become involved in World War I, and the total situation had changed. Predictably, the objective of improving the condition of Russian Jewry was lost in the shuffle. Even with a new government, bloody pogroms continued into the twenties.

A similar pattern can be discerned in the case of gaining Washington's support for the *yishuv* and the Balfour Declaration. The issuance of the declaration can only be understood by viewing it against the wartime struggle between the allies and central powers to win public opinion to their side. Ironically influenced by wartime anti-Semitism, which greatly exaggerated the importance of Jewish opinion in Russia and America, the British and German foreign offices spared no effort to gain Jewish support. The issuance of the Balfour Declaration was dictated, according to the diplomatic historian Josef Rappaport, by "the grand strategy of the battlefield." The support of American Jewry, whose antipathy toward Russia led to favoring a German victory at the outset of the war, was thought to be an important asset in London, especially after Berlin made diplomatic moves to convince Turkish leaders to make concessions to the Zionists and also promised to protect Jewish civil rights in Poland. Although Washington did not yet possess larger policy aims in the Middle East, Wilson's concession to the Zionists aroused countervailing opposition within the Jewish community and among missionary interests. The president was linked to the latter group by ideological and social, as well as family, ties. His son-in-law, Howard Bliss, was president of a major missionary institution—Syrian Protestant College. Moreover, the American missionary enterprise in the Middle East ranked second only to that in the Far East in power and influence (historians of American diplomacy call it the "vestryman" influence). The vestryman influence stems from the fact that many high officials in the foreign-policy-making establishment come from missionary families. Indeed, this influence was soon discernible. The Wilson administration dispatched the King– Crane Commission to Palestine to investigate the situation. The result was predictable. Within ten days of landing in the port of Jaffa, the commission forwarded a strongly worded anti-Zionist report to the State Department.

The same pattern can be noted in the case of Louis Marshall's struggle to gain legal protection for the Jewish minority in newly reestablished Poland by inserting a minority-rights clause into the founding treaty. That goal aroused the adamant opposition not only of certain Polish leaders but of Polish-Americans as well. The Polish National Committee, headed by Ignaces Paderewski and the notoriously anti-Semitic Roman Dmowski, were largely financed by the Polish-American community. The committee also successfully enlisted the aid of Colonel House, the most influential adviser of the president. By 1919 some Polish-Americans tried to organize an anti-Jewish boycott.

If we jump ahead for a moment, the same pattern is discernible during the bitter years of the Holocaust. Here we see the Jewish interest in having a more generous policy for the admission of refugees subsumed by the "great debate" in foreign policy between isolationists and interventionists during the late thirties. For obvious reasons, Jews strongly favored the latter position. When the great folk hero Charles Lindbergh warned the Jews and Anglophiles to stop their efforts to bring the United States into a war which he felt was against the American national interest, in his famous Des Moines speech of September 1941, the lines were clearly drawn. The linkage of the refugee issue to the "great debate" had an ominous side effect. It almost injected a "Jewish question" into the foreign-policy debate, something both Jewish leaders and Roosevelt wanted to avoid at all costs. When later the question became one of rescuing European Jews being killed in specially constructed Nazi death factories, that issue was again subsumed by the larger question: how to win the war quickly. Just as patriotic and restrictionist groups had opposed the admission of Jewish refugees in the thirties, so now, military leaders and State Department officials opposed refugee schemes like sending food packages to the camps and bombing the gas chambers and rail lines leading to them. They argued that it would take away needed resources from the war effort.

Thus, we can conclude from these examples that the Jewish interest never stands alone as a foreign-policy issue, but rather becomes part of the larger question, what is in the national interest—and furthermore, that when it is raised, it inevitably generates opposing interests, which makes the realization of Jewish objectives through the intervention of the American government problematic.

There exists yet another factor that seriously hampers the projection of a Jewish interest on the making of public policy. A look at the historical record before 1945 indicates that it is impossible to speak of a single coherent Jewish interest, something that all Jews agree upon as an objective. One rarely detects a focused Jewish voice projected on decision makers until the Zionist consensus; that has presented the Jews with some unity, at least as far as the security of Israel is concerned, although an internal debate continues to rage on how best to achieve that objective. During the first three decades of the century, the Jewish voice was continually riven by internal strife arising from religious, class, and derivative national differences. What an irony! While anti-Semites imagine the existence of a secret Jewish conspiracy to rule the world—the predominant theme of much anti-Semitic literature in the twentieth century—Jews, in fact, can rarely agree on what to do and how best to do it.

During the protracted struggle over the passport question between 1908 and 1914, the petition to the Kremlin (a major tactic of Jewish leaders) brought much acrimonious comment over its effectiveness and the way it was implemented. Nor did Jewish leaders like Louis Marshall and Rep. Henry Goldfogle—who represented an almost all-Jewish district in New York City—see eye to eye. During the struggle for support of the Balfour Declaration and the mandate, there was persistent opposition from anti-Zionists who published a virulent memorial in the *New York Times*. Divisions and disunity on virtually everything during the period of the Holocaust were even more marked.

Yet, the idea of a secret Jewish power working behind the scenes, unified and having a common purpose, persists not only among anti-Semites but among many Jews as well. It is part of what I call an "illusion of centrality," which imagines Jews to be more important and more powerful than they really are. Although Jews have a more sustained interest in influencing foreign policy and their precarious situation in the world compels them to try harder, their record in influencing foreign affairs is no better or worse than other "hyphenate" and special interest groups. The influence of all these groups on policy is circumscribed by the system itself.

It warrants repeating that, in its simplest form, the American Jewish community acts as the agent of world Jewry before the American power structure, whose influence it tries to enlist to ameliorate the condition of Jewish communities abroad. However, American Jewish interest is not confined to Jewish problems. We have seen that it maintains a high and separate interest in the broad range of problems that confront America overseas. But whereas the latter role is assumed by Jews acting as loyal, interested citizens of America, the former serves as an identifiable link to their Jewishness. It is a dual interest in which a conflict can be most vexing. The assumption behind the first role is that certain states and international agencies (the United States, the Western democracies, the Vatican, the League of Nations, and the United Nations, the International Red Cross) embody a moral force,—call it the "spirit of civilization"—which, if mobilized effectively, can compel nations that persecute Jews to mend their ways.

Although recent history presents ample evidence that the facts warrant no such assumption, it continues to inform the political culture of American Jewry. In the past, Jewish leaders have spent inordinate energy in wringing notes of diplomatic concern and direct intercession from often reluctant administrations. They have been avid in using legal devices, such as the minority rights clause, or gaining Congressional resolutions to protect Jewish communities abroad. A few examples drawn from the history of Jewish activity in the foreign-policy arena illustrate this strategy. Jews got the Van Buren administration to send such a note during the Damascus affair in 1840. They were less successful with the Buchanan administration, which rejected intercession in the Mortara kidnapping affair in 1858. In the post-Civil-War period, notes of concern were sent, at the behest of American Jews, concerning the critical situation in the Swiss Cantons, Morroco, Russia, and Rumania. Among the best known of these diplomatic notes is the one sent by Secretary of State James G. Blaine to the British Foreign Office requesting joint action against the infamous May Laws. Its renown rests on its outspoken philo-Semitism (the comparison is with fifteenth-century Spain):

> Then as now in Russia, the Hebrews fared better in business than his neighbor, then as now his economic and patient industry bred capital and capital bred envy and envy persecution and persecution disaffection . . . The Jews are made a people apart from other people, not of their volition, but because they have been repressed and ostracized in the communities in which they mixed.

The officials of the Foreign Office were undoubtedly non-plussed at such philo-Semitic passion, but it did not affect their policy. They rejected the offer for joint action out of hand.

In the early years of this century these notes, drafted by Alvey Adee, the State Department's master of good penmanship and sentiments, were strongly motivated by the desire to win political favor in the Jewish community. In July 1902, for example, after Rumania passed its infamous artisan law, which further pauperized Rumanian Jewry, American Jewish leaders requested diplomatic intercession, and a note was dispatched characterizing Bucharest's action as "repugnant to the moral sense of liberal modern peoples." Talk of "moral sense" and "liberal modern people" won the hearts of American Jews, and Hay was soon requested to campaign on the Lower East Side, where crowds of appreciative Jews came out to hear him. Actually the dispatch was written by Adee, who received kudos from Hay on 30 August 1902. "The President [Theodore Roosevelt] is greatly pleased," he informed Adee, "and the Hebrews . . . poor dears! all over the country think we are bully boys." Adee was instructed to burn the note after reading it. Another note was dispatched as the date of the congressional election approached. "Even if Russia does nothing," Hay informed Adee, "we shall have a good note to print next winter."

The Kishinev pogrom brought an emotional reaction among American Jews, which "uptown" leaders felt had to be deflected into acceptable channels. Their plan was to gather a giant protest petition to be signed by important people. The leaders implemented their plan even while aware that the Kremlin would never receive it. They viewed it more as a tactic to diffuse the anger of the "downtown" Jews, many of whom had had first-hand experience with Russian pogroms. The tedious task of collecting signatures took months and was further delayed during the summer, when many notables were on vacation. Finally the names were collected and the organizers were faced with the problem of what to do with the petition. The answer came from John Hay. Why not place the petition in the Department archives, where it could be viewed by future generations. An appropriate ceremony indicating the importance of the petition would be held. Jewish leaders welcomed the idea, and when the day came Hay delivered a speech:

> In the future when the students of history come to peruse this document, they will wonder how the petitioners, moved to profound indignation by intolerable wrongs perpetrated on the innocent and helpless, could have expressed themselves in language so earnest and eloquent, yet so dignified, so moderate, so decorous. It is a valuable addition to public literature, and it will be sacredly cherished among the treasures of the Department.

All this for a petition that was never delivered! Political leaders had learned how easy it was to buy Jews off with gestures and words. It may be that what insecure American Jews wanted as much as help for their coreligionists abroad was assurances from American leaders that they were loved and appreciated and that it could never happen here.

If the government had learned to play the "air for the Jew string," as one British observer would later put it, Jewish leaders were no less adept at manipulating Christian statesmen by citing Scriptures and Judeo-Christian morality. This proved especially effective with Wilson, who, as a son of a minister, was devout. In the early months of 1920, when France was intent on detaching the Herman and Litany rivers from the Mandate, thereby leaving the potential Jewish homeland in Palestine ecologically unviable, Rabbi Stephen Wise, founder of the American Jewish Congress, reminded Wilson of the "solemn promise of the Christian nations." Justice Louis Brandeis, whom Wilson had appointed to the Supreme Court, was more direct. He spoke of Christian "honor" and "morality."

Such reminders by Jewish leaders were not insincere. They believed that as part of the "spirit of civilization" such things as Christian morality and honor really played a role. That is why when in 1915 anti-Jewish depredations in Poland took a sharp turn for the worse, Louis Marshall naturally turned to Pope Benedict IV for redress. The assumption was that the Vatican would be concerned with such things as justice and morality.

But the reply from the Vatican was as indifferent in 1915 as it would be during the bitter years of the Holocaust.

For men like Marshall, the assumption that a "spirit of civilization" could be used to protect Jews was not as outlandish as it appears today. A Jew like Marshall, born in America, having fully savored her benevolence and being almost totally unfamiliar with the kind of virulent anti-Semitism that characterized the European scene, was in a sense disarmed by his personal history. The call to morality and the use of law worked on the American scene. All that had to be done now was to apply them universally. That is the reason he labored so hard to impose a national minority-rights clause on Poland. He continued to believe in its worth even after bitter arguments on its merits disrupted the session of the Polish Sejm. "It is our firm belief," he insisted in 1920, "that these treaties have at last absolved the Jews of Eastern Europe from the serious disabilities from which they have so long suffered and will forever end the great abuse of the past. A better era is now dawning." To a friend he boasted that "the work of emancipation has now been accomplished." But even as he wrote, bloodier depredations and legal restrictions were in preparation. He seemed totally unaware of the failure of previous attempts to guarantee Jewish rights through legal clauses. The Polish experiment was even less successful than the one attempted in Rumania by the Treaty of Berlin in 1878. It would be even more manifest during the years of the Holocaust.

One might well ask why American Jewry and its leaders clung so tenaciously to this notion. Perhaps the answer lies in the fact that survival, which requires hope, would have become impossible if all Jews possessed was the certain knowledge that they were totally vulnerable in a world that had murder in its heart. A people's sense of reality is fashioned by its history. For American Jews that optimism, that willingness to believe that morality played a role in human affairs, stemmed from Judaic roots and was strongly reinforced by their American experience. We mentioned at the outset that the assumptions a group brings to the arena of foreign policy can serve as a fingerprint of its inner value structure. American Jewry is revealed as being both quintessentially Jewish and American. The source of the heavy moral freight it bears has American as well as Jewish roots. In examining the American style in foreign affairs, George Kennan, one of the most perceptive students of American diplomacy, has observed that in the international arena Americans tend to underrate the role of naked power and overrate the role of law and morality. The "illusion of civilization" in American Jewry is especially strong because it eminates from the two principal wellsprings that determine their own behavior.

That American Jews give high priority to morality, justice, righteousness, and law will not come as news to the reader. What is so puzzling is that so many Jews who have lived in the time–space between Kishinev and Auschwitz can still be so confident about "civilization." Little in their historical experience warrants such optimism. One concludes that we are dealing with a people who either possess a genius for faith or a penchant for illusion.

Bibliography

Adler, C., and Margalith, A. M., *With Firmness in the Right: American Diplomatic Action Affecting Jews, 1840–1945.* New York: 1977.

Feuerwerger, M. *Congress and Israel: Foreign Aid Decision-Making in the House of Representatives, 1969–1976.* Westport: 1979.

Ganin, Z. *Truman, American Jewry and Israel, 1945–1948.* New York: 1979.

Gerson, L. *The Hyphenate in Recent American Politics and Diplomacy.* New York: 1964.

Hero, A. O., Jr. *American Religious Groups View Foreign Policy.* New York: 1973.

Isaacs, S. *Jews and American Politics.* Garden City: 1974.

Janowski, O. I. *The Jews and Minority Rights.* New York: 1973.

Reznikoff, C. ed., *Louis Marshall, Champion of Liberty,* 2 vols. (Philadelphia 1957).

Snetsinger, J. *Truman, the Jewish Vote and Israel.* Stanford: 1974.

Wilson, E. M. *Decision on Palestine.* Stanford: 1979.

CHAPTER XIII

Assessing Jewish Power in America:
Case Study—the Holocaust

IN the darkest hours of the Holocaust a special kind of gallows humor developed among the Jewish victims struggling to keep up their morale. Sometimes they mocked their Nazi tormentors, other times they turned their sharp wit on themselves. One example of the latter concerns the story of two inmates of the notorious death camp at Auschwitz, who succeeded in momentarily escaping. They were soon recaptured but the SS guards, in awe of their courage and ingenuity, decided that the escapees warranted a military execution rather than the normal gassing. They were placed against a wall and, as was the custom, asked if they had any last requests. One of the escapees asked for a blindfold, whereupon the other nudged him and anxiously whispered "Don't make trouble."

Most Jews of my generation understand only the humor of that reaction, but I have observed that younger audiences really want to know why Jews did not make more "trouble." Perhaps what is really desired is evidence of courage, which might redeem a fallen image of the Jewish people. It is an unfair quest, since the victims in their last agony are being asked to yield yet one more thing, heroism, so that survivors can live more comfortably with the fact of the Holocaust. The truth is that "making trouble" made little difference. Whether they hid in the attics of Amsterdam, dug their graves at Babi Yar, or offered heroic resistance in the Warsaw ghetto, the victims were ultimately overcome. So predetermined was their fate that resistance was never conceived of as a means of saving lives. It was, in fact, usually undertaken when most Jews had already been deported and when the remainder finally understood that Hitler had sentenced all Jews to death. It was undertaken to redeem Jewish honor, not to save Jewish lives.

But the case of the witnesses to the Holocaust is different. The governments of the United States, Britain, the Vatican, and the neutral nations had choices. They could have taken a more active rescue role; they could have "made trouble." Their indifference to, and sometimes seeming complicity with, the goals of the "final solution," poses a real enigma for the historian. Why didn't they act?

The answer is not a simple one. There is always the temptation to recite yet another story of man's inhumanity to man, to produce another cry of pain. Rather than do that, let us briefly examine what the Roosevelt administration did do and how American Jewry reacted to the emergency. Our examination is made more difficult by a problem faced by all researchers in this area. It does no good to scream that more might have been done since that is a self evident truth which applies to all catastrophes wrought by society itself. Holocaust researchers have not been able to agree on what the possibilities of rescue were. Some argue that after Germany invaded Russia in June 1941, joining the ideological and physical wars, the opportunity for mass rescue, especially in the East, was severely limited. That is important for our story, for if it is true, then witnesses like the Roosevelt administration and American Jewry, which was called upon to influence the administration in the direction of rescue, did not fail at all. There are others who point out that the opportunity for rescue, especially during the refugee phase between 1938 and 1941, was always there—the case of bombing is a good example—and that failures of will and of mind prevented it.

Let us begin with the refugee phase, and mention some of the actions that were taken. A good argument can be made that the failure to accept Jewish refugees between 1938 and 1941 sealed the fate of the Jews of Europe. It convinced Nazi decision makers that Europe could never be made *Judenrein* (free of Jews)

by emigration and that therefore a more drastic solution, a so-
called final solution, was necessary. In America the momentum
of inaction manifest during the refugee phase carried forward
into the liquidation phase. By the time rescue advocates were
able to reverse the notion that nothing should be done, it was
too late for the Jews of Europe.

We have already seen in our previous discussion of the restrictive immigration laws of the twenties that they proved to
be lethal for Jews in desperate need of a haven during the
thirties. These laws reversed the traditional policy of America
as a refuge for the world's "huddled masses" by means of a
quota system that discriminated against potential immigrants
from Eastern and Southern Europe. Most Jews in dire need of a
haven came from Eastern Europe. Moreover, the immigration
law made no distinction between normal immigrants and refugees who faced extinction if they did not find a haven. When
one adds to these structural roadblocks the deliberate use of
administrative strategies, conceived during the Depression, to
further limit immigration, the hopeless situation faced by Jewish refugees comes fully into focus. Despite the crying need,
only the year 1939 saw the filling of the relevant quotas. The
method used by the Roosevelt administration to build a "paper
wall" to keep Jews out are too intricate to examine here. In
general terms, however, it entailed the use of a security psycho-
sis in the American public mind, the notion that spies had
infiltrated the refugee stream. This then served as the rationale
for increasingly rigid screening of refugees by various security
agencies. By mid-1940 few refugees could negotiate these bar-
riers, and by June 1941 the American consulates were closed so
that virtually none could enter. By that year American
screening procedures were more rigid than those of Britain,
which was already at war. The story has an ironic twist. The
government policy of keeping Jewish refugees out was a classic
example of democracy at work—the very democratic process
American Jewry revered so highly. It was what the American
people, and incidentally American Jewry too, wanted in 1938
when the nation was still in the throes of the Depression. Most
researchers agree with the judgment of Rep. Samuel Dickstein,

made at the time, that an attempt to change the immigration
law, or a strategy of circumventing it, even for Jewish children,
would probably have boomeranged into even more restrictive
immigration laws.

To mitigate the effects of this cruel policy, Roosevelt em-
barked on a "politics of gestures"; a series of steps creating the
impression of good will in the Roosevelt administration, while,
in fact, little was being done for the refugees. From our previous discussion concerning the Jewish question in American
foreign policy, readers will recall that such gestures, made to
garner the Jewish vote, were well precedented in prior administrations and in fact were encouraged by Jewish leaders. One
such gesture, made in 1938, was the extension of visitor's visas.
Earlier there was a special directive to the consuls to show
"special concern" for Jewish visa applicants. After the *Anschluss*
in March 1938, Roosevelt ordered that the Austrian and German quotas be combined in order not to lose the former. The
high point of the "politics of gestures" came in the spring of
1938, when Roosevelt called thirty-two nations to meet at
Evian les Bains to bring order to the chaotic refugee situation.
Nothing much came of the conference, partly because the
American delegation came with nothing in its pockets to indicate that America was willing to do its share in absorbing refugees. It offered no lead which other nations might follow. It
proved rather an embarrassment to Roosevelt when his old
crony George Rublee, who had been made director of a new
intergovernmental refugee committee which grew out of the
conference, was actually able to reach an agreement with moderate Nazis to "buy out" German Jewry being held in hostage.
It was the first of the ransom proposals which characterized
Nazi policy towards the Jews. But then, as later, even such
cynical tactics could not be realized, because there was no place
to put the Jews so ransomed.

Instead of opening its gates, the Roosevelt administration,
acting under pressure from an isolationist–restrictionist Congress, turned its attention to resettling the Jews some place else.
They preferred unsettled areas of Africa which were then in the
British sphere: Angola, Rhodesia, even the Belgian Congo. As

many as 666 such potential "havens" were explored by a special agency but none was ever found. Ironically, while the Roosevelt administration turned to Africa for likely resettlement prospects, Britain, which had virtually closed Palestine—the most likely prospect—in the teeth of the crisis, turned to British Guiana in the United States' Latin-American sphere for the same purpose. The truth was that no one wanted the Jewish refugees, and ultimately the very term "resettlement," which Berlin had also hit upon in Nisko Lublin and Madagascar, became the code word for the "final solution." Many hapless Jewish victims boarded the cattle cars to the East desperately wanting to believe that they were simply being resettled there.

The last of these gestures was the cruelest mockery of all. The Bermuda Conference, held finally on an inaccessible island in April 1943, occurred when the news of the "final solution" was fully known and precisely at the moment of the heroic Warsaw Ghetto uprising, the first urban resistance against the Nazis. Yet at Bermuda, the conferees spoke of "surplus people" and refused even to consider any plan to do anything for the inmates of death and concentration camps. It chose, rather, to focus its attention on those refugees who had found a precarious haven in Spain and North Africa and whose lives were no longer in danger. Breckinridge Long, the Assistant Secretary of State who had taken it upon himself to thwart any rescue of Jews lest America thereby help the Nazi war effort, insisted that the IGC, created at Evian, be revitalized. Yet by 1943 it was clear that it was precisely this agency, ostensibly created to rescue refugees, that blocked their rescue at every turn.

By November 1942 word of the implementation of the "final solution" had leaked out of occupied Europe. When a Jewish delegation visited the Oval Office on 8 December 1942, Roosevelt informed them that he knew precisely what was happening to Jews in Europe. It took a full year after the news was known, however, to get the administration to act. Many people are convinced that the delay was due to the indifference of American Jewry. That charge is highly unfair and would have been uncharacteristic of American Jewry, which defined its Judaism largely by its nurture of Jewish communities abroad.

American Jewry, in fact, devised virtually every protest tech-
nique—rallies, marches, theater, use of media, boycotts—later
used by the civil-rights movement. It was not as effective as it
might have been because the war itself tended to mute a cry for
special attention emanating from the Jewish community. What
rescue advocates wanted flew in the face of strategic priorities,
which placed the defeat of the axis as the first order of business.
The rescue of Jews, whether by bombing the death camps or
the rail lines leading to them, or sending food packages to certain camps, or ransoming certain Jews, could not be accom-
modated, it was argued, because it was not consonant with that
higher priority. When, for example, Breckinridge Long got
wind of a proposal to send food packages to certain camps, he
strenuously argued against it on the basis that it would relieve
the Nazi authorities of the responsibility for feeding these inmates and thereby help the German war effort. Rescue advocates experienced great difficulties in changing these priorities
and sometimes seemed reluctant to do so because they feared to
raise doubts regarding Jewish patriotism.

By the fall of 1943, however, the demand for action had
gained considerable momentum in both the United States and
Britain. In the vanguard of the new protest was a group of
revisionist Zionists led by Palestinian-born Hillel Kook, alias
Peter Bergson. Unfettered by the bureaucratic viscosity of Jewish organizational life, and willing to give rescue total priority
even over the cherished goal of establishing a Jewish homeland
advocated by the Zionist Biltmore conference in May 1942, the
Bergson group mounted a dramatic publicity campaign from
which mainline Zionists were not spared for their supposed
lack of energy and will. The Bergson group, which had attracted such brilliant publicists as Ben Hecht and Pierre Van
Passen, possessed no mass base but demonstrated an uncanny
ability for bringing the rescue question to public attention. One
result of their publicity campaign was to push the organized
Jewish community, which had in a sense written off European
Jewry, to clamor for a special rescue agency. Congressional
hearings to establish such an agency were held in November
1943. The hearings successfully identified Breckinridge Long

and a coterie of State Department officials as principal blockers of a more successful rescue effort. To succeed, the rescue advocates would have to remove the program from the egis of the State Department where it languished.

It was not until Henry Morgenthau, Jr., Roosevelt's secretary of the treasury and probably the Jew closest to Roosevelt, presented the president with a file prepared by three department assistants—originally entitled "The Acquiescence of the American Government in the Murder of the Jews"—that Roosevelt acted. The report, retitled by Morgenthau "Personal Report to the President," briefly detailed, with devastating accuracy, the State Department's deliberate suppression of news of the "final solution" and other actions blocking rescue. The report led directly to the issuance of an executive order establishing a War Refugee Board charged with the responsibility of "rescue, transportation, maintenance and relief of the victims of enemy oppression." The order came none too soon, for in March 1944 Berlin was preparing to zero in on the last remaining Jewish community in Central Europe—the almost one million Jews of Hungary.

A desperate effort to save these Jews—using psychological warfare techniques, threats of retribution, and filtering money to the anti-Nazi underground—was initiated. In June, a special camp was opened in Oswego, New York, to house one thousand refugees. It was one of several temporary havens where refugees could find shelter. But the temporary haven in Oswego had symbolic significance for rescue advocates. It circumvented the supposedly immutable immigration law, but it happened too late to make a great difference. It was, ultimately, an unforeseen event that led to the halting of the deportation of Hungarian Jewry and saved the lives of thousands. On June 2, 1944, the railroad yards of Budapest were bombed. The raid had a devastating effect on Horthy, the Regent of Hungary, who called off the deportations on July 7. It is a good indication that retaliatory bombing alone might have been the key to mass rescue. The mere threat of retaliation proved sufficient to stop the deportations in the satellites, whose cooperation was required to transport the Jews to the death camps.

Nevertheless, within full view of the world and when the Nazis knew that the war was lost, they still slaughtered over half of Hungarian Jewry. In some measure the survivors, the Jews of Budapest and its environs, owe their lives to the new active American rescue policy. It took six years to turn the Roosevelt administration to a more humanitarian policy towards Jews. When it came it was too little and too late for the six million.

The foregoing account barely touches the full and tragic story of American inaction during those bitter years. Nor does it expose the layers of lies and half-truths concerning American Jewry's ostensible failure to act. We want to spend the remainder of this discussion examining the role of American Jewry, which has been compelled to bear the onus of guilt for not having done enough. Is that accusation historically accurate?

Our discussion is best structured by posing a concrete question: How was it that American Jewry, holding an important position in the liberal–urban–ethnic coalition that served as the political buttress of the New Deal, having many Jews in the innermost circle of the Roosevelt administration, having a longer experience in projecting pressure for their coreligionists abroad than any other group in America, emerging from the Depression faster than other group, and heading three major congressional committees—Sol Bloom, House Foreign Affairs Committee; Samuel Dickstein, House Committee on Immigration and Naturalization; and Emanuel Celler, House Judiciary Committee—nevertheless was unable appreciably to move the Roosevelt administration to rescue European Jews until it was too late?

Those who recall our previous discussions dealing with the Jewish question in American foreign policy and the character of Jewish communal organizations already know a good part of the answer to this question. The responsibilities history thrust upon American Jewry during the Holocaust were simply greater than the power of American Jewry to meet them. The idea that there existed a unified Jewish community in the thirties able to speak to the Roosevelt administration with a coherent voice is nowhere substantiated by the evidence, which

shows that on virtually every issue—from how best to counteract the Nazi threat, to the boycott, rescue through resettlement, ransoming, the question of Palestine and the White
Paper, to the centrality of the rescue question itself—American
Jewry and its organizations were deeply divided. The American Jewish Conference, an attempt to cement over these deep
fissures, never really got off the ground. The radicalized Zionist movement and the non-Zionist organizations such as the
American Jewish Committee simply could not agree on a common strategy. Even within the American Zionist movement,
which now represented the consensus within American Jewry,
there were deep divisions. That became apparent in 1944,
when an appalling clamor broke out in the American press
between the mainline Zionist organizations and the revisionist
Peter Bergson group. Even on the periphery of occupied
Europe, where Jewish organizations had established listening
posts, the Joint Distribution Committee and the World Jewish
Congress often seemed more anxious to tear each other apart
than to rescue Jews. Nothing was sadder than to watch each
Jewish organization send a delegation to Washington to plead
separately for their respective clients.

The disunity in the Jewish community, its inability to project a coherent message to decision makers, certainly lessened
the Jews' influence. But one suspects that even had they been
able to create a united front, the amount of action to save Jews
would have been circumscribed. Other factors entered the picture.

Policy makers were simply never able to fathom the meaning
Auschwitz would have for their own society. The war aims
they established ignored the Jewish question. It was simply an
unpopular minority who, rumor had it, were being slaughtered
by the Nazis in a systematic way. There was no special
significance attached to what was happening. Thus, even while
Nazi leaders in Berlin spoke incessantly about Jews, Allied
leaders took great care not to allow the war to become a war to
save the Jews. Washington developed a special euphemistic vo-
cabulary to conceal the centrality of the "Jewish question" in
the war. There is rarely mention of it in the documents con-

cerning the war effort. The three rescue agencies dealing with the fate of the Jews employ the term "political refugee." Even the executive order creating the aforementioned War Refugee Board, designed expressly to rescue Jews, does not mention them directly. When Roosevelt heard mention of it in the Oval office he expressed distress. Even Nazi propaganda's conversion of Roosevelt himself to the Jewish faith brought no reaction from the White House.

Paradoxically, despite the failure to get action from the administration, the Jewish voter maintained a deeper loyalty to the New Deal than other hyphenate groups. Many of these actually decreased their commitment after the election of 1936, when Roosevelt veered leftward. Jews, however, increased their proportion of support. It was said that Jews had *"drei Velten: Die Velt, Yenneh Velt,* and Roosevelt.* So close was the "love affair" of the Jewish voter with Roosevelt that Jewish leaders were denied the ability to threaten the President with the removal of the Jewish vote. They were compelled to depend on the less certain rewards for political loyalty. We have seen that these took the form of meaningless gestures.

Yet Jews were then and now no less successful than other subgroups in the foreign-policy arena. Ultimately they did succeed in activating the Roosevelt administration in the cause of rescue, but it took four crucial years, and by the time it happened European Jewry was already in ashes. When one considers that it was wartime and that the nation's resources were strained, that is no small feat. We have noted previously that the ability of subgroups to alter major policy decisions, once they have been made, is limited. That is even more true during wartime. Jews proved unable to change the major policy formulation of American war aims, that first priority must be given to victory. The rescue of Jews, it was argued time and again, would work against that goal. Rescue advocates were never able to successfully challenge that contention. But one ought to note carefully that in the history of American diplomacy, Irish-Americans, German-Americans, and other hyphenates were no

---

*"Three worlds: This world, the world beyond, and Roose [world]."

more successful in changing American policy to further an interest they were advocating, and they projected a far clearer voice.

Behind the failure of rescue advocates to move the American public was their inability to get the story of what the Nazis were doing to Jews believed; they failed to gain credibility. The facts of the "final solution" as they filtered out of Europe were so gruesome that they defied the imagination. Many well-meaning people were convinced that what they were hearing was simply atrocity-mongering similar to the type that had occurred during World War I. It became merely another story of cruelty in a particularly cruel war, which took its place in the American imagination beside Pearl Harbor, the Bataan death march, Katyn, Lidice, and finally Malmedy. It is in that context that the efforts of the State Department to suppress news of the "final solution" appear particularly onerous today. The absence of hard facts compounded the problem of gaining credibility. Rescue advocates failed to break through this roadblock. The public opinion polls we possess—some taken after pictures of the death camps had appeared in America's hometown newspapers—indicate that the fact that a systematized mass-murder operation of enormous scale was going on in Europe did not remotely enter the consciousness of the average American. That fact is crucial in our examination, since in order to get the Roosevelt administration to act an aroused public opinion was essential. Without it the President could do very little, since the largess of America throughout the crisis was difficult to mobilize. Yet no public opinion could be generated unless the fact of the "final solution" was believed. There was more involved here than simply the State Department's concealing of information. Even when the fact was made known, the public paid little heed to it. What we do not know is how one gets the public to believe the unbelievable. How can such an incredible fact as the "final solution" be impressed on the public conscience—assuming, of course, that there is such a thing as a public conscience.

Many people wonder why the many Jews close to Roosevelt did not do more. We need not recite lists of the many Jews in high positions, but it should be noted that the appointment of Jews to high places was so disturbing to some opponents of the New Deal that the pejorative "Jew Deal" was in common usage by 1936. What of these Jews acting as agents to push for a more active rescue effort? We have already noted that it was finally when Henry Morgenthau, Jr. pressured Roosevelt that the War Refugee Board was created. Why didn't more of these "court Jews" speak up? Not all the facts about the activities of these people are available to researchers, but it seems clear, from the little we do know, that Jews who were close to the Administration were customarily drawn from the periphery of the Jewish community. They rarely thought in terms of a Jewish interest, since they were no longer fully identified as Jews. The case of Henry Morgenthau, Jr., is particularly instructive. When he did come out with his hard "Morgenthau plan," which called for the "pastoralization" of postwar Germany, accusations that the secretary was motivated by an ethnic rather than an American interest were not long in coming. Other men, like Samuel Rosenman, the president's speech writer, rarely made an effort to speak out on the matter of the Holocaust, while Ambassador Laurence Steinhardt inadvertently played an antirescue role in an effort to protect his diplomatic career. Breckinridge Long used Steinhardt's dispatches from Moscow to prove to Roosevelt that the refugee stream presented a security risk for America. Leaders of Jewish organizations were, of course, more able to recognize a Jewish interest. But even here, the case of Joseph Proskauer, who led the American Jewish Committee during these critical years, shows that he was not immune from ambivalent feelings about his Jewishness and never totally resolved the tension he felt between it and his loyalty to America. In the end, one reluctantly concludes that the possibility of mobilizing such influence was, at least during the years of the Holocaust, more chimerical than real. That should not surprise us, since it is abundantly evident in the later case of Henry Kissinger, who held more power—with the exception of Judah P. Benjamin, "the brains of the Confederacy;—than any other Jew in American history.

If American Jewry can be said to have failed at all, it was not so much a failure of will as it was a failure of mind. That is apparent in the case of bombing the camps and railroad lines leading to them. Rescue advocates did not press for that until mid-1944, when it was all but too late. The bombing of Auschwitz was not possible until the spring of 1944, but merely the threat of retaliatory bombing might have saved lives. It would have at least opened up the question of what was happening to the Jews, it might have broken the "wall of silence," which both the Nazi and Allied authorities desperately wanted to maintain. The halting of the deportations from Hungary after a bombing raid gives us a clue that retaliatory bombing— that is, an announcement that a city like Hamburg would be bombed in retaliation for what was taking place in Auschwitz, Treblinka, or Sobibor—might have been the key to mass rescue, or at least to the saving of thousands of lives. Yet in the twelve-point rescue program of rescue advocates, publicly proclaimed at a giant Madison Square Garden rally in March 1943, bombing was omitted. Rescue advocates simply did not consider its possible use in 1943.

Finally, one ought to say something about the assumption underlying the accusation that the Roosevelt administration did not do enough. It is based on the quaint notion that a humanitarian spirit, call it a "spirit of civilization," plays an important role in the behavior of nations and can be mobilized to serve a Jewish interest. It turns out that a weak and vulnerable people, the Jews, call upon the world to be better than it wants to be or perhaps is capable of being. When their efforts prove less than successful, they blame themselves for not having done enough. But how Jews living in the twentieth century came to the conclusion that such a spirit plays a significant role in human affairs and is housed either in the Oval office, the Vatican, the International Red Cross, the corridors of the League of Nations or the United Nations, or the countless other places Jews have sought it, is a great mystery. A reading of their own history, especially, should have indicated that nations are concerned primarily with their own interest, which in wartime is interpreted as survival. Jews above all have reason to believe that when nation states act at all the result is more likely to be malignant than humane. The Jewish experience in tsarist Russia, Rumania, and many other states in Europe, might have told them that. Indifference to the fate of the Jewish people during the Holocaust should not have come as a surprise.

It is possible that the Holocaust has finally taught Jews that lesson. It may be gleaned from the difference in the Jewish reaction to Entebbe as compared with the Holocaust. In the latter case they were forced to come, hat in hand, to beseech world leaders like Roosevelt to save their brethren. They had no power of their own and were constantly worried about such questions as legality and loyalty. Their actions had in the end to conform to someone else's priorities. They were priorities which simply did not take into account the rescue of Jews. But at Entebbe their own sons, flying their own planes, carrying guns they had manufactured themselves, snatched their brethren from those who would do them harm. There was no waiting for the civilized world to act, there was no concern about the legality of the action. How many Jews would be alive today had such a feat been possible during the Holocaust years?

Bibliography

"America and the Holocaust." *American Jewish History*, vol. 68 (March 1979).

"America and the Holocaust." *American Jewish History*, vol. 70 (March 1981).

Bauer, Y. "The Holocaust and American Jewry." *The Holocaust in Historical Perspective*. Seattle: 1978.

Feingold, H. L. *The Politics of Rescue: The Roosevelt Administration and The Holocaust, 1938–1945*. New York: 1980.

Feingold, H. L. "Roosevelt and the Holocaust: Reflections on New Deal Humanitarianism." *Judaism*, vol. 18 (Summer 1969).

Feingold, H. L. "The Witness Role of American Jewry: A Second Look" in *Human Responses to the Holocaust* ed., Michael D. Ryan, New York: 1981.

Friedman, S. S. *No Haven for the Oppressed*. Detroit: 1973.

Morse, A. *While Six Million Died*. New York: 1977.

Wyman, D. *Paper Walls: America and the Refugee Crisis, 1938–1941*. Amherst: 1968.

CHAPTER XIV

Can American Jewry Survive?
A Second Opinion

EVERYONE has heard of the paradoxical announcement made by one of those unflappable pilots over the intercom to his passengers: "Ladies and gentlemen, this is the captain speaking . . . I have two pieces of news for you—one good and one bad. The good news is that we are making excellent time. The bad news is that we are hopelessly lost." That strange balance between good news and bad, between hope and despair, is common in Jewish humor because it is common in the Jewish condition. "If everything is so good," Jews say, "then why is everything so bad?" In Jewish history the two seem always to appear together. Historians call it a "dialectic tension," by which they mean that good and bad are somehow linked and may, in fact, simply be opposite sides of the same coin. What appears at one historical juncture to be an asset may develop into a liability at a later point. This discussion about the condition of American Jewry is not unlike the pilot's message. It contains both good and bad news. It observes that something is indeed dying in American Jewry but it also finds that something new and hopeful is coming to life.

We need first to illustrate that dialectic tension in the contemporary Jewish condition. We have seen the extremely high priority Jews have given to formal education. Much energy was expended in opening up the doors of the best American universities for their children, and in keeping them open. That was what the struggle against quotas at Harvard during the twenties was all about. Today, over 88 percent of Jewish children receive some form of higher education. Together with Japanese-

Americans, Jews maintain the highest percentage of higher education of any subgroup in America. Yet today some survivalists are convinced that the sending of Jewish youth to distant campuses serves in the long run to weaken their identities as Jews. The seductive campus, usually located in an idyllic natural setting, and the watered-down liberal-arts curriculum, with its persuasive universalistic assumption, combined with the heady social atmosphere of a summer camp, is something the demanding Judaic ethos cannot compete against. Many survivalists have come to consider the campus a "disaster area," where the Jewish enterprise loses its youth.

Another example, where an objective once realized had the opposite result of what was intended, can be seen in the struggle against anti-Semitism. American Jewry fought hard against it and continues to nervously monitor public opinion to discover early the first signs of the dread malignancy. By and large the Jewish defense agencies have been successful. Today it is unacceptable to propogate anti-Semitic slander openly without losing a certain respectability. To attack Jews is to attack an integral part of American society and thus outside the boundaries of acceptable behavior. But that acceptance has come at the price of loss of particularity. Jews are so well integrated into American life that many no longer recognize a distinctive subgroup differentiated by its Judaism. It may seem almost perverse, but that loss of particularism, some survivalists feel, must be regained even if it entails the threat of reawakening anti-Semitism. They instinctively perceive that nothing reminds Jews of their Jewishness faster than anti-Semitism. They consider the renewal and reinvigoration of the binding ideology of Zionism, which is central to the American Jewish civil religion, as well worth the price of the danger of being targeted for a special animus. America is too benevolently absorbent for the Jewish enterprise to survive. A similar tale might be told regarding Jewish affluence. American Jewry strove hard to achieve its current high occupational status and income. But there is a growing group which feels that the very success achieved makes Jews conspicuous and ready to serve as a target based on an anti-Semitism rooted in economic envy. Others feel that too high a price is exacted for affluence in loss of spirit, ideals, and identity. It has made the Jewish poor more invisible than most, so much so that their existence was only discovered a few years ago. What in the long proves helpful to Jewish survival is not as easily determined as one might imagine.

Determining with precision what is a threat to survival in the contemporary Jewish condition is further complicated by recent Jewish history which has naturally intensified survival anxiety. Under normal circumstances, such anxiety may itself be the surest sign of vitality, as was pointed out by Simon Rawidowicz in an essay significantly titled, "Israel, the Ever-Dying People." But after the Holocaust and over thirty years of nonacceptance of the Jewish state by its Arab neighbors, the ominous prognosis for Jewish survival affects the ability of even objective observers to see light at the end of the tunnel. Instead, Jewish survivalists are in the throes of a catastrophe perspective, which magnifies the slightest unsettling event, such as Skokie or the energy problem, into a major crisis. The paranoic vision regarding the intentions of the outside world toward the Jewish enterprise is understandable. During this last half-century, Jews have after all lived through the classic paranoic nightmare: they lived in a world that wanted to kill them and gave them no quarter. During the Holocaust one out of three of their number was murdered in the cruelest way. Such an experience cannot be cast off easily. It is not a question of seeing reality in a twisted way. For Jews, reality has in fact been twisted. It has made them sensitive to impending danger, by furnishing them with an early warning system. This was developed at a very dear price in blood and survivalists might well argue that had the German Jews of the thirties had such a catastrophe perspective, many more might have survived. Yet, at the same time, the amplification of every untoward incident into a major crisis creates a freneticism that dulls the senses and makes extraordinarily difficult the distinction between what is a real problem and what is ephemeral, a distinction that must be made if we are ever to understand what problems American Jewry really faces.

One category of problems confronting American Jewry

stems directly from the condition of the American host culture with which it has cast its lot. An old Yiddish proverb has it that when the Gentile world sneezes, the Jewish world catches a cold. That seems to hold especially true for American Jewry, which, because of its peculiar configuration, often amplifies the problem of living in· America. Thus, the processes of urban decay, inner city violence, and the general insecurity of urban life have special impacts on Jews, who traditionally favor city life. If there is a loss of confidence and a general confusion about basic principles in the general culture, that will be reflected in the Jewish community as well. The same holds true for the unresolved race problem, which ticks like a time bomb beneath the surface of American society. If America faces a contraction of its economy, a shortage of energy, or even a growing geriatric problem, its effect on Jews will also be manifest. In the most direct way, American Jewish survival is linked to the survival of America itself, and the ups and downs of its day-to-day condition are directly related to the health chart of the nation.

In addition to that linkage, the Jewish community faces distinct internal problems. The most important of these may be a demographic crisis, which some believe places its continuance in jeopardy. Jews were among America's earliest and most efficient contraceptors. Today the average 45-year-old Jewish woman has given birth to 2.3 children, below her Catholic and Protestant counterparts and perilously close to zero population growth of 2.1. Jews realized early that their overriding drive for middle-class rank required smaller family units. That drive clearly continues to take precedence over group survival. Jews, perhaps more than most, insist that the determination of the size of family is a decision made privately rather than by the needs of the group. The result has been a decline of their proportion of the population—from a high of 3.2 percent, reached in the early thirties and forties, to less than 2.7 percent today. The aging of the American Jewish population is connected with this efficient and early practice of birth control, and that problem is in turn related to the discovery of poverty among Jews. The latter is, in fact, a concealed geriatric problem.

If one adds to the low Jewish birth rate the soaring rate of intermarriage, then the problem of survival can be seen with all its ominous implications. For many it has become simply a problem of biology, which can be solved by ordering Jews to have more children. But that assumes that there is someone who can issue such an order and that there are those who would feel bound to obey. In a modern secular society of free citizens, not subjects, there can only be voluntary compliance. Nor can Jews of marriageable age be compelled to marry within the fold. Jewish men and women have become positively popular as choice of mate by non-Jews. The former are purported to be good husbands and fathers. They are well educated and usually earn a good living. Similarly, Jewish women are purported to be competent homemakers and more likely to earn an income. These are characteristics admired by Americans, whereas being Jewish, which might at one time have served as a deterrent, no longer does. Perhaps as many as one out of three Jews now marry non-Jews. Of course, not all of these are lost to Judaism, since the community has been quite successful in bringing non-Jewish mates into the fold. One demographer argues that inter-marriage combined with in-group marriage actually increases the Jewish population, if there is conversion, since it makes for more Jewish children. Each Jewish partner in effect becomes a missionary through marriage. If that is true, then some agree-ment between the three branches of Judaism on the *halakah* of conversion is crucial. That does not appear likely to happen in the foreseeable future. The question of legitimate conversion, a possible alteration of Jewish law concerning the passing of the faith exclusively through the female line, or Rabbi Schindler's proposed strategy of proselytizing among "non-churched" Jews and Christians, even if implemented, would not solve the sur-vival conundrum of those who feel that it is related to maintain-ing sufficient numbers. The question is really how much inter-marriage American Jewry can abide before an irreversible cultural dilution sets in. Such marriages are usually entered into by people already weak in their commitment. It is the end-product of acculturation, so that it is hard to see how it could produce more Jews worthy of the name. Moreover, while the

non-Jewish wife or husband may undergo conversion, the un-
cles, aunts, grandparents, and cousins on the non-Jewish side,
who act as models for the children of an intermarriage, do not.
Intermarriage, more often than not, is not only the end-product
of an assimilation process that has been going on for generations; it acts as an intensifier of that process even when the
couple calls itself Jewish.

The demographic problem is in fact of older vintage than
most survivalists realize. For generations, American Jewry has
been biologically and culturally enriched from abroad. The
original Sephardic community would have disappeared had it
not been supplemented by German Jewry, and that community
in turn would have vanished had it not been reinforced by Jews
from Eastern Europe. The waves of immigration have tended
to conceal the attrition problem. One of the hidden costs of the
series of restrictive immigration laws passed during the twenties is that it prevented that supplemental population from
reaching American shores. During the thirties the laws proved
to be catastrophic for these potential immigrants in search of a
haven, so that the tragedy is in a sense double: they desperately
needed America and, from a demographic point of view,
American Jewry desperately needed them. Hitler's "final solution" largely eliminated this population pool, and in doing so he
may have also created a large demographic hole in the population curve of American Jewry, which may yet prove fatal. Not
only was the Jewish family of Eastern Europe the most prolific
in the world, it also was host to a particularly intense Jewish
culture, which might have been tailor-made for the flagging
spirits of American Jewry.

Today some of that biological deficit is filled by *yordim* and
noshrim, emigrants from Israel and the Soviet Union, who prefer to find their Zion in America. The influx of these immigrants to supplement American Jewry's flagging growth rate
has a bitter irony for survivalists. It indicates that America has
more drawing power than the population-starved Jewish state
in the Middle East on which so much hope was projected and so
many resources spent. It is a phenomenon that increasingly
challenges the ideology of Zionism. Why create a Jewish

sovereignty when a growing proportion of its population refuses to live there and Jews in need of a haven prefer America over Israel?

At the same time, there are survivalists who do not feel that the growing biological shortfall poses a real threat to the survival of American Jewry. They note the peculiar demographic symmetry in the American Jewish population curve, which indicates that America's Jews are well on their way to becoming again the inconspicuous minority they were during the colonial and national period. They point out that world Jewry has never obeyed demographic rules and that, had it done so, Jews would have vanished as a distinct group ages ago. It matters not how many Jews there are but the quality of commitment. It is the lessening of the attachment to Judaism that poses the real problem. Yet for American Jewry, the shrinkage of numbers has some immediate consequences. It lessens Jewish political influence, which in the last analysis is dependent on the delivery of votes. More important, it may mean a diminution in philanthropic giving and general cultural energy.

It is, then, the demographic problem in combination with the general loss of particularism, a desire to be Jewish, that poses the major threat to Jewish survival in America. The latter is more conspicuous than the lessening of the proportion of Jews in the general population. The well-appointed temples that grace Jewish suburbia are more a study in bourgeois esthetics than they are symbols of a vibrant faith. The bland religiosity practiced in these houses of worship is not very successful in filling them with worshippers, who largely confine their attendance to holy days. Even here there is an alteration in traditional priorities. The two most popular Jewish holidays, according to one poll, are Passover and Chanukah rather than the Days of Awe, Rosh Hashana and Yom Kippur. It is no accident that the former correspond neatly with Christmas and Easter. Behind the acculturation process there continues to be a thinly veiled Protestantization. It continues to wear down what remains distinctive about Judaism.

Traditionally, the Jewish family played a primary role in shaping and transmitting Jewish identity. But the impact of modern secular culture, from whose effects it was once believed the Jewish family was somehow immune, has proven to be illusory. The Jewish divorce rate and the attendant number of families headed by single parents now almost matches the national average. Although Jewish divorced partners are still more likely to remarry, the weakening of the Jewish family structure is manifest, as is its enormous impact on the Jewish survival potential. Talk about giving Jewish education a new priority in funding is based on the notion that it can deliver a Jewish identity, which was formerly largely transmitted by the Jewish family. It is, however, by no means established that such a substitution can by itself generate such an identity.

Then, American Jewry faces a series of problems that might be broadly classified as political. Should American foreign policy in the oil-rich Middle East tilt more to the Arab side, there is a distinct possibility of a disinterring of the vexing dual-loyalties question, which so plagued American Jewry in the early decades of this century. On an issue like the future disposition of the West Bank or the recognition of the PLO as the legitimate representative of the Palestinians in the international arena, American foreign policy may well be in accord with the Arabs, and American Jewry may find itself out of step and even accused of forwarding a purely Jewish interest over America's. In addition, there is the possibility of an anti-Semitic fallout from the energy crisis. That did not occur during the 1973–1974 OPEC boycott, but there is some question whether one can tamper indefinitely with the love affair of the American people and their automobiles.

No less worrisome is the anemia in secular Jewish organizational life, which plays a crucial role in community bonding outside the religious congregation. With the exception of the local federations, which have assumed a leadership role, the original mass-membership organizations find it difficult to attract younger members. Those who today make up the rank and file are not less dedicated and vital, no less the resourceful Hadassah lady known in Jewish wit and fable, but they are older. The organizations do not attract the younger Jewish professionals who are the most vital elements in the Jewish population. Even while actual membership figures may periodically indicate a rise in membership, it is membership of the wrong kind and is, in fact, an increasingly smaller percentage of the Jewish population.

From the vantage of a catastrophe perspective, the situation looks bleak. One Israeli demographer (Elihu Bergman) in *Midstream* (October 1977), predicted ;that there would be only ten thousand committed Jews in America in the second decade of the twenty-first century. Such predictions are not unprecedented in Jewish history. The demographer simply replaces the ancient prophets, who were no less gloomy. One recalls the prediction of Dr. Teilhaber in 1911. That German-Jewish demographer was certain that German Jewry would have vanished before the end of the century. Teilhaber's figures could not tell him that the Holocaust would cause German Jewry to vanish well before that date. Demographic projections really say, "This will be the case providing nothing happens to intercede." But, of course, history always happens. It is especially dangerous to prognosticate about Jewish continuance, since it lies not in commonalities, things it shares with other groups of seemingly similar character, but in its idiosyncratic nature, which is wrought by an anomalous history. Like Elihu Bergman, who projected the gloomy population figures for American Jewry, the historian Arnold Toynbee too could not confront the mystery of millenial Jewish survival. They do not sense that the development of Jewish civilization follows the so-called normal laws of neither history nor demography. If it did, the Jewish presence would have passed from the stage of history long ago. That unpredictability is no less manifest in the development of American Jewry. We have noted how the Orthodox branch defied the predictions of its demise, made at the turn of the century. It appears surprisingly vital today. Similarly, the Jews of the Soviet Union did not have a good prognosis for survival after the Holocaust and the "Black Years" under Stalin. Yet we daily witness signs of a remarkable renewal. By all rules there should be no Jewish civilization today; yet it is very noticeably, and sometimes very noisily, present in history. The demographers' error is not in their statistical projections, which are accurate enough, but in their failure to account for the idiosyncratic character of Jewish historical development, which simply does not follow normal rules.

For every sign pointing to the inevitable conclusion that American Jewry is moribund, one can point to signs of renewal and continuing vitality. So complete does their acculturation appear to have been that American Jews sometimes appear to be "exaggerated Americans." Yet it is also clear that they acculturate on different terms than other groups on the American social landscape. I call this "American Jewish exceptionalism," by which I mean not its superior achievement but the distinctive way it comes to terms with the demands of the host culture. Its self-consciousness predates the current vogue for things ethnic, much of which may actually be sentimental nostalgia. It demonstrates its continued cohesiveness not so much by grouping itself in the same squares of the economic checkerboard or of living in the same neighborhoods, as once was the case, but by its continued loyalty to k'lal Yisrael (the universal community of Jewry). It is a tie demonstrated often on these pages. We mean by it a connection with the continuing stream of Jewish history, a concern for what is happening to Jews elsewhere. American Jewry virtually defines itself by this connection, whether it is the Jews of Israel, the Soviet Union, or, more recently, Iran.

That eternal group feeling seems less pronounced today, but it should not be dismissed altogether. The Gerhard Lenski studies done in a Jewish suburb of Detroit and the celebrated Lakeville studies both show that Jews are distinguished from non-Jews by their associational patterns. Even when Jews are no longer religious or concentrated in the same neighborhood, even when they do not affiliate with a religious congregation or some Jewish secular organization, 87 percent of their primary associations, the people with whom they prefer to socialize, continue to be other Jews. Jews of the third and fourth generations form "golden ghettos," at least in the socializing sense, not because they are despised by the general society and therefore forced back on themselves, but because they find something fulfilling in associating with other Jews. Whether the reason is that Jews feel that the jokes among their own kind are funnier or the food tastier or that the neighborhood schools are inevitably better if Jewish kids are in attendance, matters not. What does matter is that after generations of holding fast to a universalist–egalitarian ethos, which denied their group elan, many Jews have come to openly recognize and appreciate it. They begin to sense that the Jewish achievement in America, whether it is in business or science or the professions, has some relation to the fact of their Jewishness. In a democratic society based on the norms of a leveling popular mass culture, the need to have something that differentiates and individuates is imperative. De Tocqueville recognized it as a driving force in America. For many Jews their Jewishness, rather than a fact to be concealed, has become something of which to be proud. The recognition of Jewish elan by non-Jews may be a factor behind the growing desire to marry Jews. Certainly the number of *yarmulkahs* (skull caps) on the heads of Jewish students in our best universities indicates that something about the group's self-image has changed. Perhaps they are on the threshold of recognizing their specialness. If that is so, then an entirely new ingredient for Jewish continuance has developed.

In the passage below, Irving Howe describes how that sense of specialness worked in the move to surburbia:

> Part of the reason for moving to the suburbs had been a wish to get away from those "constricting old Jewish neighborhoods," sometimes from the people who lived in them—yet one of the first consequences was to force upon the new suburbanites major problems of their self-definition. Living on Ocean Parkway in Brooklyn or Moshulu Parkway in the Bronx meant yielding all one's senses to a Jewish ambiance . . . But moving into the suburbs required that people decide whether or not they wanted to declare themselves as Jews. At first everyone seemed amiable and anonymous, young and shining, and stamped with an encrusted ethnicity. But that was just the trouble, since merely to surrender to the ways of suburbia was in effect a declaration about what one wanted to be.

One of the first things the newly suburban Jews did was to seek

out other Jews . . . At least some of them must have been alive to
the irony that they were going to escape from "old fashioned"
Jewishness, perhaps from Jewishness entirely, but would escape
together as Jews, comforted by the presence of other, also escaping Jews.

In Jewish history an intense concern for Jewish scholarship
serves as a measure of the vitality of a particular Jewish community. That thrust to scholarship among Jews in America,
reflected in the high percentage of Jewish youth enrolled in
college and the disproportionate number who make their living
in the academy, might be considered its secular equivalent. The
tradition of learning through books has contributed much to
create the American Jewish elan. It retains the traditional aspect of talmudic scholarship as well. There are five rabbinical
academies and six additional institutes of higher learning sponsored by the Jewish community, as well as hundreds of
yeshivot and at least three hundred secular colleges with
courses and specializations in Jewish studies. At least fifty
books of serious Jewish scholarship are published yearly. Some
of the best talmudic scholars and historians do their work in
America.

Questioning officers of Jewish congregations and organizations, one gets the distinct impression that a goodly number are
Jews who have come back to their Judaism in midlife. These *baale
tshuve* (returnees or repentees) represent one of the most hopeful
signs of the continued vitality of American Judaism. One can only
guess how widespread the phenomenon of the returnee is or
what the reasons for return may be. One observer is convinced
that much of the Jewish religious and organizational life is increasingly populated and enriched by the returnees. The return
may be part of the allure of the fraternal function, which we
have seen plays a key role in the proliferation of Jewish organizations. Certainly membership in congregations is still
motivated by basic primordial religious functions, such as
birth, confirmations, marriage, and death, which traditionally
require some religious intermediary. The most important reason for a return may in fact be psychological or, more accu-

rately, spiritual. By midlife, modern men and women have had some of the stuffings, the confidence that they can make and control their own world, knocked out of them. We are speaking of the very hubris which is at the heart of Western achievement and which is intrinsically antireligious, since it places man at the center of the universe. For the middle-aged in our society, life often begins to go awry: a loved one leaves or dies, a good business fails, a child in whom much has been invested becomes addicted to drugs. Suddenly we realize that we are lonely, afraid, and not in control of our world. It is the perfect juncture for a religious sensibility to enter the picture.

Baale tshuve return to Judaism not necessarily asking a Jewish question. They want to know what Judaism can do for them, rather than what they might do for it. They want to know if Judaism has any cures for what ails them. But from a survivalist perspective the reason for their return is less important than the fact of the return. With the longer lives we are granted, there is time even after the age of 45 to bring such a returnee to the rich Jewish heritage. The very process of returning, especially the cultural and religious rebirth it entails, is part of what is being looked for. It brings a concern for something outside ourselves, which in an age of narcissism is a cure in its own right. What survivalists have yet to discover is how to broaden the trickle of returnees so that it becomes a broad stream.

Part of our gloomy view regarding the future of American Jewry is a matter of historical perspective. We suffer from an inferiority complex because our natural frame of reference is the intensely Jewish Jews of Eastern Europe. What we do not realize is that virtually all Jewish communities, including the Jews of ancient Israel, look pale in comparison with these Jews, who were perhaps the most spiritual and separatist in all Jewish history. The comparison is particularly inappropriate for American Jewry, which is really much more like the cosmopolitan Jews of the Golden Age of Moorish Spain, or the Jews of the Babylonian exile. We also tend to forget that American Jewry is relatively young. It did not establish itself as a community in earnest until the turn of this century, when the Eastern Jews arrived in numbers. Yet, although American Jewry is in many respects less than a century old, it is already entering upon its golden age, decades ahead of other Jewish communities in the long stream of Jewish history.

No midrash on American Jewry would be complete without a little prophecy. Those who see only a gloomy future have focused on what is dying in Jewish life, its corporate–collective aspect, the total Jewish environment that conditioned Jews to live with their Jewishness as if there were nothing else. Like all people of modernity, Jews no longer take their behavioral cues completely from their religious culture. But for those willing to see, something new is coming to life in American Jewry, too: secular, highly individuated, superbly educated persons, who relate to their Jewishness by sensing that they are members of the Jewish people and that this people possesses a special elan which differentiates them from others. They often awaken to their Jewishness, the source of that elan, only after they have established themselves economically in midlife. They come to Judaism by voluntary choice, since the total Jewish ambience once furnished by the Jewish family and community and total separateness from the secular environment no longer exists. To be sure they are modern people, detribalized, playing many different roles and no longer fully capable of an overriding faith dictating their daily activities. They take from the religious cultures what they think might be useful to them. They are in effect their own religious tailors. Frequently the result is a kind of civil religion in which some form of Jewish peoplehood—in the form of Zionism, plays a major role. They are more American, more secular, than ever before, but in their loyalty to *k'lal Yisrael*—which takes the form of concern for beleaguered Jewries in Israel or the Soviet Union—they are also more Jewish than ever before.

In the end we are compelled to recognize that the American Jewish condition is at once desperate and full of hope. Has it ever been otherwise with this people?

Bibliography

Feingold, H.L. "The Condition of American Jewry in Historical Perspective: A Bicentennial Assessment." *American Jewish Yearbook*, vol. 76 (1976).

Feingold, H.L. "German Jewry and the American Jewish Condition: A View From Weimar." *Judaism*, vol. 20 (Winter 1971).

Feingold, H.L. "The Jewish Immigrant Experience in North America: The Myth of Accommodation and the Myth of Survival," Council of Jewish Federations, New York: 1982.

Himmelfarb, M. *The Jews of Modernity*. New York: 1973.

Lenski, G. *The Religious Factor*. New York: 1963.

Howe, I. *World of Our Fathers*. New York: 1976.

Liebman, C. *The Ambivalent American Jew*. Philadelphia: 1973.

Rabinowitz, D. *The Other Jews: Portraits in Poverty*. New York: 1972.

Scholem, G. *On Jews and Judaism in Crisis*. New York: 1976.

Sidorsky, D., ed. *The Future of the Jewish Community in America*. Philadelphia: 1973.

Strober, G. *The American Jews: Community in Crisis*. New York: 1974.

Index